+LA21 .H54

Hill, Brian Victor/Education and the end
LA21 .H54 C.1 STACKS 1973

LA   **Hill, Brian Victor.**
21   Education and the
H54   endangered individual

LA   **Hill, Brian Victor.**
21   Education and the
H54   endangered individual

DATE DUE	BORROWER'S NAME	ROOM NUMBER
JUN 3 1992		

education and the endangered individual

education and the endangered individual

A CRITIQUE OF TEN MODERN THINKERS

Brian V. Hill
Murdoch University
Western Australia

Teachers College Press
Teachers College, Columbia University
New York & London

© 1973 by Teachers College, Columbia University
Library of Congress Catalog Card Number: 73-82283

Manufactured in the United States of America

Foreword

It has frequently been remarked that the distinctive feature of modern Western civilization is its preoccupation with man. Earlier epochs have been concerned more with nature or with God. Beginning with Descartes, modern philosophy has sought to plumb the meaning of human experience and has essayed a variety of answers to the most fundamental questions of man's origin, nature, and destiny. It is now widely recognized that only through our knowledge of the human person and the human condition is it possible to justify and explicate our understandings of any realm of being, whether of nature, of society, or of the divine.

These concerns about man are not merely important to philosophers. They are crucial to every person as he seeks to make sense of his life and to direct his activities into the most significant channels. In particular, they are fundamental to all who are charged with making policy decisions that affect the welfare of others. Among such persons are educators — teachers, parents, administrators, publicists, and others — the quality of whose contributions depends in no small measure on what they believe about persons and the conditions for fostering their optimum development.

Brian Hill speaks with admirable clarity and insight to

these basic concerns of modern thought. The central theme is the human individual and his worth. If the dignity of persons is to be sustained against the array of depersonalizing forces in modern technological civilization, it is essential that belief in the sanctity of the individual be more than a sentimental posture inherited from a humanistic tradition no longer sure of its sources. It must be grounded in deep convictions resting on a framework of ideas that command the assent of thoughtful persons. The pages to follow make a splendid contribution to the development of such well-founded and critically defensible convictions.

Hill's method is consistent with his theme. He traces the idea of the sanctity of the individual in the thought of ten important thinkers of the nineteenth and twentieth centuries, including men of widely divergent points of view. Each figure is treated with the insight and respect that are his due not only as a great thinker but also as an individual to whom sanctity is ascribed. But these seminal thinkers are not left in the isolated splendor of their thought. Rather, with consummate skill the author relates their ideas to their lives and times and generates through his sympathetic yet critical interpretations a dialogue out of which emerges in the course of the book a progressively deeper understanding of the meaning of individuality, of the value of persons, and of the relation between the individual and society.

In the analysis of each thinker the import for education is indicated, and in the final section of the book Dr. Hill elaborates his own position on the central theme, together with consequences for basic educational issues such as aims, curriculum, and the organization of schools. The result is a valuable personal synthesis growing out of the author's own experience as an educator in Australia and as a scholar both in his own country and in the United States of America, criticized and enriched by his sustained and deeply informed reading of the seminal thinkers whose ideas constitute the main subject matter of the book.

After a period of concentration on highly technical matters of analysis, many philosophers of education are again con-

Foreword

cerning themselves with substantive questions of personal and social values and with the competing ideologies that people use to guide their conduct. Professor Hill's book is an important contribution to the discussion of these pressing human issues. In a time when the life-giving role of thought is often ignored or denied and when many trust only the narrow rationality of specialists, a book like this one, exhibiting the power of reflection on comprehensive themes under the inspiration of great minds, is singularly needed and welcome.

PHILIP H. PHENIX

preface

The present study is an attempt to illuminate a major problem of values in educational theory: the standing of the individual to be educated.

Three convictions have influenced my choice of this topic: one, that not only has present-day improvement of techniques and material conditions outdistanced our understanding of purposes, but in a changing, pluralist society one can no longer assume that aims and values will take care of themselves; two, that one must draw on many disciplines to appreciate the scope of such problems, without granting to one the final right to make pronouncements in the area of values; and three, that translation of the democratic consensus into practical statements of purpose within educational theory is one of the responsibilities of the philosopher of education.

Initially I pose the question whether there is any kind of consensus amongst influential Western thinkers as to what is understood by "the sanctity of the individual"; and, because this enquiry includes testing their definitions against other aspects of their thought, I limit myself to a sample of ten thinkers to secure reasonable depth of analysis. Assuming that the selection is to some degree helpfully representative of contemporary Western thought, the investigation reveals a widely held conviction that the individual should be regarded as an end in himself, and that social and educational organization should honor this value.

The degree to which thinkers are successful in sustaining this valuation seems, however, to depend markedly on their views of human individuality, and on their willingness to recognize several different levels of discourse. A severely behavioral orientation is as cramping as a militantly existentialist one. Hence, in the concluding section of the study (Part Six) I seek to construct a statement about the sanctity of the individual, profiting from these insights, in terms that can be related to specific areas of educational theory.

The claim that this work belongs to philosophy of education may seem presumptuous to some, and it is defended in the first chapter. But whichever way the battle of labels should go, one would hope for little dispute on the need for someone to do this kind of job. Education has to do with values in action; the educationist theorizes with a view to immediate application of his findings in a going concern. Insofar as these findings relate to prescriptive value judgments, he must commit himself to them in advance of assured results such as are available when dealing with methodological findings. This must be my defense for the speculative propositions put forward in Part Six. Ostensibly what plausibility they may possess derives from the analyses in earlier parts, though it cannot be claimed that a logically necessary implication has been established. The weighing of views has more in common with what a historian of ideas does, when he tries to assess the ideological power and theoretical fertility of a concept or system of thought. The ultimate verdict on this study, then, will derive from its power to stimulate clearer and more effective theorizing at the normative level in education.

One verdict is not in doubt. This book owes much to a variety of persons other than the author. Philip H. Phenix, who so generously consented to write a foreword, has in his own writings deepened my appreciation of the need for enquiries into the theories of man which underlie curriculum proposals. W. E. Andersen at the University of Sydney super-

Preface

vised the original study on which this book is based, and his friendship and wise counsel over many years place me forever in his debt as a scholar and a person. Laura Whitehall's diligence and care in editing the manuscript for Teachers College Press have constantly evoked my respect and admiration. And finally, to Margaret my wife I give public thanks for her comradeship throughout a task that levied tax on many domestic priorities. It would, however, be unfair to such great friends to suggest other than that the interpretations put forward in this book are on my head alone.

B. V. H.

Perth, Western Australia
1973

CONTENTS

Foreword by Philip H. Phenix — v
Preface — ix

PART ONE
INTRODUCTION: DEFINING THE PROBLEM — 3

PART TWO
PRODIGAL SONS OF HEGEL — 19

Søren Kierkegaard — 23
Friedrich Nietzsche — 41
Karl Marx — 59
Kierkegaard : Nietzsche : Marx — 77

PART THREE
SOCIAL SCIENTISTS AT ODDS — 83

T. Percy Nunn — 87
Karl Mannheim — 97
Nunn : Mannheim — 117

PART FOUR
SCIENTIFIC WORLD-VIEWS — 125
- John Dewey — 129
- Alfred North Whitehead — 149
- Dewey : Whitehead — 169

PART FIVE
MODERN RELIGIOUS THINKERS — 179
- Martin Buber — 183
- Jacques Maritain — 203
- Reinhold Niebuhr — 221
- Buber : Maritain : Niebuhr — 241

PART SIX
TOWARD ADEQUATE EDUCATIONAL THEORY — 255
- The Sanctity of the Individual — 257
- Education and the Individual — 271

Bibliography — 297

Index — 311

Part One:

Introduction – Defining the Problem

DEFINING THE PROBLEM

Education has to do with the individual in society. "Developing the powers of the individual" has become a cliché in statements of educational aims. Assumptions concerning the nature of man orient research into educational methods. Educational doctrines invariably honor—on paper—the intrinsic worth of the individual.

Yet in the present day the sanctity of the individual is being eroded from all sides. Industrialization has absorbed the craftsman into vast labor pools, mass media have begun to homogenize cultural patterns, mechanization has destroyed the tightly knit community by increasing the mobility of the individual, and collectivist responses to political issues have become increasingly common. Interpersonal relations lack concern and permanence, and the individual is losing his identity because of pressures to conform. Even the social sciences, committed as they are to the study of such phenomena, tend, through assumptions that define the individual in terms of entities such as "the group" or "the role," to disparage his uniqueness.[1] In the face of such trends, educational slogans of the kind mentioned sound hollow and utopian.

[1] Gordon W. Allport initiates his notable study *Personality: A Psychological Interpretation* (London: Constable, 1938) with a chapter in which he chides social scientists for obscuring unique personal experiences with studies of a generalizing and statistical nature alone.

Either such trends are to be accepted docilely as facts of modern life which make the old slogans irrelevant because vague, or they are to be resisted with more precise definitions that provide clearly operational objectives for the educational process. Can the second alternative be embraced?

IDEOLOGY AND EDUCATIONAL THEORY

We must first establish the relevance of the whole enquiry to educational theory, because of the current debate concerning the nature of "educational theory" and "philosophy of education."

Clearly a notion like "the sanctity of the individual" presupposes a philosophical plane of discourse. It implies metaphysical discussion of the nature of man and value judgments concerning his status in the world. In the long history of philosophical system-building, the place of man in the system has always been a primary concern; and inevitably this has affected studies in many other fields, including education. Compare for example the classical Greek view of man as a rational animal and the medieval Christian view of man as a spiritual being. In the first instance, education was geared to the development of the physical and rational powers of the individual so that he might control his natural and social environments more effectively.[2] In the second, education aimed to produce individuals whose goals and values were other-worldly and for whom the earthly life was essentially probationary.

Speculative philosophy reached a peak with Hegel in the nineteenth century, just as its shroud was being prepared by positivistic science. At the same time the chief responsibility for education was passing from the church to the state. The confluence of these trends brought into being academic studies in education, studies which reflected the tension between philosophy and science. On the one hand, an amalgam of Christian supernaturalism and philosophical Idealism pre-

[2] I do not speak here of Plato's other-worldly vision for the education of the philosopher but of the "liberal" education which actually obtained in his day.

Defining the Problem

scribed educational aims and curricula of a traditional kind, reflecting the ideological homogeneity of the times. On the other, the experimental temper of science was being reflected in the improvement of educational method. Thus Pestalozzi, Froebel, and Herbart laid the foundations for the systematic study of educational psychology and teaching methods. With the establishment in 1895 of the National Herbartian Society for the Scientific Study of Education in the United States of America, the distinction of being pace-setter in educational reform passed from Europe to the New World. In the process, the scientific movement in education came into its own, breaking away from the leading strings of European speculative philosophy.

"The Scientific Movement in Education" became not only a description of trends in the developing discipline of education, but the slogan of an influential body of thinkers. The trends were ably demonstrated in the labors of E. L. Thorndike and the McMurrys, especially during their time as members of the illustrious Teachers College of Columbia University. Advances in learning theory, studies of child development, methodology for teaching the school subjects, and improved measuring techniques came thick and fast, all the more so because the criteria were behavioral rather than ontological.

The slogan emerged in the writings of those who preached that the way to solve all the problems of educational theory was by the scientific method. At its most naive this included the claim that there was no need for philosophical speculation, that all their data were available in social science as such. However, this attitude could only be maintained in a period when there was still a relatively unified world-view residual from the previous era. Once the impact of scientific progress began to be felt in society at large, the need for fundamental overhaul at a philosophical level as well seemed to be called for.

In John Dewey these conflicts met and were resolved at a high level of sophistication in favor of science. Dewey came out of the Hegelianism in which he was initially steeped into an evolutionary naturalism which he called Pragmatism.

Within this frame of reference he proceeded to exalt scientific method (as he saw it) as the keystone of experience, epistemology, and value theory. It therefore became, not merely the paradigm for insight into learning and pedagogics, but a new way of life, a militant world-view: an "ism" indeed. For although Dewey asserted in 1917 that "the chief characteristic of the pragmatic notion of reality is precisely that no theory of Reality in general . . . is possible or needed," [3] it has been well said that a metaphysical position can only be rejected from another metaphysical position. Pragmatism (or Experimentalism, to use Dewey's later preferred term) is a speculative "ism" and by no means the only one derivable from science, as is apparent from the alternative postulations of such thinkers as F. S. C. Northrop and A. N. Whitehead.

Educational theory as conceived within the scientific movement in education therefore took a further step. It was now seen as the outcome of deriving educational implications from Experimentalism, the philosophy for a scientific age. As Dewey said, "the most penetrating definition of philosophy . . . is that it is the theory of education in its most general phases." [4] For a time this view commanded wide support because its attack on sterile, traditional school practices attracted many followers from the ranks of that wider reforming agency, American Progressivism,[5] who were not at first conscious of the philosophical assumptions of its leaders. Henderson's comment on the strong Pragmatist element in the policies of the Progressive Education Association, set up in 1919 to hasten reform, is apposite:

> It is doubtful whether many teachers really understood its philosophical foundations. Certainly, few had studied Dewey's

---

[3] Quoted in J. Donald Butler, *Four Philosophies and Their Practice in Education and Religion,* New York: Harper and Bros., 1951, p. 429.

[4] John Dewey, *Democracy and Education* (New York: Macmillan, 1916), p. 386, obviously meaning by "philosophy" that which he considered to be the only live option.

[5] Cremin carefully discriminates between the general reforming spirit and that particular, institutionalized form of it, the Progressive Education Association, which functioned from 1919 to 1957. See Lawrence A. Cremin, *The Transformation of the School: Progressivism in America, 1876–1957,* New York: Alfred A. Knopf, 1961.

Defining the Problem

philosophy against any background of other philosophies . . . To some extent the movement was popular because it constituted a revolt against the boring formalism of the traditional school.[6]

During the Depression years of the thirties, when criticisms of Progressivism multiplied, there were those who blamed its failings on the Experimentalist rationale and sought to provide other rationales which, though still progressive and in keeping with the modern age, reclaimed some traditional insights.

Thus: in 1935 Herman Horne brought Idealism up to date; in 1938 the Essentialist Committee was set up, pledging itself to maintain "values embedded in the cultural heritage"; Adler and Breed popularized revivals of forms of Realism; and Catholic theorists entered public debate after the publication in 1929 of a notable papal encyclical on education.

For educational theory the net result was confusion, but the stalemate of the "isms" which succeeded the pragmatic-progressive epoch did at least reveal one thing: it pointed up the failure of speculative philosophy to command general agreement. Thus Experimentalism's ideological character had been laid bare by its rivals and critics, who themselves continued to reflect the belief inherited from Hegel's century that one could erect a philosophical world-view and then derive from it an educational theory.

Since the Second World War there have been two types of attack on this belief, in the interests of educational theory. The first has questioned the validity of the notion that one educational theory is necessarily implied by a philosophical "ism." The second has stemmed from the English revolution in pure philosophy. For the sake of clear statement in the ensuing discussion, we shall cease to speak of "philosophies" or "isms" and refer instead to "ideologies." [7]

[6] Stella van Petten Henderson, *Introduction to the Philosophy of Education*, Chicago: University of Chicago Press, 1957, p. 250.
[7] As used here, "ideology" means a coherent set of speculative ideas and values, and does not imply disapproval of ideologies and ideological structures as in Karl Mannheim's analysis of the term in *Ideology and Utopia: An Introduction to the Sociology of Knowledge*, trans. Louis Wirth and Edward Shils, New York: Harcourt, Brace and Co., n.d.

The first attack represents a philosophical doubt that any ideology, no matter how well articulated, can imply one and only one educational theory. McMurray fired the first salvo in 1955. Advocating that education should be an autonomous discipline, he pointed out that

> while educational "philosophers" engage at second hand in the controversies of systematic philosophy and in finding implications for education, practical educators with no training in theory proceed with their own tasks of constructing and changing school programs.[8]

This is not the place to trace the debate that has since ensued, except to say that it is becoming clear that the case for a necessary logical connection between speculative ideology and educational theory cannot be sustained. Equally, however, it is clear that educational theory cannot be strictly autonomous because it is involved with norms at both the ideological and sociological levels.[9] Burns insists on the existence of "some kind of organic connection between philosophy and educational practice" [10] and proposes a "pragmatic implication" — a concept whose fruitfulness remains to be seen. Latterly the practice has been growing in the United States of examining what are now called "theories of education" [11] in order to clarify concepts, check consistency, and expose underlying philosophical assumptions (which may or may not cohere with some major ideology).

The second attack suggests that all the foregoing is somewhat irrelevant, because philosophy itself has long since left the arena of ideological speculation and is now a properly technical discipline of language analysis. Whereas most

---

[8] Foster McMurray, "Preface to an Autonomous Discipline of Education," *Educational Theory*, vol. 5, July 1955, p. 131.

[9] Note for example Philip G. Smith's exposure of the concealed empiricist theory of value in McMurray's article, in "Philosophy, Educational Theory and Pedagogy," *Educational Theory*, vol. 6, July 1956, p. 132.

[10] Hobert W. Burns, "The Logic of the 'Educational Implication,'" *Educational Theory*, vol. 12, Jan. 1962, p. 63.

[11] See my review of John P. Wynne's book by this title, in *Australian Journal of Education*, vol. 8, Oct. 1964, pp. 262-63.

Defining the Problem

"philosophy of education" is still neo-Hegelian in method, "true philosophy" is post-Wittgensteinian. A growing body of educational philosophers is coming over to this view and defining "philosophy of education" essentially as O'Connor does here:

> Philosophy is not in the ordinary sense of the phrase a body of knowledge but rather an activity of criticism or clarification. As such, it can be exercised on any subject matter at all, including our present concern, the problems of educational theory.[12]

O'Connor goes on to summarize the problem of how to justify value judgments, reaching a conclusion which is now generally endorsed: that no academic discipline as such possesses the methodological tools whereby value judgments may be both described and justified.[13] Hence the philosopher of education is not entitled to be, as Dewey was, an ideologist or (synonymous in the eyes of an Analyst) speculative metaphysician.

What then is the status of educational theory? O'Connor describes some senses in which "theory" is employed and commends the usage which is closest to physical science theory. Hirst detects in O'Connor's analysis an implicit bias towards a positivist view of knowledge which annuls his claim to objectivity. In particular, he claims that O'Connor has neglected the distinction between scientific theory and educational theory, which derives from the difference between knowledge organized "for the pursuit of knowledge and the understanding of our experience" and knowledge organized "for determining some practical activity."[14]

In Hirst's view, educational theory is inescapably involved with values, both in clarifying the use of various value judgments in the educational context and in constructing opera-

---

[12] D. J. O'Connor, *An Introduction to the Philosophy of Education*, London: Routledge and Kegan Paul, 1958, p. 4.

[13] Page 71. See also I. Scheffler, ed., *Philosophy and Education*, Boston: Allyn and Bacon, 1958, p. 4; and Henry D. Aiken, "Moral Philosophy and Education," *Harvard Educational Review*, vol. 25, Winter 1955, pp. 39–59.

[14] Paul H. Hirst, "Philosophy and Educational Theory," *British Journal of Educational Studies*, vol. 12, Nov. 1963, p. 60.

tionally useful ones. The theorist therefore seeks not only the benefits of philosophical analysis in the modern sense, but also substantive insights regarding the nature and origins of value judgments which many Analysts tend to eschew. The subject matter to which he applies these tools is the vast body of normative judgments and doctrines which has been and is being built up around the educational process. While it is clear that ideologies are not the only determinants of a community's value patterns, they are, as surveys like that of Northrop [15] have shown, major determinants. Hence part of the task of the educational theorist must be the study of ideologies and ideologists that appear to be having an impact on educational theory-building.

It is of course possible by a manipulation of definitions to insist that "educational theory" shall be a strictly analytic and empirical discipline, but this only pushes the problem further back. One must then find a new *nom de plume* for that researcher who, denied such titles as "philosopher of education" or "educational theorist," seeks to relate ideology to current educational theory. Indeed, such are the evils of specialization that he would soon lose touch with the philosopher and the theorist, to whose understanding he is as essential as they are to his.

If, then, the study of ideology is necessary to the development of theory in the applied field of education, how is it to be pursued? Put in this form, the question finds little in the current literature to suggest an answer. One must pursue a course between the Charybdis of speculative educational philosophizing in the grand synoptic manner and the Scylla of being an Analytic "gadfly without a stated point of view." [16] Thus it is not satisfactory to attempt to derive an educational theory direct from a major ideology. Nor is it legitimate to seek a fully articulated theory from one ideologist, since educational

---

[15] F. S. C. Northrop, *The Meeting of East and West: An Enquiry Concerning World Understanding*, New York: Macmillan, 1947.

[16] The phrase is borrowed from John Paul Strain's caustic article, "Critique of Philosophical Analysis in Education," *Educational Theory*, vol. 14, July 1964, p. 191.

Defining the Problem

theory is a compound of both normative and empirical elements and must arise from a team assault on the task, incorporating the skills of philosopher, sociologist, psychologist, historian, and others.

One trend in modern philosophy may point the way, though it must be recognized that philosophy of education is not necessarily pursuing the same objectives as pure philosophy, and is not bound to take its cue slavishly from that source. However, the trend is of interest because it represents an attempt to open up a similar middle way in philosophy. We refer to Strawson's "descriptive metaphysics." Thus Strawson's book *Individuals* undertakes to establish the family of meanings for a familiar metaphysical category and explore the basic structure of language so as to arrive at a general conceptual core.[17] He avers that this is a different style of research from that of the "revisionary metaphysicians" (whom we are calling ideologists); but Burtt gives reasons for believing that ultimately no line can be drawn between the two approaches, however chastened Strawson's may appear in comparison with the nineteenth-century synoptists.[18]

Serving different purposes from "descriptive metaphysics," the present study may yet appropriate certain elements in Strawson's approach. First, there is the desire to describe the family of meanings surrounding a concept that is in wide use. Strawson's concept is located in common speech, ours in the theorizing of some influential ideologists. Hence his result is descriptive, whereas ours will contain normative elements even though the method is descriptive, because the concept under examination is normative (i.e., value-loaded). Second, Strawson seeks to define a use which he believes tallies with the essential structure of ordinary language, so that "we" will not be misled by impermanent idiomatic uses.[19] Similarly, we shall seek to discover whether competing ideologies in the

---

[17] P. F. Strawson, *Individuals: An Essay in Descriptive Metaphysics*, London: Methuen and Co., 1961, p. 10.
[18] E. A. Burtt, "Descriptive Metaphysics," *Mind*, vol. 72, Jan. 1963, p. 31.
[19] As Burtt points out, it is at this point that Strawson passes from the role of "describer" to that of "recommender."

present time concur sufficiently on "the sanctity of the individual" to provide clear guidance for educational theory, or, if they do not, why they do not. In both cases clearer thinking and communication are the goal.

There, however, comparisons cease. Strawson is a trailblazer in his field and may safely reason in the first person. Ours is the humbler task of investigating and comparing the insights of other pioneers in modern thought, men whose impact has been, in most cases, of such magnitude as to influence assumptions and research orientations in such diverse fields as psychology, history, economics, biology, and even educational theory.

For our purposes, then, it seems best to work backwards from educational theory rather than forwards from an ideology, by taking some concept or slogan relevant to educational objectives and seeing what part it plays in current ideologies. One can then come forward again and see if a working agreement is (*a*) possible between contending theorists, and (*b*) useful in defining goals. The answer will not only clarify uses of the concept but may have implications for the debate as to whether one unified educational theory is possible. The concept we shall study is "the sanctity of the individual."

SELECTION OF IDEOLOGISTS

Sheer abundance of material makes selection necessary, and it is proposed to confine our attention to ten contemporary thinkers. What sample would have some prospect of representing major ideological tendencies in the Western world?

The present day is characterized by ideological diversity and conflict. Nations are opposed on grounds which are often ideological before they are political or economic. Within Western cultures there are conflicting points of view which compete for disciples not merely in academic cloisters but in the marketplace; scientific humanism crosses swords with liberal humanism, and both pour scorn on resurgent Christian viewpoints. A doctrine of moral aloofness and alleged neutrality produces in many academic institutions "a peculiar

Defining the Problem

malaise and impotence . . . a lack of any clear, agreed sense of purpose."[20] Many observers do not hesitate to speak of the present day therefore as one of cultural crisis, whatever reasons they compound to account for it.

If this is so, at what point did the fragmentation which characterizes contemporary life come to the surface? The turning point, in our view, was the mid-nineteenth century. In philosophy there was Hegel; in science Darwin and Spencer; in education, Rousseau's Teutonic admirers, Pestalozzi, Froebel, and Herbart. At the beginning of the nineteenth century Europe and America were member cultures of "Christendom": homogeneous in standards of public morality, latitudinarian in religious sentiment, and largely oblivious to both social distress and scientific advance. By the end of the century, social change and schism were fairly launched, technology and democracy had come in with a rush, the Establishments episcopal and aristocratic were objects of contempt, and a naive Englightenment optimism concerning the progress of mankind was marching full tilt into the catastrophe of a fiendishly well-equipped war which would complete the demolition of widely held world-views.

It is not only because our interest is mainly philosophical that Hegel is the appropriate figure to single out in the prologue. In him were past and future. On the one hand he represents the culmination of speculative metaphysics and formal Christendom,[21] the last great attempt at a rational synthesis of a Christianized culture. Yet he scattered the seeds of many modern ideological developments in his dialectical methodology; Marxism found in it the logic of history, Pragmatism the reality-category of "becoming," and liberal humanisms the omnipotence of objective reason.

It is not only for his congeniality to modern thought that Hegel is notable, but even more for the hostile reactions he

[20] Sir Walter Moberly, *The Crisis in the University*, London: SCM Press, 1949, p. 21.
[21] Thus Karl Löwith, *From Hegel to Nietzsche: The Revolution in Nineteenth-Century Thought*, trans. David E. Green, London: Constable, 1964, pp. 49ff. "Hegel is the last Christian philosopher before the break between philosophy and Christianity."

sparked off. Marx and Dewey substituted Naturalism for his Idealism, Kierkegaard and Nietzsche rebelled against his devotion to universal reason, and Moore and Russell rejected his metaphysical speculation. However, because the grounds of hostility were different in each case, there was no rapprochement of the rebels, no cultural resynthesis. Since Hegel there has arisen no prophet with even a meager majority in the Western world,[22] and diversity and conflict are the hues of contemporary thought.

The choice of thinkers is therefore post-Hegel. From the nineteenth century are drawn three who may be described as prodigal sons of Hegel because they reflect his intellectual paternity while rejecting major elements of his system. Kierkegaard becomes the father of modern Existentialism as he reacts against Hegelian rationalism. Marx turns Hegelian Idealism upside down to create the ideology of Dialectical Materialism. Nietzsche replaces cool universal reason with passionate will-to-power, thereby offering a rationale to those who in the next century promoted super-race ideologies.

To represent the present century, we seek a balance of scientific and religious ideologists, four of the first and three of the second. This also provides a counterpoint of absolutist and relativist theories of value, though it would be a mistake to make an easy equation of absolutism with religion and relativism with science. A debate between social scientists in Britain is first examined, involving Sir Percy Nunn and Karl Mannheim. The veneration of Nunn is largely a British phenomenon, and he is perhaps relatively lightweight compared to others in our sample. But he is a valuable foil to the views of Mannheim, which find on the whole a more sympathetic audience in America. Then follows a comparison of John Dewey and A. N. Whitehead. Dewey's eminence is assured both in philosophy and education, while Whitehead's star is rising in both spheres also; and a contrast is made especially interesting by the different concepts each has of the

---

[22] Unless we bestow the mantle on Marx, who has recruited his "majority" from Asia, where already revisionism and nationalism are creating divergent sects.

Defining the Problem

scientific method to which his allegiance is strong. On the philosophicoreligious front, two Continental philosophers — the German Jew Martin Buber and the French Catholic Jacques Maritain — and American Lutheran theologian Reinhold Niebuhr have been chosen.

The sample also exhibits the geographical diversity which appears in Western thought. The Old World speaks in the nineteenth-century thinkers and in Buber. Mannheim and Maritain illustrate transitions from European to Anglo-American cultures, the one bringing with him European social science, the other European Catholicism. Nunn and Whitehead speak for British science, though the latter migrates to America. Dewey and Niebuhr constitute diametrically opposed American viewpoints. While the sample cannot hope to be comprehensive, it is meant to be helpfully representative, and may be expected to shed light on the problem in a variety of ways.

MODE OF ENQUIRY

It remains now to set up an interpretive schema whereby we may compare systematically what each of the thinkers has to say about the concept under discussion; and here a preliminary definition is needed. What is meant by "the sanctity of the individual"?

The term "sanctity" is widely (as here) employed to signify the intrinsic worth of the individual, the respect to which he is allegedly entitled before any discussion is entered upon concerning his relation to other individuals and things, since such discussion calls for generalizations, and generalizations obscure uniqueness. Thus used, the term does not have a necessarily religious connotation, though it has been borrowed from religious discourse where it has the sense of something "set apart" or having special worth. It is a matter of common observation that most men pay lip service to the sanctity of human life, the rights of man, the integrity of the individual, and so forth. The problem is to know whence this intrinsic value derives.

Hence "individual" requires to be defined, and immediately we are in the midst of the problem. Strawson has shown how concepts like "individual" and "person" are primary particulars in human discourse, but this does not help materially to solve the normative problem. For example, if "individual" is simply taken to mean an entity which occupies different space, or a different body from other individuals, does this imply any sanction, even pragmatic, of his right to autonomy of any kind? And what then of such derivative concepts as "self" and "person"? Another basis of definition is functional rather than locational. Individuality is regarded as emerging from the unique pattern of neuromuscular behavior, or from the role-concepts, that a person develops; that is, identity is established and maintained by activity. What then of the continuance of "self"-identity? And is the inactive individual or, at one remove, the contemplating individual, of less worth? Or if what an individual does is wrong or unhealthy, does he thereby forfeit intrinsic worth? A third basis of definition is essentialistic. In essence the individual is a self-conscious animal, or a rational being, or an embodied spirit. Then is a baby as much of an individual, or person, as an adult is? Which component—body, mind, spirit—is the ground of his intrinsic worth?

In general, scientists lean to functional definitions, philosophers and religious thinkers to essentialistic ones. When scientists turn philosopher, as with Whitehead, or philosophers go scientific, as with Dewey, complexity increases. In short, it would be a prejudgment of the outcome of this study to attempt to define "individual" at any length now; for it emerges that we are dealing with a metaphysical concept, and any such attempt will reflect suppositions about reality and humanness which it is our duty to explore, not assume. Therefore, for the sake of arriving at a starting point we appeal to primitive common use and define "individual" as simply "a human being." Note that although "person" is often used as synonymous with "individual" in common speech, we shall not so use it, because it is also commonly employed in several more sophisticated ways, as well as having specialized conno-

Defining the Problem

tations for ideologists.[23] "Personality" and "self" are also loaded words which derive their meanings from the thought systems to be studied, belonging *in* context rather than *defining* the context.

The method of enquiry will be as follows. In each of several parts, two or three thinkers will be dealt with, among whom internal comparisons are especially fruitful. Each writer is introduced by a comment on his life and times and general ideological views. His attitude to "the sanctity of the individual" will then be investigated through the posing of a standard set of questions:

On defining "individual":
What distinguishes the individual from nonhuman entities? And from other individuals?

On the sanctity of the individual:
On what normative grounds is respect for the sanctity of the individual commended?

On society and the individual:
How is society defined in relation to the individual? Does this preserve the sanctity of the individual?

For each group of thinkers, following the chapters treating them separately, a comparative evaluation will be offered, summing up what each believes to be the nature of the theoretical vocabulary required to talk about the individual. With the twentieth-century thinkers this will include a résumé of the explicit contributions each has made to educational theory, the intention being not to discuss all their educational doctrines but only those which relate directly to concern for the individual.

Part Six seeks to draw on the earlier material to move towards the goal of more adequate statement of educational theory in the light of the sanctity of the individual.

---

[23] Allport distinguishes fifty variant meanings attached to the word, in *Personality*, p. 48.

PART TWO:

Prodigal Sons of Hegel

*I*n Part Two, three nineteenth-century thinkers are singled out: Kierkegaard, Nietzsche, and Marx. After chapters dealing in turn with each man, a further chapter essays a comparative analysis.

SØREN KIERKEGAARD

1813-1855

Biographers usually find it necessary to apologize for the uneventfulness of Kierkegaard's life in its outward aspect, as though a great man must needs be credited with great deeds as well as great thoughts. Yet it is precisely Kierkegaard's scorn for homage paid to "world-historical figures" (external and objective)[1] and his insistence on the transcendent importance of the inwardly existing subject that make his personal biography so fitting.[2]

He was born in Copenhagen, the intellectual center of Scandinavia at the time, to a prosperous but melancholy merchant with a guilt complex aggravated by an austere brand of Lutheranism. As Søren commenced his university studies, four deaths in the family increased the introspective tendencies of the surviving members and produced in Søren a reaction against religion which made him one of the most frivolous and critical students on the campus. However, his mind was

---

[1] For example in his commendation of Lessing because "he did not permit himself to be deceived into becoming world-historic and systematic." See *Concluding Unscientific Postscript to the Philosophical Fragments*, trans. David F. Swenson and Walter Lowrie, London: Oxford University Press, 1945, p. 61.

[2] This summary is derived from details given by three distinguished disciples and translators, in: Dru's introduction to *The Journals of Søren Kierkegaard: a Selection*, London: Fontana, 1958; Walter Lowrie, *Kierkegaard*, New York: Harper and Bros., 2 vols., 1962; and David F. Swenson, *Something About Kierkegaard*, Minneapolis: Augsburg Publishing House, rev. ed., 1956, chaps. 1–3.

reacting keenly to his studies, which were dominated by Hegelianism, and already his originality was becoming apparent. Constant procrastination held up the theological studies his father wanted him to pursue until a rapprochement with his father signified a resolution of conflict in his thinking which was climaxed by a personal religious conversion a week later.[3] Some months after this, his father died and Kierkegaard was spurred on to complete his studies. Just after the presentation of a thesis on "Socratic Irony," he became engaged to be married; but the singularity of his family and personality led him to break the association in 1841 and thereafter to plunge into an amazingly productive writing schedule.

With extraordinary dexterity he used many literary forms to promote his views. In 1845 a fashionable scandal paper, *The Corsair*, lampooned him and added to his scorn for "society." The abortive revolutions of 1848 outside Denmark seemed to him to be reversals of the Reformation. In later years he began to attack formal Christianity and became involved in acrimonious controversy which emptied his purse and broke his health. He collapsed in a Copenhagen street and died in hospital at the age of forty-two.

While biographical details help to account for a man's initial interest in a subject, and may even clarify the import of some of the views he expresses (and they do both in the case of Kierkegaard), they do not suffice to explain the durability of his ideas or the force of his logic. To be sure, the times produce the man; but the man may well give new direction to the times. Kierkegaard was interred in Denmark both literally and philosophically until the ideological collapse of France, Germany, and Italy, after the First World War brought into the open the disintegrative tendencies Kierkegaard had foreseen. It took a like catastrophe in Britain, which had been less affected by the First World War but reeled under the Depression of the thirties and the Second World War, to make Kierkegaard a talking point there; and he is still something of an intellectual pariah in secular American circles, though recent anxieties associated with international unrest and social con-

---

[3] See his account in *The Journals*, entry for 19 May 1838.

formism have paved the way even there for more serious consideration of his views.

His two great foes in Danish life and thought were Hegelianism and the soured formalism of the state church in Denmark. In the first he saw the danger of objective thought overreaching itself and dehumanizing man, and his remedy was to focus emphasis on inward existence, the subjective being of the individual. In the second he detected the sham of external observance coupled with inward disinterest, and again stressed inwardness by describing religious faith as a personal leap into the unknown as opposed to the taking up of a rational position. When Danish society pilloried him (despite the fact that many privately agreed with his criticisms), he saw the individual being betrayed by the crowd. In opposition to all these trends, he defended in life and works the supreme significance of the individual. He coined the term "existential"[4] to characterize that emphasis, and gave new meaning to the word "exist" and all its derivatives.

Of no other thinker in our selection is it so necessary to be cognizant of the whole body of writing as with Kierkegaard. Every work belongs in the mosaic which he must have had in mind at the commencement of his published output. The pseudonymous works, which are most widely known, must be put alongside his religious discourses, and the developmental plan on which they are all founded must be taken into account. Not all commentators appear to honor these obligations. We assume that no one major work represents the whole Kierkegaardian view and therefore consult all the key works.

DEFINING "INDIVIDUAL"

Kierkegaard stands clearly in the mainstream of European thought with his assumption that the individual's primary significance resides in the operation of his consciousness, rather than in his biological or social functions. This assump-

[4] But not "existentialism." That word does not occur in any of Kierkegaard's writings, so far as I have observed, and I am supported in this by Peter Rohde, *Søren Kierkegaard: An Introduction to His Life and Philosophy*, trans. Alan Moray Williams, London: George Allen and Unwin, 1963, p. 37.

tion, shared by such diverse thinkers as Hegel, Schleiermacher, and Freud, continues to characterize much European thinking in what is often termed its "existential psychology" or "philosophical anthropology." It is frequently claimed that one of Kierkegaard's achievements is to have formulated an introspective depth psychology capable of providing significant insights neglected by positivistic psychologies which presuppose that mental life is a peripheral phenomenon.[5] To those who superficially dismiss Kierkegaard's psychology as disguised theology, Rohde replies that it makes a genuine contribution to psychology *per se*, because of the way in which it makes the "individual" the focus of concern, averting that loss of his uniqueness which occurs when behaviorist sciences concede no basic difference between human beings and animals.

Definitions of "individual" are therefore readily obtainable in his writings. Primarily, an individual is an "existing," knowing "spirit" or "self." Man is differentiated from other entities because he knows that he exists; indeed he knows that he knows he exists. In a double act of reflection he outdistances other creatures by his capacity for not merely consciousness but self-consciousness. Self is a "derived, constituted relation"[6] arising from the interaction of body and spirit. Man's advantage over the beast is to be able to know the despair of being at once finite and infinite. In a formidable paragraph which, in an abridged form, may become the text for our exposition, Kierkegaard says:

> Man is spirit. But what is spirit? Spirit is self. But what is self? The self is a relation which relates itself to its own self. . . . Man is a synthesis of the infinite and the finite, of the temporal and

[5] Kaufmann less than justly compares Kierkegaard's "sundry observations" with Freud's and Nietzsche's systems (Walter Kaufmann, *The Owl and the Nightingale: From Shakespeare to Existentialism*, London: Faber and Faber, 1959, p. 169). Kierkegaard did aim at comprehensiveness, and he is coherent and consistent. More importantly, he sought to make the reader take stock of himself, and in this he succeeds admirably. This much even Kaufmann concedes.

[6] Søren Kierkegaard, *The Sickness Unto Death*, trans. Walter Lowrie, Princeton: Princeton University Press, 1941, p. 18.

the eternal, of freedom and necessity, in short it is a synthesis. A synthesis is a relation between two factors. So regarded, man is not yet a self.[7]

Kierkegaard lays himself open to the accusation that he belittles scientific endeavor by the very vehemence with which he promotes the notion of man as spirit and the concept of "existential truth," especially in his *Concluding Unscientific Postscript*. But this is not entirely just; his point is that, valuable as scientific endeavor is, the study of man has a different locus because man is spirit. One may study the biosocial entity objectively for certain purposes, but a different universe of discourse is needed to do justice to man as man.

> All honour to the pursuits of science, and all honour to everyone who assists in driving the cattle away from the sacred precincts of scholarship. But the ethical is and remains the highest task for every human being.[8]

That is, the "existing" individual's primary concern is ethico-religious truth, and his experience must be interpreted from this standpoint.

In the book that earned him immediate fame, *Either/Or*, Kierkegaard presents the contrast between a variety of postures based on an aesthetic approach to life, and the views of a practicing ethicist. It emerges that the aesthete strives to be a spectator, detached from moral involvement with or commitment to other people. He takes his pleasures as they come, but is not able to rise above an inward melancholy. As portrayed in this book the aesthete is simply a hedonist, whether by inertia or design. However, taking his writings as a whole, it is clear that Kierkegaard regards the academic researcher also as an aesthete, insofar as he concentrates on speculative *wissenschaft* to the extent of adopting a life-pose of objectivity and rational detachment. Brunner comments that:

[7] Bretall comments: "Here we have S. K., almost with tongue in cheek, expressing himself with great precision in the terminology of that Hegelianism which he hated above all else." (Robert Bretall, ed., *A Kierkegaard Anthology*, London: Oxford University Press, 1947, p. 340.)

[8] *Concluding Postscript*, p. 135.

In the main what Kierkegaard says against Hegel applies to every scientific form of existence which means every such understanding of man . . . determined by objective science. Wherever one sees himself scientifically there one doesn't see himself at all.[9]

A book published two years later, *Stages on Life's Way*, takes the analysis a step further by postulating an existence level beyond the ethical, that is, the religious. The mark of this stage is that the ethicist has come to realize the impossibility of attaining his moral ideal, and has lost his erstwhile sense of achievement in a dawning sense of estrangement and despair. *The Sickness Unto Death*, four years later, differentiates religiousness A from religiousness B. The first is a state of despair in which one realizes the continuity of one's spirit with the divine, but is shackled by the finitude of the body. The second is paradoxical and specifically Christian, because it is the despair of a sin-consciousness on which has dawned the knowledge that God is transcendentally different. At this point the psychological analysis shades over into theology. The fully enlightened despair of man can only be lifted by personal faith in, and creaturely submission to, God.

The linch-pin of Kierkegaard's analysis is the claim that all men experience a nameless despair or dread, and that therefore no psychological investigation is adequately aligned which does not employ this existential insight. He defends this thesis throughout his works but especially in *The Sickness Unto Death*. Here he begins by showing that even the mass of men, who are not conscious of despair because of the immediacy of their living, are sick, just as one may find people who think they are healthy when their physician knows they are not. However, with a

> certain degree of self-reflection begins the act of discrimination whereby the self becomes aware of itself as something essentially different from the environment, from externalities and their effect upon it.[10]

---

[9] Emil Brunner, "The Message of Søren Kierkegaard," *Neue Schweizer Rundschau*, vol. 38, 1930 (here trans. by H. Dymale).
[10] *Sickness Unto Death*, p. 86.

And then the fat is in the fire—"the more consciousness the more intense the despair." When a man probes the enigma of his existence he exposes a sense of alienation and estrangement. This is a truth fundamental for psychology and yet a truth only personally discovered; hence Kierkegaard's reiteration to the point of overstatement: "Truth is subjectivity."

Some of Kierkegaard's examples of despair and its practical effects are experiences relating to death, immortality, and marriage. Of the last he gives a most unsatisfactory account, but his comments on death are acute. We have in common with animals that we will one day die. Unlike them, we know that we will die. This is not merely objective speculation but subjective truth. "All men die" is an objective proposition, but "I will one day die" is a personal exigency. As such it imparts a new seriousness to the life we live, and it is to this dimension of consciousness that Kierkegaard seeks to call us. The influence of what Jaspers, from a psychiatric background, has termed "boundary-situations" like death, guilt, and suffering is a major component of the "existential psychologies" of the Continent, to which Kierkegaard as much as Freud may be said to have contributed.

The individual is most clearly identified not in reflection but in decision. This principle provides Kierkegaard with a new point of entry to the old but evergreen debate on determinism. He seeks to demonstrate by the employment of existential dialectic that man possesses a freedom to make choices, and that in fact it is in choosing that he lives.

The proof pivots on Kierkegaard's treatment of the logical category of "becoming." All Hegelian students were aware of this category because of Hegel's efforts to obtain a logical tool that would cope with dynamic realities for which classical deductive methods were inadequate. Hegel's answer was "dialectic"—in his special sense of a cyclic, cumulative series of "theses." Kierkegaard takes up the problem but rejects Hegel's solution. Hegel's "introduction of movement into logic," he asserts, "is a sheer confusion of logical science." [11]

---

[11] *Concluding Postscript*, p. 99. Dewey's "logic of enquiry" comes under the same existential criticism, in that it confuses the necessities of logic with the contingencies of experiment.

Thought is objective reflection, exercised on that which is now past. But existence is subjective decision exercised on that which is present now, this instant.

Hence (anticipating Sartre): existence comes before essence; "life can only be explained after it has been lived"; man is the only being aware of the "present" as a moment rather than a continuum.

> Time is infinite succession. The life which is in time and is merely that of time has no present. . . . On the other hand if time and eternity are to touch one another it must be in time — and with this we have reached the instant. . . . Only in the instant does history begin . . . and now begins spirit.[12]

This is the basis of Kierkegaard's discontent with the orientation given to research about man by Cartesianism. He first makes the logical point that when Descartes says "Cogito, ergo sum," he is not proving the primacy of thought but the primacy of existence; for *cogito* equals not "thought" but "I think." To realize this is to see the tautology in the proposition. It becomes "I am thinking, *ergo* I am; but if I *am* thinking, what wonder that I *am*."[13] Thought is subsequent to existence, and reality is located not in objective reflection but subjective decision. Far from being an intellectual embarrassment, the fact of human freedom is the key to understanding. Swenson pinpoints the radical cleavage between Kierkegaard and Descartes at this point:

> In Kierkegaard we have a thinker who completely reverses the Cartesian distribution of emphasis: he reflects where Descartes accepts and accepts where Descartes reflects. He took his point of departure in something deeper than an abstract intellectual doubt, namely, in a concrete personal despair.[14]

Consequently the truth that concerns Kierkegaard is the subjective truth of ethicoreligious decision. The discovery of

---

[12] Søren Kierkegaard, *The Concept of Dread: A Simple Psychological Deliberation Oriented in the Direction of the Dogmatic Problem of Original Sin*, trans. Walter Lowrie, London: Oxford University Press, 1946, pp. 77–80.
[13] *Concluding Postscript*, p. 281.
[14] Swenson, *Something About Kierkegaard*, p. 111.

this sort of truth is not an academic option but a necessity for the existing individual, whose self-identity is molded by his appropriation of it.

> Had not Pilate asked objectively what truth is, he would never have condemned Christ to be crucified. Had he asked subjectively, the passion of his inwardness respecting what in the decision facing him he had *in truth to do,* would have prevented him from doing wrong.[15]

At this point Kierkegaard also takes issue with his admired Socrates, on the ground that Greek intellectualism obscured the primacy of will in determining human conduct. Observing that for Socrates "sin is ignorance," he insists that, on the contrary:

> It is will, defiant will. The Greek intellectualism was too naive . . . to be able to get it sinfully into its head that a person knowingly could fail to do the good, or knowingly, with knowledge of what was right, do what was wrong.[16]

The seat of will of course is ethical decision, the moment of choice.

So much is the category of choice fundamental to the study of the individual that Descartes' suspect proposition is completely replaced by the neo-Kierkegaardian "I choose, therefore I am." [17]

Kierkegaard's expressions may be at times "verbose and repetitious," [18] but they maintain an impressive consistency of definition. This point needs to be made to protect his use of paradox, as in the statement that man is a self but not yet a self. That is, in addition to the notion of "self" spelled out above, there is a secondary sense which he does not confuse with the first.

In this sense, selfhood is something to be achieved. Human existence according to Kierkegaard, says Swenson, is both

---

[15] *Concluding Postscript,* p. 206.
[16] *Sickness Unto Death,* p. 145.
[17] The phrase is George F. Kneller's, in *Existentialism and Education,* New York: Philosophical Library, 1958, p. 67.
[18] Kaufmann, *The Owl and the Nightingale,* p. 161.

"a status and a task ... a synthesis of the temporal and the eternal which posits a process of becoming and hence involves an incessant striving."[19] It is a problem of *becoming* who we *are*. This is not to say that Kierkegaard ignores completely the influence of natural and social factors, though he does provide eager disciples with some grounds for doing so. He concedes that "every individual begins in a historical nexus, and the consequences of natural law are still as valid as ever," [20] but he insists also that

> the choice itself is decisive for the content of the personality, through the choice the personality immerses itself in the thing chosen, and when it does not choose it withers away in consumption.[21]

Self-development occurs least in those who live at a level of immediacy, lacking even the reflectiveness of the aesthete and willingly borne along by the crowd. Next on the scale is the aesthete, whether hedonist or Hegelian. For even the Hegelian is betrayed by the effort he makes to objectify his subjective experience in some description of "world-soul." He contributes to the leveling process in society as effectively as the public press, both of them working against respect for the individual. The enhancement of "inwardness" is to be coveted, rising through the ethical insight to the religious, facing the dread of existing at a fully conscious level, taking responsibility for one's own decisions, and finding full bloom in faith in God. "An existing individual is constantly in process of becoming." [22] In the words of Heinemann:

> The mere fact that we are born as men does not imply that we are human. On the contrary, it lulls us into pretence. We are in constant danger of becoming inhuman. . . . To be human is not a fact, but a task.[23]

---

[19] Swenson, *Something About Kierkegaard*, p. 129.
[20] *Concept of Dread*, p. 65.
[21] *Either/Or*, quoted in Bretall, *A Kierkegaard Anthology*, p. 102.
[22] *Concluding Postscript*, p. 79.
[23] F. H. Heinemann, *Existentialism and the Modern Predicament*, London: Adam and Charles Black, 1953, p. 39.

SANCTITY OF THE INDIVIDUAL

It will be apparent from the foregoing that Kierkegaard's point of view is shot through with a belief in the sanctity of the individual. No lip service this; it is the keystone of his edifice. However, if communication is to take place we must look for something more than passionate personal preference or inspired dogmatism. Does Kierkegaard offer philosophical justifications for the assertions he makes? Does he provide normative grounds for the sanctity of the individual which are of a kind to carry weight with the uncommitted as well as those in sympathy with his Protestant theology?

The first point that needs making is that his existential dialectic is a philosophical weapon wielded against Hegelian dialectic. Whereas Hegel is in search of a mediating principle that will resolve antinomies and incorporate them in the neat web of reason, Kierkegaard elevates paradox, particularly the paradox that logic and life, thought and being, are opposites which the individual can only reconcile in the act of existing.

> If a man occupied himself, all his life through, solely with logic, he would nevertheless not become logic; he must therefore himself exist in different categories.[24]

If dialectic is philosophical discourse, then Kierkegaard is here offering a new mode of discourse in direct opposition to the logicoscientific mode then held in such high esteem, and by implication equally opposed to the analyticopositive mode of present-day British philosophy. If it is a genuine mode of discourse it may be expected to shed new light on the traditional concerns of philosophy, particularly those related to man's being and knowing.[25]

[24] *Concluding Postscript*, p. 86.
[25] Roubiczek insists on this by describing the respective spheres of "objective method" and "subjective method," claiming that Kierkegaard has developed the latter consistently and with adequate reliability criteria. He stresses that critics evade the cogency of Kierkegaard's case by using "subjective" only in the sense it sometimes has of "biased" or "prejudiced," or to connote "wishful thinking." See Paul Roubiczek, *Existentialism: For and Against*, Cambridge: Cambridge University Press, 1964, especially chap. 6.

Consider the metaphysical problem of the relation of the individual to reality. Kierkegaard insists that for the existing individual the particular takes precedence over the universal. His own subjective existence is the fundamental datum; all else is derivative. Hence the value of the individual is primary to himself, though the reason why he should respect another's autonomy is not yet apparent.

For the further step there must be an existential recognition of the God-man axis. Kierkegaard offers no proof in the systematic sense for the existence of God—indeed, says Swenson, he brands the attempt blasphemy:

> as if one were to assume to demonstrate, in the presence of someone, that he exists; for existence is higher than demonstration, and requires a more adequate form of acknowledgement.[26]

But one may discover a form of existential induction in Kierkegaard which enhances the probability of God's existence. This is found in those analyses, mentioned above, in which Kierkegaard establishes the infinitude of the human spirit and the experience of dread. When an individual obtains the maximum level of self-awareness (Religiousness B), he is brought to recognize the root of his despair in estrangement from God,[27] and he may then take the qualitative leap of faith which for him clinches the reality of God—but for him only; truth is subjectivity.

Once the existing individual has come into right relationship with God, normative problems fall into place. The existential value I place on myself is derived from God, from whom all other individuals are likewise derived. Man exists not in scientific categories but in ethicoreligious categories; therefore, when he begins to live true to himself, he will "acknowledge the given independence in every man, and after the measure of his ability do all that can in truth be done to help someone preserve it." [28]

[26] Swenson, *Something About Kierkegaard*, p. 155.
[27] "Hence this deliberation ends where it began. So soon as psychology has finished with dread, it has nothing to do but to deliver it over to dogmatics." (*Concept of Dread*, p. 145.)
[28] *Concluding Postscript*, p. 232.

Søren Kierkegaard

In his introduction to *The Concept of Dread,* Kierkegaard calls for a new science of ethics, since the old relied on intellectual ideas, which in themselves were powerless. His will start with reality rather than ideality, enlisting the will by demonstrating the dialectical relation of faith and despair. One may say that Kierkegaard sees no safeguard for individuality in those who are victims of despair, for even their self-valuation is being corroded by defiance or death-wish. Only in the faithful will perspective and moral power arise.

It is for this reason that Kierkegaard is easily misjudged, even by so partial a critic as Martin Buber, because little evidence of a social ethic appears in his best-known writings, the pseudonymous works. The pseudonyms indicate that he is representing a spectrum of viewpoints which fall short of completeness. It is in his religious works that he proceeds to develop ethical and social themes, most especially in his *Works of Love,* built around the gospel injunction: "You shall love your neighbour as yourself."

There would seem to be some reason for terming this a new approach to ethics, in contrast to the ostensibly new approach of Analysis. Heinemann suggests that the latter has taken the Cartesian mode to its limit and obtained a nil result. He asks:

> Is the analysis of ethical statements really the only function of a moral philosopher? Is it not more important to clarify the condition of man, to reveal the danger in which the persons find themselves, to appeal to them to make their own decision and to discuss the criteria on which the rightness of an action is based? [29]

It transpires, therefore, that the source of one's knowledge of values is one's own spirit. Kierkegaard writes not to construct a neat bundle of knowledge, objectively stated and verified, but to awaken the subjective truth in individuals.

---

[29] Heinemann, *Existentialism and the Modern Predicament,* p. 171. He is having his cake and eating it as well, surely. The discussion of criteria, which he mentions last, is precisely the point at which the Analyst's contribution is most needed. Indeed Thomas asserts that Heinemann's point is anachronistic, and adds that Kierkegaard is in effect doing a job of profound analysis, albeit in a realm of experience eschewed by many modern Analysts. See J. Heywood Thomas, *Subjectivity and Paradox,* Oxford: Basil Blackwell, 1957, pp. 135f.

He claims to imitate Socrates' maieutic method, with the intention of provoking the reader to look at himself, to become personally involved in the investigation; and in this even Kaufmann concedes that he is successful. Swenson suggests that there is considerable justification for Kierkegaard's self-comparisons with Socrates, because in his own era he fulfilled an ethical task analogous to that which Socrates fulfilled in Greece.

In sum, then, Kierkegaard rejects attempts to justify by rational systematization our obligation to respect the individual. Nevertheless he is thinking philosophically in the way he discusses the issue, seeking to show that his existential dialectic copes with the metaphysical and epistemological aspects of the problem as well as the normative. Existentially, he feels he can offer an incentive to the reader to recognize and develop his own self-respect. He believes, however, that both this task and the task of having respect for other selves as individuals await for their fulfillment the emergence in the individual of the Christian response to existence. In this author's view his position coheres philosophically, rather than being shored up by imported theological dogmas. He speaks as a Christian, but he gives existential grounds for the faith that is in him. His case still remains to be tested in philosophical debate, but it may not be summarily dismissed as "mere" theology.

SOCIETY AND THE INDIVIDUAL

While his profoundly introspective nature equipped Kierkegaard admirably to investigate the unique individual, it worked against an equally searching analysis of society and social relationships. He was by no means unskilled in social encounter, having been an active leader in student life at university, a swift and successful suitor, and a "man about town" in the early years of his literary output. His *Either/Or* portrayed social behavior with a skill that won acclaim, and he constantly sought the company of ordinary people as a stabilizer for his reflections and discourses. Yet the prophet of involvement was essentially a solitary man, aloof from his fellows, playing a part in company designed to hide his true feelings. Consequently, while his negative strictures against society are pungently realistic, his positive recommendations tend only to be insightful abstractions.

Kierkegaard's encounters with the press and public opinion gave point to his antipathy to formal religion and philosophical fashion. He asserted without qualification that identification with the crowd invariably rots one's personal identity.

> Wherever there is a crowd there is untruth, so that (to consider for a moment the extreme case), even if every individual, each for himself in private, were to be in possession of the truth, yet in case they were all to get together in a crowd ... a voting, noisy, audible crowd—untruth would at once be in evidence.[30]

There is undoubtedly ground here on which to fight the contemporary giants of mass culture, conformism, and group-oriented social science.

The root of Kierkegaard's interpretation of his age was its attitude to organized religion. He regarded it as doubly damned. On the one hand, the cultural revolution called the Enlightenment had secularized European tradition; on the other, the church had failed to represent the Christian gospel with sacrificial integrity. The result was an age without conviction in which personal relationships and commitments were evaded.

> The abstract levelling process, that self-combustion of the human race, produced by the friction which arises when the individual ceases to exist as singled out by religion is bound to continue, like a trade wind, and consume everything.[31]

His remedy was to promote an understanding of true Christianity so that individual Christians might once again become the humanizers of society.

[30] *The Point of View for My Work as an Author* ..., trans. Walter Lowrie, London: Oxford University Press, 1939, p. 112.
[31] *The Present Age and Of the Difference Between a Genius and an Apostle*, trans. Alexander Dru, London: Fontana, 1962, p. 61.

However, one looks in vain for any substantive appraisal of social organizations that might supply a positive antidote on a wider plane. Bretall says truly that

> It can hardly be maintained that Kierkegaard's sympathies were democratic. . . . He remained an "unpolitic man" to the end of his life, in the sense that the value of individuality was for him supreme and could neither be enhanced, nor on the other hand impaired, by any change of social organisation.[32]

And Swenson quotes him as saying in a letter: "I have never concerned myself with Church and State, these things are too high for me." [33] The political revolutions of 1848 only invited his comment insofar as they caused the devaluation of some of his investments and the conscription of his manservant.[34]

This is hardly good enough. It is myopic of Kierkegaard to neglect the questions of authority and value in social groups if he is so concerned about shielding the individual from "leveling." One must surely work outwards as well as inwards. The work that apparently does this is *Works of Love;* but even here the emphasis is on the individual realizing the Biblical love ideal in his relations with others rather than on any practical programs of group action. The *Works of Love* leaves one up in the air, for example, in its commitment to an absolute love ideal. Thus Bretall observes about this book:

> We know, for example, that he was no pacifist; but his only escape from pacifism would seem to be via the dubious distinction between individual and social morality.[35]

In short, Kierkegaard's great omission is some operational definition of social interaction, having regard to his point of view. This constitutes a weakness, in that while Kierkegaard provides impressive justification for preserving the sanctity

[32] Bretall, *A Kierkegaard Anthology*, p. 259.
[33] Swenson, *Something About Kierkegaard*, p. 31.
[34] Lowrie, *Kierkegaard*, vol. 2, p. 393. Löwith points out how Kierkegaard mistakenly and naively predicted that the "catastrophe" of 1848 would turn from a political into a religious movement. Löwith, *From Hegel to Nietzsche*, p. 113.
[35] Bretall, *A Kierkegaard Anthology*, p. 283.

of the individual, he does not face squarely the need for the individual to exist in a social nexus. This is after all a reflection of Kierkegaard's personal flight from creative social involvement, and particularly from the intimacy of marriage. Perhaps it was necessary that his plea on behalf of the unique individual should be presented so starkly, so that it might later resist facile amalgamation with the doctrines of sociality so prevalent in our "century of the common man." Undoubtedly it has been partly responsible for Reinhold Niebuhr's new light on the social problems of Great Society in America.

FRIEDRICH NIETZSCHE

1844-1900

In Nietzsche we have another thinker whose intellectual leanings were fed by inwardly intense personal experiences. More intelligent and sensitive than most of his associates, and introspective to a fault, he was predisposed to that rejection of existing mankind which later criticism was to intensify. But pathology does not necessarily invalidate ideology, and we begin by sketching his biography, the better to interpret his views and to justify the selection of certain writings for detailed attention.[1]

Nietzsche was born into the family of a Lutheran pastor in Saxony. After his father's sudden death in 1849 he went with his mother and sister to live with female relatives in Naumburg. Aloof from most of his schoolmates, he acquired a classical education first in a *gymnasium* and later, on scholarship, in a famous school at Pforta. His interests were adult and cultural, even at so early an age as fourteen, at which time he wrote an autobiography referring to the three stages in the

---

[1] Biographies of Nietzsche tend to be either banally chronological or gleefully psychoanalytic. However, a helpful standard treatment is H. A. Reyburn, *et al.*, *Nietzsche: The Story of a Human Philosopher*, London: Macmillan, 1948; and Gerald Abraham, *Nietzsche*, London: Duckworth, 1933, is short and still useful. Exceptionally insightful in tracing the development of Nietzsche's ideas over the years of his life is F. A. Lea, *The Tragic Philosopher: A Study of Friedrich Nietzsche*, London: Methuen and Co. 1957. A re-evaluation which takes advantage of the latest scholarship is R. J. Hollingdale, *Nietzsche: The Man and His Philosophy*, London: Routledge and Kegan Paul, 1965.

development of his thought! In the same period he was questioning the faith of his family; and when at twenty he entered the University of Bonn to study theology, it was only out of a sense of duty. After a "wasted year" devoted to the revels of the student association he followed philologist Ritschl to Leipzig and became a keen philology student. The break with his Lutheran background was made irrevocable by his discovery of Schopenhauer's *The World as Will and Idea*, in which the "will-to-live" is made the ground of existence, and all truth, happiness, and deity are branded protective myths invoked by reason. Lea does not hesitate to call Nietzsche's reaction to this discovery a religious conversion. A brief period in the Prussian artillery ending in a fall from a horse returned him convalescent to Leipzig in time to meet Richard Wagner. In 1869, in his twenty-fifth year, as a result of some brilliant philological papers and Ritschl's warm recommendation, he was offered the chair of classical philology at Basel. There he was able to become an intimate of the Wagners, in whom he saw the epitomization of Schopenhauerian will and Greek-style genius. Richard Wagner deemed himself to be on a crusade for new criteria in art and music which would represent the energy of life and passion; and Nietzsche made the cause of Wagner his own in the first period of his mature writings.

In 1871 he published *The Birth of Tragedy from the Spirit of Music*, which was less a philological study than the employment of philological data to sustain the thesis that the proud spirit of Greek humanism needed to be revived in a Europe grown cold and egalitarian. Next, lecturing on *The Future of Our Educational Institutions* (1872), he contrasted popular and state education with Greek patterns and decried the academic cult of objectivity, using philology as an example. Culture, he affirmed, required personal engagement, not merely study. In retrospect we may appreciate Nietzsche's prescience in identifying the culpable detachment of the German universities from cultural concerns;[2] but at the time his

[2] See Fred Lilge, *The Abuse of Learning* (New York: Macmillan, 1948), where this trend is traced through to the capitulation of the universities to Nazism.

Friedrich Nietzsche 43

manner of presenting his views spelled professional doom. The hostility of philologists and other academics served only to confirm him in his stand, and the essays which then appeared (now grouped in *Thoughts Out of Season*) enlarged his criticism by maintaining that Hegelian philosophy had allied with national aspirations to produce a culture of philistines.

> I believe there has been no dangerous turning-point in the progress of German culture in this century that has not been made more dangerous by the enormous and still living influence of this Hegelian philosophy. . . . Such a point of view has accustomed the Germans to talk of a "world-process" and justify their own time as its necessary result. . . . If each success have come by a "rational necessity," and every event show the victory of logic or the "Idea," then—down on your knees quickly. . . . Look at the religion of the power of history, mark the priests of the mythology of Ideas, with their scarred knees.[3]

This comment might just as easily have come from the pen of Kierkegaard, whom Nietzsche never met or read. Meanwhile Nietzsche's attachment to Wagner was cooling because of Wagner's willingness to be lionized, as at the Bayreuth festival.

Nietzsche's health was poor at this time, revealing inner turmoil; and he convalesced in Southern Italy with Paul Ree, a young Jewish positivist. Such company was congenial, for beyond his emotional problems was an epistemological concern which was leading him into the nihilistic conviction that all truth and morality were mirages imposed upon phenomena by man to preserve his own sanity amid the flux. Later he was to say, *"Truth is that kind of error* without which a certain species of living being cannot exist."[4] An accidental meeting with Wagner revealed to Nietzsche that Wagner was turning to Christianity, and this intensified his antagonism to moral

---

[3] *Thoughts Out of Season*, ii, pp. 71-72. (All references to Nietzsche's writings are based on *The Complete Works of Friedrich Nietzsche*, ed. Oscar Levy, New York: Russell and Russell, 1964. The succession of volume titles is listed in full in the bibliography at the end of this book.)
[4] *Will to Power*, II, p. 20.

absolutes and his belief that Christianity denied the joy of life. In successive unpopular works he sought to demonstrate that philosophical absolutes were *Human, All-Too-Human* (1879), that the Christian foundation of morals must yield to *The Dawn of Day* (1881) in the light of which we realize that "life may be an experiment of the thinker—and not a duty, not a fatality, not a deceit!" If this be so, then we have been liberated by *The Joyful Wisdom* (1882) of "Life as a means to knowledge." Lea reminds us that it is incorrect to describe this phase as positivist, as some do, for Nietzsche was probing beyond positivism, and was later to say:

> In opposition to Positivism, which halts at phenomena and says, "There are only *facts* and nothing more," I would say: No, facts are precisely what is lacking, all that exists consists of *interpretations*.[5]

The improvement in Nietzsche's health in Italy, subsequent to his being pensioned by the university in 1879, accounted for a more high-spirited tone in the second and third of the above works, but his epistemological discovery had entered his soul; for Nietzsche not only thought new thoughts but, as he admonished academics and artists to do, lived them. A young Russian intellectual introduced to him at this time, Lou Salomé, testifies to his loneliness and sense of horror, and to her he confided the doubts of his adolescence, the alleviation of his first skepticism by Schopenhauer and Wagner, and the deeper skepticism he now knew. Subsequent intriguing by his jealous sister sundered him from Paul Ree and Lou Salomé; his works were ignored by academics and friends; and he began to take drugs to secure sleep. He has been called the first atheist, for at this time he not only came to believe that the concept "God" was "dead" but lived by that belief. A former associate, meeting him again, exclaimed, "It is as though he came from a country where no-one lived." [6]

The third phase was ushered in by the great prose-poem *Thus Spake Zarathustra* (1883–85) in which Nietzsche de-

---
[5] *Will to Power*, ii, p. 12.
[6] Lea, *The Tragic Philosopher*, p. 219 (originally in italics).

clared his new faith; and all subsequent works were commentaries on its themes, mostly derived from notes for the synoptic exposition of *The Will to Power*, which he never completed for publication. It was a message for the élite,[7] calling for the development of a superman who would rise *Beyond Good and Evil* (1886) to become an incarnation of the will-to-power: the Antichrist who would bring on *The Twilight of the Idols* (1888) by exposing *The Genealogy of Morals* (1887). Nietzsche came to terms with his nihilism by finding in "will-to-power" an organizing principle for all experience; he compensated for the loss of objective and long-term goals by committing himself to a doctrine of "eternal recurrence."

At last his own logic and circumstances spelt his personal doom. *Ecce Homo* (1888) was a megalomaniac autobiography; two months after its completion Nietzsche suffered a mental collapse. He was removed some months later to the care of his sister, and died eleven years later. By the time of his death his views were already attracting wide interest in Europe. The rise of Nazism in Germany led to Nietzsche's being pressed into service — as a prophet of race-superiority, anti-Semitism, and wars of aggression — by dint of selective quotation of the more intemperate utterances of his third phase. Eclipsed in the fall of Nazism, he has nevertheless in recent years been rehabilitated as a perceptive forerunner of existentialist criticism. His influence on Sartre and Heidegger in particular is indisputable, and Kaufmann claims for him a wider relevance still as the restorer of an image of "the noble man" which a post-Christian world needs to see.[8] Since such estimates derive in the main from the work of his third period, this is also the source of our analysis.

It is important not to let oneself be so bemused by Nietzsche the artist that one underrates Nietzsche the sociologist and philosopher. His writing is at all times passionate and personal, and it is sometimes fragmentary — as when, forced by ill health, he jotted down aphorisms without sustaining arguments. Furthermore, myths like the figure of Zarathustra

---

[7] Only 40 copies of *Zarathustra* were at first printed (privately).
[8] See especially Kaufmann, *The Owl and the Nightingale*, chap. 11.

and the doctrine of eternal recurrence invite hasty dismissal when in fact their real utility is to publicize Nietzsche's profound appraisals and postulates. It behooves us to pose our questions at two levels: first in relation to Nietzsche's diagnosis of current trends, and second in relation to his own corrective ideology.

DEFINING "INDIVIDUAL"

Copleston subtitles his study of Nietzsche "Philosopher of Culture" in recognition of the fact that Nietzsche's concern was with the ideological dimension of society. By temperament and certain childhood associations he was early involved with the fine arts, and classical studies steeped him in the Greek culture. Such training, coupled with his antipathy to the feminized Lutheran respectability of his home, sharpened the critical gaze he turned on contemporary European culture. Fundamentally what he discerned was the absorption of the individual identity in the "herd." What he sought was opportunity for superior individuals to be free of the constrictions of herd morality.

It was Nietzsche's contention that false estimates of the nature of man had given rise to a situation in which there was nothing to admire in man — to a culture that was despicably smug and nondescript.

> What produces today our repulsion towards "man"? — for we *suffer* from "man," there is no doubt about it. It is not fear; it is rather that we have nothing more to fear from men; it is that the worm "man" is in the foreground and pullulates.[9]

What had brought this about? The answer was Christianity and its offspring, European philosophy and European science. Christianity had sprung from Judaism, which had opposed to the more natural and sensual cultures of Greece and Rome a view of moral man which inverted the true state of affairs. It had successfully taught that man was a "soul" whose goal

[9] *The Genealogy of Morals*, p. 43.

was happiness and peace, obtainable by self-abnegation and the promotion of the ascetic ideal. It had erected a moral absolutism sanctioned by an unanswerable God to lay the blight of "sin" on all man's natural pleasures and ambitions. "We modern men," lamented Nietzsche, "inherit the immemorial tradition of vivisecting the conscience, and practising cruelty to our animal selves." [10]

Consequently philosophy, even when with Kant it threw off Christian dogma, inherited the habit of stressing the conscious life of man and elevating reason far above the lowly function which it in fact performs. Presupposing a soul operating in a transcendental realm, philosophers spoke of freedom of will and moral absolutes, ignoring the instinctive and physiological nature of man. The result was a false psychology of man which, stressing as it did the authority of external criteria, subjugated his true individuality. The end result of such views was totality-embracing Hegelianism with its exaltation of the state.

A further sin of philosophy was its detachment from life. Nietzsche himself could not experience a shift in thought without a change in life; and he saw in the solemn speculations of the philosophers only posturing, with no intent to practice what they preached should it be inimical to present mores. Zarathustra's diatribe against "scholars" included this:

> I am too hot and scorched with my own thought: often it is ready to take away my breath. Then have I to go into the open air, and away from all dusty rooms. But they sit in the cool shade: they want in everything to be merely spectators.[11]

The result was paralysis of the will and a culture of philistines.

Out of the embers of dying philosophy was rising positivistic science, "the declaration of independence of the scientific man." But emancipation from the unbridled transcendental speculation of the philosopher had not rescued the scientist from that other scourge, the loss of spiritual nerve.

[10] *Ibid.*, p. 115.
[11] *Thus Spake Zarathustra*, p. 149.

> The objective man, who no longer curses and scolds like the pessimist, the *ideal* man of learning in whom the scientific instinct blossoms forth fully after a thousand complete and partial failures, is assuredly one of the most costly instruments that exist, but his place is in the hands of one who is more powerful. He is only an instrument; we may say, he is a *mirror*—he is no "purpose in himself." The objective man is in truth a mirror: accustomed to prostration before everything that wants to be known, with such desires only as knowing or "reflecting" imply.[12]

In short, all the authorities of contemporary society were wrong in their estimate of man and, despite the praise they lavished upon him, were engaged in depriving him of his true stature and remodeling him into a characterless uniformity within a system—be it theological, philosophical, or scientific.

Convinced, especially by his admiration for genius, that there must be some other premise that did justice to the individual, Nietzsche obtained clues from the Greeks and Schopenhauer. In Greek culture he discerned a parallelism between terms like "good" and "bad" and a man's social position, which led him to reject the Judaeo-Christian account of morality. In Schopenhauer he found a nonmoral principle of value in the will as opposed to the mind. To these clues he applied his personal determination not to believe in God, and produced a naturalistic account of the nature of man which aims to reinstate the individual.

Man is continuous with the whole evolving cosmos. His emergence from animality was signalized by the beginning of consciousness, but he took a false (though developmentally necessary) turning in imputing more importance to consciousness than was warranted. Especially did he err in objectifying it as "soul." There is no soul atom.

> The greater part of conscious thinking must be counted amongst the instinctive functions. . . . Behind all logic . . . there are . . . physiological demands.[13]

---

[12] *Beyond Good and Evil*, p. 140. These sentiments find perhaps a more sympathetic audience since Hiroshima.
[13] *Ibid.*, p. 8.

Friedrich Nietzsche

Self dwells within the body, indeed *is* the body. Spirit and ego are its toys. The activity of an individual owes very little to his conscious intellect. How little we really know about what precedes an action; "How fantastic our feeling, 'free will' and 'cause and effect' are."[14] Nietzsche anticipates the Freudian exploration of the subconscious, but adopts as his base concept not sexuality but will-to-power.

Commentators tend to discuss the slogan "will-to-power" without sufficient regard to context. It is for Nietzsche not merely an expression relating to conscious willing or to social power but the keystone of his whole world-view. Metaphysically he locates reality not in ideas or "facts," but in will-to-power, which has come to consciousness — albeit partial — in man.

> The world seen from within, the world defined and designated according to its "intelligible character" — it would simply be "Will to Power," and nothing else.[15]

> Man is an assemblage of atoms absolutely dependent, in his movements, on all the forces of the universe, their distribution and their modifications — and yet unpredictable like every atom, a being in itself.[16]

Furthermore, because consciousness is "a newcomer among the organs," man must himself be in a transitional state. "Man is a rope stretched between the animal and the Superman."[17] His species is not fixed, and man as we know him is something that must be surpassed.

That which animates man is not the will-to-truth hypothesized by priest, philosopher, and scientist, and not the will-to-live of Schopenhauer and Darwin,[18] but the driving force

---

[14] *Will to Power,* ii, p. 149.
[15] *Beyond Good and Evil,* p. 52. Lea comments: "Nietzsche's theory marks a complete break with both Idealism and Materialism. . . . In the beginning was the event. Nietzsche's theory excludes from the outset the Cartesian 'substance' in both its forms, mind and body — and there with the Cartesian dualism." (Lea, *The Tragic Philosopher,* p. 259.)
[16] Quoted by Lea (p. 265) from an unavailable translation.
[17] *Thus Spake Zarathustra,* p. 9.
[18] See his detailed criticism of Darwinism in *Will to Power,* ii, pp. 126ff.

to subdue and rule. We do not merely will to live, for existence is a given; it is how we realize our existence that matters.

It now becomes possible to locate the individual's place in Nietzsche's thought. In contrast to Darwin's thesis that the evolutionary trend is towards the general elevation of a species, Nietzschean evolution assumes that it is towards the production of distinctive specimens. Nietzsche draws support for this view from history, which

> pays tribute to *outstanding individuals*—warriors, statesmen, saints, artists, and philosophers—who have raised themselves above the crowd and transcended the limits of average human nature.[19]

His symbol for the individual thus regarded is the Superman, whom Zarathustra awaits in the last section of the book, scornful of the "higher men" of his own time who were too weak to hold steadfastly to their hope of his coming. It is not appropriate to impute individuality to the herd, whose value is determined "simply and exclusively by their material usefulness to the *élite*." [20] To the extent that the will-to-power obtains self-expression in a human being, to that degree is he an individual. In moral terms he may be greatly creative or greatly destructive, but in Nietzsche's scale of values, if he contributes to defining the as yet unrealized species of higher man, he will be an individual worthy of honor.

Modern culture is submerging the individual despite the apparent respect accorded him, says Nietzsche, because it sets out to define him from false premises. His main attribute should be defined not as soul or reason (as by Christianity, Hegelianism, and science) but as will-to-power. Setting out afresh from this new premise, we discover the definition which makes of the individual an incarnation or articulation of that driving force which animates and is the cosmos. On this definition man is a living body possessing a little consciousness of its existence, and the term "individual" is best re-

---

[19] Paraphrase, in James Collins, *A History of Modern European Philosophy*, Milwaukee: Bruce Publishing Co., 1956, p. 779.
[20] *Will to Power*, ii, p. 312.

served for those few who attain an eminence in human affairs which is not to be accounted for in rational or moral terms.

SANCTITY OF THE INDIVIDUAL

Nietzsche speaks, as we have seen, of the "individual" as opposed to the "herd." In these terms there would appear to be two ways of protecting the autonomy of the individual. One is to guarantee equal rights for all—the egalitarian solution. The other would be to elevate the worthiest and thereby limit the privileges of individualism to the few—the aristocratic solution. It is apparent that Nietzsche, in his biocultural analogy, preaches the second and deplores the first.

Surveying the democratic liberalisms of his day, Nietzsche observed: "The two traits which characterise the modern European are apparently antagonistic—*individualism and the demand for equal rights.*"[21] He accused the sociologists of naiveté in supposing that "the growing autonomy of the individual" was being fostered by socialistic policy. On the contrary: "The individual grew strong under quite opposite conditions: ye describe the extremest weakening and impoverishment of man."[22] He credited socialists with desiring a society with the "means of making many individuals possible," but pointed out that in this the socialists were obeying an instinct of which they were not fully conscious, since individualism is a first stage towards the open expression of the will-to-power. However, should they realize this and counter with an altruistic frame of reference accenting service to others, they would then be reverting to the defense of the herd.[23] Their logical dilemma then is that they must either eventually disavow democracy and become Nietzschean, or resubmit to the pernicious Christian morality from which they supposed themselves to be breaking free.

[21] *Will to Power*, ii, p. 225.
[22] *Ibid.*
[23] Of the English utilitarians he says elsewhere that they were "ponderous, conscience-stricken herding-animals (who undertake to advocate the cause of egoism as conducive to the general welfare)" (*Beyond Good and Evil*, p. 115).

The great foe of true individualism in Nietzsche's eyes was Christianity. It had taken hold of mankind with an inversion of values that resulted in a subtle and sustained campaign against the truly noble man. It had invented morality. Nietzsche in his third phase embarked on a natural history of morals which claimed that the reward-punishment connotation of words like "good" and "bad" was an invention of the Jews,[24] skillfully designed to undermine the authority of their oppressors.[25] Primitive society had been "pre-moral," in that social behavior was subject to the balance of power, which usually resulted in societies with a power élite ruling over a subject class. Within the power élite, gradations of rank depended again on the proportionate power of individuals. "Good" and "bad" were originally related to class. That is:

> "aristocrat" "noble" (in the social sense) is the root idea, out of which have necessarily developed "good" in the sense of "with aristocratic soul" . . . parallel with that other evolution by which "vulgar," "plebian," "low" are made to change finally into "bad." [26]

Judaism, which in Christianity overcame Europe, was the revolt of the masses, accomplished by bestowing on such attitudes as submission, love to one's neighbor, and hope of reward in the hereafter the moral mantle "good" (thereby espousing qualities exactly the opposite of "good" in the master-morality), and by the priestly invention of the category "evil" with which to wreak vengeance on the masters. As part of the shrewd inversion a new power élite of "saints" was born, obtaining scope for their will-to-power through the promotion

---

[24] It is important to reiterate that Nietzsche was not an anti-Semite, and whilst hard things are said about Jews in his writings, so are they about other groups, while many tributes are paid both to individual Jews and to the race. See also Hollingdale, *Nietzsche*, p. 211.

[25] Collins comments: "Nietzsche states explicitly that a discussion of the *origins* of moral beliefs is different from a critical evaluation of their *validity*. But, in practice, he overrules this distinction and thus commits the 'genetic fallacy' of deciding the worth of a moral principle in function of a psychological guess about its genesis." (Collins, *History of Modern European Philosophy*, p. 792.)

[26] *Genealogy of Morals*, p. 22.

Friedrich Nietzsche 53

of the ascetic ideal. The resentment at the heart of this slave morality was epitomized in the "far-seeing revenge" labeled Christian love. God was then created by man to provide the sanction for these moral imperatives and the guarantee of ultimate redress of wrongs.

This middle phase in the development of values had led to the contemporary malaise, because the ascetic ideal was basically self-denying and will-decaying. Now requisite was a transvaluation by which the moral basis for value judgments would be rendered obsolete. Slave morality robs man of dignity:

> Like the father,[27] so also do the teacher, the class, the priest, and the prince still see in every new individual an unobjectionable opportunity for a new possession.[28]

The Renaissance had been a sophisticated rediscovery of the master-morality, but Judaea had counterattacked with the Reformation. Christianity made the herd comfortable at the expense of those with true individuality. Modern society possessed no noblemen — even kings felt they must placate the herd.

For Nietzsche the remedy was to set up the conditions that would give the Superman opportunity to emerge. Nietzsche could hardly have had any great confidence in the inevitability of this emergence, for his philosophy denies purpose in the cosmos, or direction in evolution, or any future goal beyond the austere notion of eternal recurrence. On his view, the age could just as easily produce the Last Man as the Superman, for the Voluntary Beggar from Judaea had done his work well. Indeed, as his friends dropped away from him and his alienation increased, Nietzsche became more the revolutionary than the prophet, writing only, in his last works, for initiates, and counseling drastic measures.

His declared motive in writing is to awaken the higher men

---

[27] Or mother? Löwith quotes studies showing Nietzsche's mother's influence on his later attitude towards Christianity, in Löwith, *From Hegel to Nietzsche*, p. 369.
[28] *Beyond Good and Evil*, p. 117.

now living to the philistinism and decadence of society, and to re-establish the aristocratic approach to value which is beyond the moral categories of good and evil. He professes no desire to interfere with the morality of the masses, for it is a good bulwark against trouble from them (one is reminded of Marx's reference to religion as the "opium of the masses"). His appeal is to those who should have resisted the seduction of slave morality because they are biologically of a better breed. He challenges them to come out and be separate. For them there shall be new tables, new commandments that emphasize the hard virtues. *"Be not considerate of thy neighbour!* Man is something that must be surpassed,"[29] he tells them. This is their new beatitude: "Blessedness to write upon the will of millenniums as upon brass. . . . This new table, O my brethren, put I up over you: *Become hard!"*[30] They are to relearn the contempt of Aristotle's noble or great-souled man for the populace. The aristocrat is a man too big to reflect such traits as resentment or pity, for he has the power to be the creator of value and law.

At first Nietzsche locates his hope for this renaissance in the philosophers. Castigating his contemporaries as levelers who chant "equality of rights" and seek to justify "the universal green-meadow happiness of the herd,"[31] he calls for a rank of genuine philosophers who will rise beyond the Kantian-critical stance and become the creators of values. "The real philosophers . . . are commanders and law-givers."[32] Towards the end he looks rather to men of violence, war lords of the Napoleonic cast, and speaks in revolutionary terms. At all costs victory must be won from The Crucified.

SOCIETY AND THE INDIVIDUAL

Inasmuch as the Nietzschean "individual" is the member of an élite, we must investigate the social safeguards of individuality at two levels: first as applied to the "individual" in

[29] *Thus Spake Zarathustra*, p. 243.
[30] *Ibid.*, p. 262.
[31] *Beyond Good and Evil*, pp. 223ff.
[32] *Ibid.*, p. 152.

Nietzsche's usual sense, and second as applied to the "individual" defined for the purpose of this study as "any human being."

In *Thus Spake Zarathustra* Nietzsche designs Part Four around the cry of distress from the higher man. We are to infer from this that though it is adversity and suffering rather than a congenial environment which produce the resilient toughness of the noble yea-sayers to life, we are at a perilous point in the evolution of man because slave morality has seduced even the aristocratic classes. They, in whom breeding and social position are conjoined, instead of being properly proud of their station, have succumbed to the blandishments of the priests and unfitted themselves to rule. The later Wagner is the personification of this capitulation. This is why Nietzsche gave full reign to his artistic temperament in writing attention-getting critiques like *Thoughts Out of Season* and *Thus Spake Zarathustra*. When he found that he was coldly ignored by those from whom he had hoped for a response, his reaction was to become more revolutionary in the means he recommended.

It is apparent in *The Twlight of the Idols: or, How to Philosophise with the Hammer* and *Ecce Homo* that Nietzsche's creative proposals have yielded place to the urge to desecrate and destroy, so that, even if it be through the invocation of open class warfare between the "Dionysians" and the "Judaeans," the resolution of the struggle will one way or another be brought on.[33] Later notes for *The Will to Power* reveal increasing regard for the achievements of warfare. "I am delighted at the military development of Europe, also at the inner anarchical conditions,"[34] he says. And again.

---

[33] This despite Zarathustra's repudiation of the "Fire-Dog" of anarchy and revolution. (*Thus Spake Zarathustra*, pp. 155f.)

[34] Most of the quotations following draw on the section in *The Will to Power*, ii, headed "The Will to Power as Exemplified in Society and the Individual" (pp. 183–238). Hollingdale protests that we should honor the distinction between Nietzsche's published works and those he did not make public. On this ground he objects to any weight being given to the *Will to Power* notes collected and published posthumously. However, I would contend that (*a*) they account for much of Nietzsche's influence, and (*b*) they are consistent with the logic of his ideology. I do not seek to quote isolated fragments but

> The maintenance of the military state is the last means of adhering to the great tradition of the past.... By means of it the superior or strong type of man is preserved, and all institutions and ideas which perpetuate enmity and order of rank in States, such as national feeling, protective tariffs, etc., may on that account seem justified.[35]

In such circumstances he expects the emergence of a new Napoleon, who will constitute in himself all the justification needed for social revolution. Then at last will the rebuilding of society take place on the right lines.

Nietzsche gives some hint of what will constitute the "right lines." He quotes frequently and with evident approval the *Laws of Manu*, which are geared to the rigid caste society of Brahmin-dominated India. The élite

> should therefore accept with a good conscience the sacrifice of a legion of individuals, who, *for its sake*, must be suppressed and reduced to imperfect men, to slaves and instruments.[36]

He goes on to declare: "We are the *noble!* It is much more important to maintain *us* than *that* cattle."[37] He proceeds to note certain social principles that would apply, with special emphasis on selective breeding. Medical certificates, leasehold or experimental marriages, and castration of poor types like the "physiologically bungled and botched"[38] are advocated, together with the right to experiment on criminals of a degenerate type.[39]

---

sustained themes. Note also that Roubizcek makes similar points to those developed here, drawing mostly from earlier works whose publication Nietzsche had himself arranged. Roubizcek suggests that Nietzsche in his last sane years came to view his own remorseless nihilism as a warning rather than a gospel, and his proposals for social engineering as dire prophecies of the direction in which his century was moving. (See Roubizcek, *Existentialism: For and Against*, pp. 45f.) I feel this is a very charitable reading.

[35] *Will to Power*, ii, p. 189.
[36] *Beyond Good and Evil*, p. 225. Note that Nietzsche here uses "individuals" in our sense, which is for him only a secondary usage for the term.
[37] *Will to Power*, ii, p. 312.
[38] *Ibid.*, pp. 192–94.
[39] Cited by Lea, in *The Tragic Philosopher* (p. 312), from an unobtainable source.

Friedrich Nietzsche 57

But these are hints rather than thoroughly worked out policies. What is more serious is the way Nietzsche reverts in these later writings to the blond beast of prey who had expressed the will-to-power in the "pre-moral" phase of culture. His championship of militarists, says Lea, begs the fundamental question: "whether the artists of dissolution and destruction are always, or even often, artists of reconciliation and creation?"[40] Furthermore, it is not possible to exonerate Nietzsche completely from the charge of being implicated in the development of Nazi fascist theory, when one has regard to his later views.[41] Nor is it deniable that these later views may be regarded as legitimate offspring of his earlier and more temperate views, for there are no logical safeguards against such deductions in the will-to-power ideology. One must wonder whether even the yea-saying Superman of *Thus Spake Zarathustra* has not been swallowed up by the monsters of militarism and barbarism.

It is apparent that the human individual as such is afforded neither respect nor protection in the society of Nietzsche's dreams. The traditional values imputed to human existence are inverted completely. It is for him a joyful wisdom to discover in happiness, in security, and in the virtues of obedience, chastity, piety, and justice the life-negating ideals of slave morality—"the meanest mode of existence that has ever been."[42] His denunciation of the flight from the responsibility of "becoming what you are" that he discerned constitutes Nietzsche's most acute criticism of the European scene. The solution he proposes, however, is not to challenge the masses but to leave them in their soporific state so that they will be more amenable to control by the élite. He is content to believe that the masses have become what they are, whereas the élite, who are different in kind, need yet to do so, at the expense of the masses. "It follows again, that the value of the

[40] *Ibid.*, p. 300.
[41] See for example the charges laid by C. E. M. Joad, *Guide to the Philosophy of Morals and Politics*, London: Victor Gollancz, 1948, pp. 629ff., and supported by Löwith, *From Hegel to Nietzsche*, p. 200, and Roubizcek, *Existentialism: For and Against*, pp. 25–37.
[42] *Joyful Wisdom*, p. 77.

majority of mankind will be determined, simply and exclusively, by their material usefulness to the *élite*." [43]

As we have seen, this could imply slavery in every sense, including the power to maim and exterminate. In this view the individual possesses no intrinsic worth. By the measures he advocates for the elevation of the exceptional individual, Nietzsche lets loose dogs of strife which endanger all that is genuinely creative in society.

[43] *Will to Power*, ii, p. 312.

KARL MARX
1818-1883

Marx appears to have experienced few inner tensions of the kind that compounded the most significant experiences of Kierkegaard and Nietzsche. There is passion in his writing, but it is not the agony of a mind coming to terms with itself; it is the ardor of a completely convinced social planner. Ironically, the man who preached so firmly that social conditions create personality is himself relatively opaque to psychological analysis. Perhaps he was shamed by the ideological expediency of his father; undoubtedly he was disgusted by the blatancy of repressive measures carried out by the ruling classes; yet his intellectual pilgrimage was brief and his viewpoint settled before he was twenty-five. Furthermore, though intellectually committed to the cause of the proletariat, he displayed little affection for individual representatives of it and was dictatorial in the promotion of his own views. His intellectual honesty is hardly to be doubted, but the inner springs of his conduct are obscure. Our biographical notes [1] serve mainly, therefore, to indicate which writings have been selected for close attention, and to place them in the context of their times.

[1] Biographical information is drawn from the standard work by Marxist Franz Mehring, *Karl Marx: The Story of His Life,* trans. Edward Fitzgerald, London: George Allen and Unwin, 1948. Of the non-Marxist sources the neatest short account is I. Berlin, *Karl Marx: His Life and Environment*, London: Thornton Butterworth, 1939.

Marx was born into the family of a German-Jewish lawyer living in the Rhineland. He pursued studies at the Universities of Bonn and Berlin, initially in law but later in history and philosophy. His shift of interest was due to the attraction which Hegelianism held for him, and he became one of the radical group known as the "Young Hegelians." Loyal as to method, Marx increasingly opposed Hegel as to content, becoming convinced that the motive forces of history are not spiritual but material. Consequently he welcomed Feuerbach's criticisms of philosophical and religious ideologies, and wrote on such themes in the *Rheinische Zeitung*, a radical journal of which he became editor at twenty-three, just after his father's death. It was suppressed for political reasons in 1843 and Marx migrated with his bride Jenny to Paris. Despite poverty, hardship, and the untimely death of three of their children, Karl and Jenny Marx remained staunch in their love until Jenny's death.

In Paris, Marx found himself surrounded by social, political, and artistic ferment, and by exiles from European and Russian countries, at a time when the 1830 revolution was a memory of failure and class conflict the topic of debate. He now read thoroughly the works of political economists like Adam Smith and Pierre Joseph Proudhon, and began to criticize socialism as lacking in historical sense. Together with Friedrich Engels he adopted the label "Communist" and developed a "Historical Materialism" applying Hegelian dialectic to economics. Expelled from Paris in 1845 because of his provocative journalism, he went to Brussels and there wrote all and published part of *The German Ideology* (attacking Hegel, Feuerbach, Max Stirner, and those calling themselves "True Socialists") and *The Poverty of Philosophy* (attacking Proudhon).

In 1847 he joined the Communist League and went to London as a conference delegate. He and Engels were instructed to prepare a manifesto. The *Manifesto of the Communist Party*, published in the year of revolutions, 1848, helped to cause his expulsion from Brussels, and he went to Cologne to edit a *Neue Rheinische Zeitung*. Engel's collaboration led to an improved style; and after the *Manifesto*, with the exception of the first volume of *Capital*, the respective responsibility of the two authors for what was published is hard to determine. Expelled from Cologne and then Paris, Marx sought temporary refuge in London but stayed there for the rest of his life.

Under conditions of extreme poverty he wrote newspaper articles and revolutionary pamphlets with Engels, while corresponding on an increasingly wide scale with Communists in other countries. His *Critique of Political Economy* (1859) foreshadowed the vaster contribution to economic theory on which he was working constantly. Untouched by the English culture in which he lived, he nevertheless found the data with which to fill out his thesis in the official records housed in the British Museum. In 1864 he participated in the founding of the International Working-Men's Association in London and quickly became its dominant figure, working successfully to reduce the influence of powerful rivals such as the German Lassalle and the Russian Bakunin.

The publication in 1867 of the first volume of *Capital* guaranteed that Communism would be first of all an ideological movement. As Berlin puts it: "No social movement has laid such emphasis on research and erudition."[2] It is this volume which has been the history-maker, the remaining two being published posthumously through Engel's editing of Marx's notes. Undisputed authority that he was, Marx was heavily involved in correspondence in later years; and he found himself somewhat astonished by the aptitude of disciples who wrote from Russia, a country he had considered too backward to envisage an imminent revolution by the proletariat but which now began to appear ripe with promise. In 1881 his wife died and then in 1883 another daughter. Sadness and exhaustion claimed him in that latter year. The loyal, self-effacing Engels, whose pocket and pen had ever been at his disposal, spoke at his funeral.

Subsequently Lenin and Trotsky utilized Marxist principles in establishing the Bolshevik party which captured the Russian revolutionary movement for Communism and commenced the march of Communism in twentieth-century politics. As has

[2] Berlin, *Karl Marx*, p. 219.

often been observed,[3] the theory devised by Marx to characterize advanced industrial capitalism in western Europe has taken root in semifeudal Russia and China, and in the technologically backward cultures of Southeast Asia, while the countries he deemed ripe for class warfare have modified the outlines of classical capitalism as he described it and look less like revolution than ever. But of the vitality of Marxism-Leninism in the modern world there can be no doubt, and it is urgent that we put to Marx the questions on which this enquiry is based.

DEFINING "INDIVIDUAL"

Discussing the philosophy and social theory of Marxism, Cohen asserts that "Karl Marx devoted his life to investigating the nature of man, to discovering the human essence." Acknowledging that Marx hoped to develop a science of society on the assumption that man never exists in himself, he goes on to declare that "even this may have been subordinate to his simple goal of attaining the truth about man." [4] This may seem an absurd judgment in the light of the common picture of Marx as the prophet of Communist collectivism and social determinism. Yet it contains much truth, for Marx did consider that he was bringing true individualism to the fore by the application of social science. He did protest at the absorption of individuals into Hegel's abstract "man," and claimed that he by contrast was theorizing from the initial datum of "real, active men." [5]

---

[3] E.g., by ex-Communist leader Milovan Djilas, *The New Class: An Analysis of the Communist System*, London: Thames and Hudson, 1958, p. 8.

[4] Robert S. Cohen, "On the Marxist Philosophy of Education," in National Society for the Study of Education, 54th Yearbook, Part I, *Modern Philosophies and Education*, Chicago: University of Chicago Press, 1955, p. 177.

[5] Karl Marx and Friedrich Engels, *The German Ideology: Parts I and III*, ed. R. Pascal, London: Lawrence and Wishart, 1938, p. 14. Paul Nyberg indeed brackets Marx with Kierkegaard, Nietzsche, Mannheim, Tillich, and Riesman in respect of his concern for the individual, in an overstated chapter of Paul Nash *et al.*, eds., *The Educated Man: Studies in the History of Educational Thought*, New York: John Wiley and Sons, 1965, pp. 277–304.

Karl Marx

The whole point of his analysis was that men were being dehumanized and oppressed because philosophers had mistaken the nature of human life and ideals and had therefore been unable to see the realities of social change and to work toward a solution that would bring in truly individual living. Marx's intention was to re-align the pursuit of philosophy so that it would issue in social science. Thus his famous aphorism: "The philosophers have only *interpreted* the world differently; the point is, to *change* it." [6] The action philosophy that he expounded to accomplish this was "dialectical (or historical) materialism."

Sidney Hook suggests that "no two names are at once so suggestive of both agreement and opposition as are the names of Hegel and Marx." [7] This becomes apparent when we analyze Marx's historical materialism, where undoubtedly the reading of human nature is at issue. In the first place, the Hegelian dialectic was a tool chiefly devised to handle human history as distinct from natural science. Hegel and Marx were in agreement that German rationalists, English empiricists, and French materialists had united to apply Newtonian scientific method to human behavior. Thereby "man" had become a concept within a theory, a cog in a closed system, an abstract entity with "natural rights" which were flouted at every historical moment. Hegel insisted that a new science was needed, a history of culture as an organism, and Marx, agreeing, made this the basis of his criticism of "True Socialists" with their neat, abstract utopias.

Further, Hegel's philosophy of nature is built on the dialectical triad of mechanics, physics, and organics, with man at the apex of organic development because in him consciousness has become free ego, that attribute which takes nature across into absolute spirit. Marx accepts the premise that man is unique but declines to go on into Idealism. Instead he locates this uniqueness in the capacity to labor for a living.

[6] *Ibid.*, p. 199.
[7] Sidney Hook, *From Hegel to Marx: Studies in the Intellectual Development of Karl Marx*, London: Victor Gollancz, 1936, pp. 15f.

> Men can be distinguished from animals by consciousness, by religion or anything else you like. They themselves begin to distinguish themselves from animals as soon as they begin to produce their means of subsistence.[8]

Hence the cycle of nature is broken by the entry of human behavior, and sciences of closed systems must give way to a methodology that copes with an open system, where change takes one into novelty. It is Hegel's and Marx's conviction that the Hegelian dialectic provides a scientific way of understanding the changes that are bound to occur. But whereas Hegel's application of dialectic to ideology is complex and esoteric, Marx considers that he has turned Hegel right side up by applying the method to the material relations of men.

> In considering such transformations a distinction should always be made between the material transformation of the economic conditions of production which can be determined with the precision of natural science, and the legal, political, religious, aesthetic or philosophic — in short, ideological forms in which men become conscious of this conflict and fight it out.[9]

This therefore constitutes Marx's historical materialism, distinguished on the one hand from empiricist materialism because it is historical, and on the other from Hegel's dialectical Idealism because it is materialistic. The implications for a definition of "individual" are considerable.

Individual consciousness according to Marx is a late arrival on the scene of human life. It arises within the on-going process of productive labor.

> The mode of production in material life determines the social, political and intellectual life processes in general. It is not the

---

[8] *German Ideology*, p. 7.

[9] From the Preface to *A Contribution to the Critique of Political Economy*, quoted in Karl Marx, *Selected Works*, vol. 1, New York: International Publishers, n.d., p. 354. The Preface contains an oft-quoted definitive statement of Marxist ideology and will be referred to again, but the Critique itself has not been consulted, since Marx devotes the first part of *Capital* to an improved summary of it, as he himself indicates. See *Capital: A Critical Analysis of Capitalist Production*, trans. Samuel Moore and Edward Aveling, ed. Friedrich Engels, London: William Glaisher, 1912, p. xv.

consciousness of men that determines their being, but, on the contrary, their social being that determines their consciousness.[10]

The primacy of the social nexus in the formation of the individual's ego is stressed by Marx when criticizing the views of Max Stirner, a nihilist who in *Der Einzige und sein Eigenthum* rejected all ties with society, and who was read with interest by Nietzsche. It follows that subjective states such as — in his view — ideologies do not interest Marx. This is not to say that he ignores their existence or their influence, but that he considers them to be subordinate to the economic patterns which govern human relations.[11] Unlike many of his lesser disciples, Marx is fully aware that he is abstracting from the total life situation. He prefaces the *Capital* with this clear comment:

> Here individuals are dealt with only in so far as they are personifications of economic categories, embodiments of particular class-relations and class-interests. My standpoint from which the evolution of the economic formation of society is viewed as a process of natural history, can less than any other make the individual responsible for relations whose creature he socially remains, however much he may subjectively raise himself above them.[12]

However, he cannot altogether escape the charge that he himself is promoting not merely a scientific hypothesis but a declared ideology; nor is he coldly objective in the descrip-

---

[10] *Selected Works*, vol. 1, *op. cit.*, p. 354.

[11] Subsequent Leninist-Stalinist modification has mitigated Marx's rigorous materialism by prescribing a constructive and creative role for ideology in the Communist state, with visible implications in the present day for Russian education; but I submit that this is a modification of Marx and not merely an expansion. See the section entitled "Dialectical and Historical Materialism," in A Commission of the C.C. of the C.P.S.U.(B), *History of the Communist Party of the Soviet Union (Bolsheviks)*, Sydney: Current Book Distributors, Australian Education, 1942, esp. p. 116. A latter-day Marxist writer supports my view when discussing "consciousness" by declaring that Marx's necessary concentration on "the socio-economic isolate" prevented a clear statement of the interaction of thought and action until Lenin. See Jack Lindsay, *Marxism and Contemporary Science: or, The Fullness of Life*, London: Dennis Dobson, 1949, pp. 57-68.

[12] *Capital*, p. xix.

tions he applies to members of the capitalist stratum, despite his explicit acknowledgment that they are helpless victims of the economic determinants of their class.

It follows from the premise that personality is molded by social relations, that human nature is not something constant or abiding but is being constantly transformed. Rebuking Proudhon for his alleged utopianism, Marx says brusquely: "M. Proudhon does not know that all history is nothing but a continuous transformation of human nature." [13] That is, whenever the dialectic of history has brought into being a new class, there emerges also a new human type, together with new associated ideologies. Hence Marx applauds the principle enunciated in Hegel's *Logic* that "merely quantitative differences beyond a certain point pass into qualitative changes," [14] because it accounts for existential novelty not only in logic but in history.

Up to this point there appears to be little scope for the exercise of human will or the acknowledgment of individuality. This is to be expected because while society continues to be composed of classes, the general behavior of classes will largely determine and wholly outweigh the choices of individuals within those classes. However, with increasing understanding of the "economic law of motion of modern society" [15] and the eventual emergence of the classless society there will come true individuality and the opportunity for men actively to transform their own natures. This requires that we appreciate the nature of human freedom.

Marx is concerned to define the issue of freedom because he believes that the formulations of philosophers like Kant and Hegel are both naive and hypocritical, giving rise amid conditions of class uniformity and oppression to utopian abstractions. The usual approach in obtaining one's definition of freedom is to work from some premise about human selfhood, blithely ignoring the actualities of the conditions under which

---

[13] *The Poverty of Philosophy,* London: Martin Lawrence, n.d., p. 124.
[14] *Capital,* p. 296.
[15] *Capital,* p. xix.

men live. Marx claims instead to be using these very conditions as his starting point.

He posits two kinds of restriction on human freedom: natural law and the state. Nature is governed by law, and man is under the necessity of understanding natural law in order to gain power over nature. With the coming of the industrial revolution he has reached the point where the abolition of poverty is a genuine possibility. "Freedom is the recognition of necessity," and by discerning the laws of nature man is being freed from the total bondage to nature of lower animals. The other hindrance is the state, that is, the political entity characterized by controls and a ruling élite. The bourgeoisie created by the industrial revolution has of necessity imposed on that revolution's other creature—the proletariat—a bondage more complete and inhuman than any previous interclass struggle has ever produced.

> It has pitilessly torn asunder the motley feudal ties that bound man to his "natural superiors," and has left no other bond between man and man than naked self-interest. . . . In one word, for exploitation, veiled by religious and political illusions, it has substituted naked, shameless, direct, brutal exploitation.[16]

Hence, while classes remain, only the ruling class is free from oppression, and even its members are not really free because their behavior as a class is predictable. The emergence of individuality awaits the coming of the classless society. In Berlin's paraphrase:

> Bourgeois society is the last form which these antagonisms take. After its disappearance the conflict will disappear forever. The pre-historical period will be completed, the history of the free human individual will at last begin.[17]

Marx's vision of the free, human individual is apocalyptic and somewhat unclear. It is contingent on the successful revolution of the proletariat and the withering of the state,

[16] *Manifesto*, p. 11.
[17] Berlin, *Karl Marx*, p. 123.

leaving behind a genuine society, that is, a free association of individuals who by an educated self-consciousness are able to discern the areas of creative action available to them. This in itself is perilously vulnerable to Marx's own scathing label "utopian," and will be further discussed at a later stage.

There yet remains some doubt as to the nature of the activities whereby this freedom is to be demonstrated as real. Cohen deduces from his reading of Marx that the symbol is work: "Labor is the very touchstone for man's self-realization . . . and it is labor which should make him happy." [18] He will be alienated from his work as long as he is regarded as a factor in the production line while another reaps the reward. The optimum will be mass participation in social democracy when men and women "freely recognize the desirability of their labor." [19]

Schlesinger's reading is different. He quotes Marx as saying:

> The realm of freedom actually begins only where drudgery, enforced by hardship and external purposes, ends; it thus quite naturally lies beyond the sphere of material production proper.[20]

This, says Schlesinger, implies that the ideal of every worker having a genuine area of decision-making power in the industrial complex is chimerical. Therefore he suggests that Marx must mean that it is in the increase and creative use of leisure time that full self-realization is achieved,[21] which would include participating in the forums of social democracy. The doubt remains because Marx did not in fact do much more than hint at the shape of the society-to-come, and the views of Lenin on the subject go beyond commentary on Marx and therefore are of doubtful help in interpreting him.

In summary, there are good grounds for assuming that Marx is particularly concerned to understand human individuality. His account is governed by the axioms of what he calls histor-

[18] Cohen, "Marxist Philosophy of Education," p. 190.
[19] Ibid., p. 192.
[20] Rudolph Schlesinger, *Marx: His Time and Ours*, London: Routledge and Kegan Paul, 1950, p. 411.
[21] Ibid., p. 407. He adds the evaluative comment: "Present socialist experience does not yet supply a satisfactory answer."

ical materialism. He insists that the individual cannot be defined as some abstract *esse* but must be understood within the particular social nexus. What sets man apart from the animals is his productive capacity, and economic factors are the primary element in social relations. There is therefore nothing fixed about human nature. Religious, philosophical, and aesthetic judgments in the culture are relative and subsidiary. The much-vaunted freedom of the individual is conditional on his being obedient to the necessary laws of nature and liberated from the oppression and thought forms of a class-structured state. Both conditions are about to be realized as the dialectic of history carries us into an industrialized and classless society through the fires of the proletarian revolution. The free, human individual is not yet realized, but by inexorable historical development will be.

SANCTITY OF THE INDIVIDUAL

It was apparent to Marx that the sanctity of the individual was being outraged as never before. His diagnosis that this was an inevitable result of the dialectic of history did not preclude his waxing bitterly eloquent about the inhumanities being inflicted on the working classes in advanced industrial societies. His remedy called for a revolutionary party which, understanding the laws of the dialectic, would be able to "shorten and lessen the birth pangs"[22] and hasten the emergence of the classless society. Since respect for the sanctity of the individual normally arises from moral and spiritual convictions, it is salutary to observe the functioning of ethical elements in Marx's ideology.

In the *Manifesto* Marx summarized his reading of history by saying: "The history of all hitherto existing society is the history of class struggles."[23] And he went on to characterize "the epoch of the bourgeoisie." It was, he said, involved in the penultimate struggle·

[22] *Capital*, p. xix.
[23] *Manifesto*, p. 9.

> Our epoch, the epoch of the bourgeoisie, possesses, however, this distinctive feature: It has simplified the class antagonisms. Society as a whole is more and more splitting up into two great hostile camps, into two great classes directly facing each other — bourgeoisie and proletariat.[24]

And that bourgeoisie, he added, was of all classes in history the most ruthless and shameless, and knew it.

> It has drowned the most heavenly ecstasies of religious fervour, of chivalrous enthusiasm, of philistine sentimentalism in the icy water of egotistical calculation.[25]

However determinist and academic in theory, Marx could not restrain his indignation at the deliberate villainies of the capitalists. Even in his most academic study, long sections described with close documentation the sins of many individual capitalists against their workers. He did not seem quite able to swallow his own line that they were "doing what comes naturally." His rage was deeply moral.

Nevertheless he labored elsewhere to divest himself of all morally toned judgments. Berlin remarks how his manuscripts still bear

> the strokes of the pen and the fierce marginal comments with which he sought to obliterate all references to eternal justice, the equality of man . . . and other such phrases which were the stock in trade . . . of the democratic movements of his time.[26]

So far as Marx was concerned, "morality" had always signified the morality of the ruling class, functioning as much to intimidate the oppressed classes as to guide the rulers. In the eyes of the modern worker: "law, morality, religion, are . . . so many bourgeois prejudices, behind which lurk in ambush just as many bourgeois interests";[27] the worker's criterion of value and truth is summed up in the pragmatic [28] test of how success-

---

[24] *Ibid.*
[25] *Ibid.*, p. 11.
[26] Berlin, *Karl Marx*, p. 17.
[27] *Manifesto*, p. 20.
[28] Note the repetition of the term "praxis" in the Theses on Feuerbach (appendix to *German Ideology*). It is partly obscured in the English translation.

fully his material needs are met. Even the bourgeois ethos of family is alien to the worker, for "the proletarian is without property; his relation to his wife and children has no longer anything in common with bourgeois family relations." [29] Some of Marx's sharpest barbs were reserved for religion, which he described as "the opium of the people." [30] For example, he traced the defense of the status quo by the followers of Hegel to the fact that Hegel taught the Absolute Idea toward which the state inexorably moves, thereby enlisting the Christian God on the side of reaction. Marx also attacked the Christian commendation of suffering and forgiveness because, he said, it encourages the proletariat to be content with its lot; and he accused the "True Socialists" of promulgating a "religion of self-abasement" and sentimental altruism. Shades of Nietzsche!

Marx's nonmorality emerges most clearly when he describes the policies to be pursued by the party of the proletariat, in its endeavors to quicken the tempo of change.[31] In the revolutionary interregnum one ideal remains: the achievement of a proletarian victory, and all means are justified by this end. It would seem that the sanctity of the individual must be in complete abeyance during this time. The outstanding example of this attitude is the alacrity with which Marx seized on the bloody debacle of the Paris Commune in 1870 as a landmark in proletarian revolutionary history.[32] In his

[29] *Manifesto,* p. 20. See also *Capital,* p. 496.

[30] In the introduction to *Criticism of Hegel's Philosophy of Right,* which Joad quotes, adding that English Christian Socialist Charles Kingsley had already employed the phrase! See Joad, *Guide,* p. 672.

[31] In his famous comments on the *Manifesto,* Laski endeavors to maintain that Marx and Engels were "opposed to any separate Communist party" and that Communism since the Russian revolution has been a "denial of the spirit of the *Manifesto.* . . ." (Harold I. Laski, *Communist Manifesto: Socialist Landmark,* London: George Allen and Unwin, 1959, p. 87.) In my view, however, the behavior of both men in the years subsequent to the *Manifesto's* appearance, especially in their willingness to expel opposers like Lasalle and Bakunin, bespeaks an impatience with sectarian disagreements and muddling by the masses, and a readiness to develop a party élite. Lenin hastened this development but did not need to initiate it.

[32] See Mehring, *Karl Marx,* pp. 447–454. When to their existing antipathy towards the ruling classes was added the shame of their king's capitulation to Prussia, the workers of Paris erected barricades against the national forces of

panegyric he made no moral judgments, confessed no crimes against humanity. Pragmatically the revolt was an instructive revolutionary model.

It may be urged that, as a revolutionary, Marx repudiated the cloak-and-dagger methods of many of his followers and worked rather for an openly recognized and organized party. But again, as Berlin observes, this was less because he thought conspiratorial procedures unworthy than because he believed them obsolete and ineffective.[33] Life would be cheap until the age dawned when life could be sweet. The fearful thing about this view is that Marx and Engels tended to foreshorten their time estimates, and it would seem apparent that the interregnum might be of considerable duration, together with the nonmoral policies it "justified," perhaps extending well beyond even this present day.

As has been intimated, there are few clues as to the standards that might be expected to obtain in the society-to-come. Berlin observes that Marx makes no plea for a change of heart in men, since subjective states have little effect on the outcome, and one might add that in Marx's view any change of heart would come automatically with the change in material circumstances. In a later comment Berlin unmasks the presupposition concerning man which buoys up Marx's millennial vision:

> For Marx, no less than for earlier rationalists, man is potentially wise, creative and free. If his character has deteriorated beyond recognition that is due to the long and brutalising war in which he and his ancestors have lived ever since society ceased to be that primitive communism out of which, according to the current anthropology, it has developed.[34]

France. Their protracted stand exhibited not only a bravery born of desperation but a savagery born of anarchical conditions. The former enlisted the sympathies of many liberal individuals and groups in Europe, but the volume of condemnation gradually became general as the latter came to the fore. In the circumstances, Marx's championship of the Commune-ists was not without danger to himself.

[33] Berlin, *Karl Marx*, p. 24.
[34] *Ibid.*, p. 131.

Karl Marx

Some things can be inferred about the new social relations. A hint is given that the functions of the family as a social group would to some degree be taken over by the "collective working group . . . composed of individuals of both sexes and all ages."[35] Education would be geared to producing not specialized detail workers but

> the fully developed individual, fit for a variety of labours, ready to face any change of production, and to whom the different social functions he performs, are but so many modes of giving free scope to his own natural and acquired powers.[36]

Political life would be identical with social life, because, having no class interests to defend, one would be at liberty to enter into voluntary associations whenever social purposes required group decision.

SOCIETY AND THE INDIVIDUAL

It is not the function of this study to examine the long term practical effects of the ideologies being examined, but to test their theoretical adequacy in relation to the place they give to "the sanctity of the individual." Marx's theory rests on the ability of philosophy and social science to give him the kinds of answers he claims to get.

In taking up the position that social science has the task of unraveling the dialectical laws of history, Marx falls under the strictures of Popper in the latter's closely reasoned *Poverty of Historicism*. Popper brackets Marx with "historicists" — in his sense, social scientists who adopt a holistic approach towards social data and endeavor to locate and employ the laws of social progress for predictive purposes.[37] He highlights as the theoretical error the misuse of the word "law," and as the practical problem the resulting overconfidence in one's capac-

---

[35] *Capital*, p. 496. This has been given educational form in the work of A. S. Makarenko.
[36] *Capital*, p. 494.
[37] Karl R. Popper, *The Poverty of Historicism*, London: Routledge and Kegan Paul, 1957, pp. 3ff.

ity to plan society. One may add that in the case of Marx it is not the pure scientist who speaks, but an ideologist whose metaphysical axioms exercise great influence over his selection and verification procedures. Hence "science" becomes an ideological prestige word and "utopia" a loosely defined swear word in Marx's writing, to the detriment of clear thinking.

The crux of Marx's historicism is his claimed ability to predict social change. As we have seen, this bears directly on the treatment meted out to "the individual," for at the worst we might discover that the moral nightmare of the interregnum is with us forever. In fact the most frequent criticisms of Marx are leveled precisely at his predictive powers. For example, the time element was consistently astray in his calendar of European events, as even Mehring occasionally concedes, and to this day indigenous Communist revolution has bypassed the most advanced countries of Europe which were the subjects of most of his predictions. His postulate that under capitalism the capitalists would get fewer and richer and the proletariat more numerous and depressed has not been vindicated; this is due in part to socialist group action and collective capitalist monopoly procedures. There would also appear to be grounds in the contemporary Communist world for doubting the accuracy of the prophecy that a postrevolutionary proletarian society would be classless,[38] and this suggests a misreading of human nature back at the start of his hypothesizing. But if what Popper says about the boundaries of social science is true, then Marx's "scientific predictions" are no more than hunches, many inspired, some not; a serious matter when the manipulation of human beings is at stake.

Social planning which involves imposing an ideology on society through official power channels is a hazardous pursuit. Firstly it requires that the planners be correct in their theories, yet we are now realizing that it is beyond the power of any scientific discipline as such to supply the requisite certainty. Secondly it is hazardous because if the planners consider they

---

[38] See Djilas's refutation in *The New Class*, already cited.

are correct, they will be sorely tempted to override the sanctity of the individual, for example with respect to his right to criticize their plans. The problem is aggravated when the ideologist arrogates to himself the label "scientific" — as Marx does — for the right of lay dissent is thereby automatically excluded.[39] It is so easy for collectivism to become totalitarianism. Another Communist fighter whom Marx caused to be expelled from the International spoke presciently:

> We believe power corrupts those who wield it as much as those who are forced to obey it . . . . Intellectuals, positivists, doctrinaires, all those who put science before life . . . draw the inevitable conclusion that, since such theoretical knowledge is at present possessed by very few, these few must be put in control of social life.[40]

In summary, as a scientist Marx gave a valuable lead to several disciplines, but he overrated the power of his methodological tool. Consequently he made predictions and on the basis of these predictions drew up plans which were overambitious. With the intention of freeing the individual for creative living, he in fact placed him in jeopardy. The interim development of collectivism under party control and censorship does not seem as certain to proceed dialectically into classless society and social democracy as Marx supposed.

[39] One must in fairness acknowledge that Marx said, "Every opinion based on scientific criticism I welcome" (*Capital*, p. xx), and that his followers have been far more dogmatic than he; but even so he defines "scientific" in such a way as to preclude much genuine dissent. For him "science" is that mode of investigation which uses Hegel's dialectic as method and his own materialism as manifold. By definition hypotheses handled in other ways are ideology-bound and unscientific. However, in practice Marxism distorts science as it is more generally understood because it expects scientific hypotheses to buttress what may fairly be called the Marxist ideology. Reference has often been made in this connection to the Lysenko school in biology which (until recently) received the stamp of official approval because it stressed environmental as opposed to genetic factors, and this was considered to be supportive of Marx's views on cultural determinism. Similarly it has been pointed out by W. E. Andersen how Russian psychology has been impoverished by its ideological shackles (*Ideological Education*, unpublished thesis, University of Sydney, 1965, pp. 168–179).

[40] Bakunin, quoted in Berlin, *Karl Marx*, pp. 205–206.

COUNTERPOINT
KIERKEGAARD : NIETZSCHE : MARX

DIAGNOSES

The context of the views we have been examining is European culture of the mid-nineteenth century. Each thinker serves an intellectual apprenticeship under the thought of Hegel, but for all three in their twenties Hegel has become the symbol of what is amiss in society; and the crux of the matter is disregard for the individual. All three detect the alliance between rational philosophy and formal religion [1] which provides ideological support for a status quo of mediocrity and oppression. Kierkegaard hits on the defection of the church from its mission to promote personal concern, and traces some of the guilt back to Cartesian rationalism; Nietzsche detects the debasement of morality to a "safe" code of middle-class comfort and hypocrisy, and blames the Judaeo-Christian heritage; Marx agrees with Nietzsche that conventional morality cloaks much injustice and hypocrisy, but casts the capitalist, whose initiative might have been expected to appeal to Nietzsche, in the role of villain.

Interestingly, all these men challenge the philosopher to be more existential in approach, and in this they are most nearly at one in their criticism of Hegelianism. Be subjective, says Kierkegaard, so that the individual may re-enter your scholarly

[1] Löwith (*From Hegel to Nietzsche*, p. 45) shows how explicit this association was in Hegel himself.

vision. Add willing to knowing, says Nietzsche, so that you may be alert to recognize the higher individual. Stop theorizing about the "free ego" while all men are in chains, says Marx, and become architects of change by virtue of your understanding of the dialectic of history.

Again, each takes issue with the absolutism that came to fullest flower in Hegel. Nietzsche and Marx accept the idea of cultural evolution from Hegel and use it to puncture the pretensions of his Idealism, the one from a biological and the other from a sociological premise. But even Kierkegaard, though retaining his faith in the absoluteness of Christian revelation, resists its extension to an ecclesiastical institution and revives the Reformation insistence on truth subjectively appropriated. On either count, axiological relativism is encouraged, and Kierkegaard's failure to guard against this stems from the psychological rationale he applies to religion.[2] Paradoxically, Marx comes nearest to preserving absolutist elements, in the self-confidence he bequeaths to the revolutionary party and in the certain emergence he predicts for the classless society.

The three thinkers vary in their reactions to the force of science in human affairs. At the time they were writing, it was becoming part of common life, through the introduction of technology in industry. Kierkegaard gives science but a passing glance. He does not fully appreciate its impact on society because he is absorbed with the private existence of the individual, yet he does make a comment from which modern disciples have taken their cue: he stresses that man treated only as an object of scientific investigation is not man. Nietzsche is more aware of the cultural impact of science and goes through a period of near-positivism, while acquainting himself with the biological sciences, from which he emerges stressing that the organic life and consciousness of man carry

[2] His heirs among modern theologians are notably Paul Tillich and Rudolph Bultmann. Roubiczek makes an impressive attempt to rescue Kierkegaard from the charge of relativism in values, in the course of arguing generally for moral absolutism. His own construct is more effective than Kierkegaard's in fact, because he relates the subjective "ought" to an objective order of things. (*Existentialism*, pp. 92ff.)

more meaning for human existence than diligent "fact"-finding by narrow specialists. It is Marx who of the three grasps the scientific factor most firmly, and he builds his diagnosis around the boost that science has given to economic productivity. It is also Marx who uses "science" as a prestige word for his exposition and embarks on just that course which Kierkegaard feared—the pigeonholing of the individual in scientific categories.

Ultimately the divergencies in diagnosis stem from different conceptions of what constitutes the true nature of the crisis. For Kierkegaard it is an ethicoreligious crisis, not because in his view Christian norms are faulty but because men have lapsed from the ethicoreligious level of living that Kierkegaard considers the measure of properly human existence. Nietzsche also considers it an ethical crisis, but blames contemporary ethics as such because on his view they inhibit the emergence of the best men. Marx belittles the importance of ethical considerations and considers that the crisis is economic. In the remedies that each from his vantage point prescribes, the common objective is an improved human individual; but there the resemblance ceases.

PRESCRIPTIONS

We may compare the prescriptions of the three thinkers for restoring the sanctity of the individual by noting three things: the social viewpoints from which they write, their views on human consciousness, and their attitudes to moral attributes.

Kierkegaard ignores questions of social structure and seeks to educate the individual maieutically through his books. Yet, although his Edifying Discourses are more simply written than most of the pseudonymous works, his writings are on the whole aimed at an élite; to this extent, though he does not intend it to be so, he is conforming to a class-structured society. Nietzsche unashamedly opts for an aristocratic viewpoint. He writes for an élite and withholds the privilege of individuality from all but the few. He would have the masses educated in the slave morality already dominant, but vacillates between his biological hypothesis that the higher man will emerge, regardless of our help or hindrance, and his desire to re-educate the élite in the master morality so that it will welcome the higher man.

Marx deliberately throws in his lot with the proletariat, which he believes holds the future in its hands. He seeks to educate its members through the formation of an élite versed in his dialectic—the algebra of revolution.[3] Insofar as he is optimistic about the growth of the Party in the period before it can embrace all members of society, he too creates a class whose assumption of authority over the masses is aggravated by its conviction of scientific infallibility. In short, all three men misjudge the relation of man in society and bequeath to the twentieth century a problem more sharply defined, not tenable solutions to it.

The problem includes debate on the conscious life of man. Nietzsche and Marx regard it as subsidiary to the main functions—as an epiphenomenon. But whereas Marx puts first the social relationships arising from material needs, Nietzsche stresses the biologically based drive of will-to-power, which in the first instance is neither conscious nor social. Kierkegaard, in contrast to both, considers that self-consciousness is the core of human being, and therefore in principle every individual rates respect. Indeed, if we are to choose between these thinkers, it would seem that Kierkegaard offers the best safeguard for individual autonomy. Marx's apocalyptic society of free, human individuals is theoretically insubstantial, and Cohen's summary of the ideological influences behind Marxism identifies the Christian world-view as the source of this concept,[4] which brings us back to Kierkegaard's theism.

This explains why it is not safe summarily to dismiss Kierkegaard's insistence on a personal change of heart as a necessary step in safeguarding the sanctity of individuals. Even Nietzsche, who like Marx envisaged militant social planning, seeks to ensure a moral conversion in noblemen, to fit them

[3] Hook, *From Hegel to Marx*, p. 74.
[4] Cohen, "Marxist Philosophy of Education," p. 175.

for their task. Man as he is, is unready. Kierkegaard takes very seriously the caliber of the conscious personal responses of men, and at the least we are thereby warned that together with social and intellectual education there must be a careful attention to moral and perhaps religious (whatever that may mean) education.

None of the three thinkers was an educationist, and no attempt is here made to explore the question of moral education in detail. But one question needs to be asked: What moral attribute is considered to be most important? The answer for Kierkegaard is "choosing" as exercised in faith toward God and love toward one's fellow men: the traditional Judaeo-Christian answer. He defines love as acknowledging the "given independence"[5] of every man while endeavoring to help him preserve it. Nietzsche counsels his disciples to "become hard,"[6] to spurn the beggarly altruism of Christians and promote the growth of their own ego first of all—"the wholesome, healthy selfishness, that springeth from the powerful soul."[7] Marx ostensibly promotes no ethical ideas, since such things belong to a merely subjective realm. Yet one may deduce some norms from the possibility of cooperative life inherent in the call "Workingmen of all countries, unite!" and the promise of collective compatibility in a classless society. As we have observed, however, the great obstacle is the preaching of revolution. This is the first ground for unity of the working classes, and it is the state of affairs which is to dominate the interregnum. If Marx's own behavior is a guide, it would seem that ruthlessness and revenge are dominant attitudes. Both Marx and the later Nietzsche anticipate great gain from class war, whereas for Kierkegaard the battle must be fought within the soul, in order that we may look with benign charity on all men. In the modern world, Protestant theology has promoted theistic existentialism, Communism has instigated a chain of revolutionary wars, and

[5] *Concluding Postscript*, p. 232.
[6] *Thus Spake Zarathustra*, p. 262.
[7] *Ibid.*, p. 232.

Nietzsche has been grist to the Fascist mill. Insofar as Nietzsche has a part in modern existentialism, it is by transmission through the nihilistic pages of Sartre and Camus.

It is with the outlines of a problem brought into focus rather than with the beginnings of a solution that we move on from the nineteenth century. Is the Western world to move further away from the Judaeo-Christian ethic toward the power politics and neo-Hellene ethic of Nietzsche or the nonmoral materialism of Marx, or are other options available? In ensuing chapters we look for answers in the study of seven twentieth-century ideologists.

part three:

social

scientists

at odds

In Part Three we contrast the views of Nunn and Mannheim. Nunn did not develop a detailed world-view of the kind found in the writings of our other nine thinkers, nor did he write very much at the ideological level. Two historical facts alone account for his inclusion: first, he exemplifies that brand of bourgeois individualism which characterized Britain at the turn of the century and insulated her from Europe's ideological collapse; second, the continuing popularity of Nunn's primer on education provoked Mannheim into expressing contrasting views of the educational process. Furthermore, since Nunn derives his model of explanation, insofar as he has one, from physiological psychology, whereas Mannheim writes as a sociologist, the cleavage between their views of the individual, especially when defining the part that education should play, is an interesting case-study of a philosophical problem posed by social science.

T. PERCY NUNN

1870-1944

Sir Percy Nunn was a busy practitioner who dabbled eclectically and brilliantly in several fields outside his own specialism, being thereby representative of a still persisting British tradition of scholarly amateurism.[1] McDougall acknowledged a debt to Nunn for the psychological concept of "horme,"[2] and Bertrand Russell at one time described himself as being "in close accord with [the Realist position] of Dr Nunn."[3] He was in close touch with the mathematical world and published a not inconsiderable work entitled *Relativity and Gravitation: An Elementary Treatise upon Einstein's Theory*, which reflected his association with A. N. Whitehead. Between 1915 and 1924 he was president of the Mathematical Association, the British Psychological Society, and the Aristotelian Society, and a university examiner in philosophy, psychology, and—lest we forget—education. For Nunn was primarily an educationist.

Born in Bristol the son of a headmaster, Nunn continued university studies after graduation, while teaching mathematics and physics in various schools. Taken into the new London Day Training College when he was thirty-three, he was its

[1] Biographical details are gleaned from sundry sources where they occur incidentally, but principally from J. W. Tibble, "Sir Percy Nunn: 1870-1944," *British Journal of Educational Studies*, vol. 10, Nov. 1961, pp. 58-75.

[2] William McDougall, *An Outline of Psychology*, London: Methuen and Co., 7th ed., 1936, p. 72.

[3] Bertrand Russell, *Mysticism and Logic*, Penguin Books, 1954, p. 120.

principal in 1922. By this time he had his doctorate, based on a dissertation entitled "The Aims and Achievements of Scientific Method," and also held a professorship in education at London University. He continued thus until retirement in 1936. The years were full, for apart from his administrative load he retained responsibility for methods courses in the college, in mathematics and science. Under the circumstances his publications list is slender—and weighted on the side of teaching methods.[4]

His writing, however, exercised an influence in all three of the theoretical fields we have mentioned. Through papers presented before the Aristotelian Society, he maintained a philosophical position known as New Realism, and Passmore asserts that his output "had an influence out of all proportion to its modest dimensions."[5] He was especially concerned to defend a Realism which countered both Idealism and mechanistic science. Insisting on the existence of the objective world outside our perceiving, he nevertheless considered that real objects were more various than just the data which the physical sciences seek to explain. For example, "consciousness" was beyond a strictly mechanistic interpretation yet undoubtedly a datum.[6] He was equally opposed to Pragmatism because of "the want of security of the relations between ideas and the reality beyond which some of us find in other presentments of Pragmatism."[7] The doorway that he thus opened to psychic events was important to Nunn; it amounted to letting in the science of psychology, the second field in which he was deeply interested. He greatly admired the instinct psychology of McDougall, though also keeping his mind open to advances in Freudian psychoanalysis. His

---

[4] See the near-complete listing in Tibble, p. 75.
[5] John Passmore, *A Hundred Years of Philosophy*, London: Duckworth and Co., 1957, p. 259.
[6] "On Causal Explanation," in *Proceedings of the Aristotelian Society*, New Series, vol. 7, 1906–1907, pp. 72–80.
[7] "The Aims and Achievements of Scientific Method," *Proceedings*, New Series, vol. 6, 1905–1906, p. 176. Compare Bertrand Russell's comment on Pragmatism in *History of Western Philosophy*, London: George Allen and Unwin Ltd., 1957, p. 845.

views in both fields predisposed him to individualism in theorizing about the human animal.

This he did in his third field of interest, educational theory. Here abstract dimensions drawn from philosophy and psychology mingled in Nunn's mind with the practical insights of such innovators in education as Pestalozzi and Montessori. The outcome was *Education: Its Data and First Principles,* which (first published in 1920) went into reprints annually till the Second World War and has been reprinted five times since.[8] The development of specialisms in the present day makes this book appear discursive and uneven, but it has a firm underlying structure and represents virtually the only substantial attempt at theoretical synthesis in British education before the War. It set out to expound this view:

> The primary aim of all educational effort should be to help boys and girls to achieve the highest degree of individual development of which they are capable.[9]

Clearly Nunn has something to say to the theme of this study. We will discuss him, albeit more briefly than the other thinkers, under the same rubrics.

DEFINING "INDIVIDUAL"

Realist philosophy and instinct psychology are the handmaids of Nunn's educational theory. His Realism accords equal standing to things and ideas as reals, his psychology maintains the continuity between man and animal, and both begin with the experience of the human individual — as observer in the one case, as actor in the other. Together with Nunn's repudiation of scientific positivism [10] goes his repudiation of Watson's

---

[8] In Britain. The only ripple Nunn caused in the American pond was his year as a visiting professor at Teachers College, Columbia University, in 1925. We shall work from the third edition of *Education* (London: Edward Arnold, 1945), representing Nunn's final revision, which undoes little of what was expounded in the first.

[9] *Ibid.,* p. 5.

[10] Which he referred to, before this label was common in England, as "materialism."

behaviorism, due to the conviction that there is a datum neglected by both which in physics is called energy [11] and in psychology consciousness.

Our starting point is therefore the autonomy or independence of the individual organism. This is not to be seen as an attribute confined to man. Quoting biologist Jennings concerning a protozoan, Nunn insists that "the humblest creature is autonomous" and that man is simply the highest development in autonomous organization. He brings this out repeatedly by the way he identifies modes of the conscious life as particular expressions of preconscious or biological traits. For example, purposive thinking or "conation" is a subclass of *horme,* the general purposive drive of the organism. "Throughout the whole range of life this attitude prevails, from the amoeba in which it is but a bare, unconscious 'will to live,' to man who consciously claims a share in the moulding of his own destiny." [12] Similarly, conscious memory is part of *mneme,* that genetically preserved record of the past, built up into "engram-complexes," which all organisms inherit and add to during their life span. And the general tendency to imitation in humans is the conscious level of *mimesis* in all creatures.

Consciousness is only one of the organism's means of "conducting that intercourse with the environment by which and in which it lives." [13] Having said this, Nunn proceeds to pay homage to many mental events that would be slighted by more thoroughgoing naturalists. Scientific method as a mode of thought naturally fares well, but the "moral law within," the religious sentiment, and aesthetic creativity are also given high status.

It is clear that in the circumstances human will is bound to present a problem to Nunn. His biological model would seem to suggest that a kind of "biological predestination" [14]

---

[11] Here, in a mechanistic era, he was aligning himself with the dynamic world-views of Whitehead and Einstein. See "Animism and the Doctrine of Energy," *Proceedings,* New Series, vol. 12, 1911–1912, p. 25.

[12] *Education,* p. 32.

[13] *Ibid.,* p. 63.

[14] The gloss comes from Robert R. Rusk, *The Philosophical Bases of Education,* London: University of London Press, 1929, p. 41.

is inevitable. Certainly he asserts that the engram-complexes are all present in the fertilized germ cell, and that there is no training of the will apart from the building up of the engram-complexes or sentiments. Yet he also stresses creativity in human life. "The human organism, body and mind, is a centre of creative energy that uses endowment and environment as its working material." [15] He insists that "nothing good enters into the human world except in and through the free activities of individual men and women." [16] His way of escape from the looming dilemma is to leave the definition of *horme* vague by imputing to it both creative and conservative elements. But by causing incompatibles to subsist within the one concept he confuses the issue, especially when in one place he attributes the sense of "personal identity" to *horme* and elsewhere describes persisting "self"-experiences as *mnemic*. As other commentators have recognized, Nunn cannot say all he wants to say within his biological model, and inconsistency arises because he is resolved to say it nevertheless.

Indeed, in chapters relating to the development of selfhood, where he is getting down to educational business, he frequently forsakes the biological analogy. In one context he begins:

> The growth of the self may be described as a process in which the impulses that have their roots in instinct and appetite become organised into a permanent hormic system wielding imperial authority within the organism.[17]

Well and good, but in the same context morality is recognized as something mainly environmental, incorporating certain proven truths of "permanent validity," i.e., truths with roots elsewhere than in the individual's instincts. Furthermore, while insisting that there is no difference in principle between animal and human consciousness, Nunn discusses the development of intellect and those powers of abstract reasoning

---

[15] *Education*, p. 118
[16] *Ibid.*, p. 12.
[17] *Ibid.*, p. 183.

of which he says *"only* men are capable." [18] Of the dubious status of society in his biological model of self-development it will be more appropriate to speak later.

SANCTITY OF THE INDIVIDUAL

There can be no doubting the intention behind Nunn's declaration that his view denies

> the reality of any super-personal entity of which the single life, taken by itself, is but an insignificant element. It reaffirms the infinite value of the individual person; it reasserts his ultimate responsibility for his own destiny.[19]

As we have seen, however, doubt may well arise as to the ability of his theoretical model to support his emphatic conclusion about the aim of education, stated in the opening pages of his major work. He has been variously called a naturalist and an Idealist [20] in relation to his normative theory, reflecting a confusion among his critics analogous, as Curtis has observed, to that caused by Rousseau in *Emile*.

Despairing of getting agreement on "ideals of life," Nunn

---

[18] My italics. Tibble highlights this inconsistency (p. 72), and Rusk comments: "Nunn fails to recognise that this creative capacity is distinctive of man and of God, and cannot, like individuality, be attributed to all organisms" (*Philosophical Bases*, p. 42).

[19] *Education*, pp. 12–13.

[20] The use of labels without definition of terms results in theorists' talking past each other. Rusk claims that Nunn is naturalistic because he despairs of discovering any universally acceptable ideals (Rusk, *Philosophical Bases*, p. 14), thereby meaning by "Idealist" an ethical absolutist. Curtis and Boultwood claim that the significance of the moral aspect in Nunn's thought prevents him from being a true naturalist, and suggest that he does have an "ideal" in view, of perfect individuality (S. J. Curtis and M. E. A. Boultwood, *A Short History of Educational Ideas*, London: University Tutorial Press, 4th ed., 1965, p. 327). This confuses a popular and a technical usage. Nunn disclaims the label Idealist and calls himself a Realist; but the context of this assertion is metaphysical. Rusk compounds the confusion by elsewhere referring to Nunn's "idealistic views of life" (Robert R. Rusk, *The Doctrines of Great Educators*, London: Macmillan, 2nd ed., 1957, p. 298), because he plumps for poetry and philosophy. Insofar as the use of these vexed terms belongs to a lean period in the development of educational theory as a field of study, we are better advised to eschew them here.

identifies the basic debate as swinging between education for self and education for society, and he opts for individuality as "the ideal of life." [21] Since there is no universal mind such as Hegel proposed, but only the interaction of many individual minds, one may therefore assert that the pursuit of individual excellence best satisfies the claims of society also. On the basis of his model, Nunn's view of the good is summed up in the development of individuality.[22]

However, having cleared his house of absolutes, Nunn proceeds to re-admit them when he discusses moral development. He begins in the fashion of Rousseau by describing the growth of the child self from infancy to adolescence, passing through narcissism and pleasure/pain judgments to the reality principle and the herd instinct.

> Hence the morality which the child first adds to the simple ethic of family life is the law of his pack: the club-law, which remains, with the majority, the most powerful influence on conduct throughout their days.[23]

However, in adolescence a "'social consciousness' of a truly ethical or religious character" emerges, due to the operation of the gregarious instinct; and moral standards arise in consequence of this.

Two criticisms must be made at this point. The first is, as Tibble has pointed out, that Nunn's attempt to justify his argument on the grounds of the social instinct is vitiated by the fact that "the social instinct is one of the concepts of early instinct theory which has stood up least well in the light of later investigations." [24] The second is that in no way can the

---

[21] *Education*, pp. 9 and 18.

[22] Of which the keystone is self-assertion, according to the analysis of Nunn's view in W. J. McCallister, *The Growth of Freedom in Education: A Critical Interpretation of Some Historical Views* (London: Constable and Co., 1931, p. 495). Interesting parallels could be drawn between Nietzsche's will-to-power and Nunn's *horme*, and it is McDougall himself who suggests that "Schopenhauer's 'will-to-live,' Professor Bergson's 'élan vital,' and Doctor C. G. Jung's 'libido' are alternative expressions for the purposive or hormic energy . . ." (McDougall, *Outline of Psychology*, p. 72).

[23] *Education*, p. 194.

[24] Tibble, "Sir Percy Nunn," p. 72.

model be made to carry the weight of references to the "permanent validity and supreme worth" of duty and neighborly love,[25] and to the "search for the universal principles of conduct which *must* be followed though the sky fall."[26] Rusk even hails Nunn as a champion, as against Spencer and Dewey, of the spiritual values of life, quoting convincing evidence from a speech delivered by Nunn to the British Association in 1923.[27]

SOCIETY AND THE INDIVIDUAL

Enough has been said to indicate that, whatever may be the outcomes of his model, Nunn is no extreme individualist. He recognizes throughout his book that social factors are significant. Clearly "a man becomes what he becomes mainly as the result of his reactions to his social environment," he says, but adds: "Yet when the inferences that too many thinkers have drawn from them are considered, one sees that one's admissions must be carefully safe-guarded."[28] The sufficient safeguard he recommends is the placing of individual development above all other goals. This is not to ignore society, for "the most clearly 'social' conduct always implies a strong self behind it."[29]

In short, Nunn believes firmly in the infinite worth of the human individual, to a degree far beyond what his model will allow. The moral code that enshrines this belief ostensibly hinges on the uniqueness of the individual but in fact follows the main outlines of the social heritage to which Nunn himself was heir and which was Christian-classical-humanist. The

[25] *Education*, p. 196. This is not to assert that Realism may not be capable of doing so, in the manner for example of John Wild, in "Education and Human Society: A Realistic View," in N.S.S.E. 54th Yearbook, pp. 17–56. However, I am saying that Nunn does not offer the philosophical justifications for such assertions that as a Realist he might well have done, nor does he arrive at them from his naturalistic biological model.
[26] *Ibid.*, p. 244.
[27] Rusk, *Doctrines*, p. 297.
[28] *Education*, p. 11.
[29] *Ibid.*, p. 248.

social safeguard that protects his belief is an education geared to the fostering of individuality.

Nunn's reputation in other fields proved that he was capable of rigorous and original thought, but his educational theory is a classic example of British compromise. We have already offered several criticisms, and need only refer here to other commentaries made on Nunn by his contemporaries. Campagnac and Sir Fred Clarke, the latter his successor at the Institute of Education, feel that Nunn fails to appreciate the social changes that were relegating individualistic Victorianism to the past.[30] In view of the attention the problem of human nature receives in other pages of this study, it will be sufficient here to mention that one may also level serious criticism at Nunn for the vagueness of his concept of the human individual and for the optimism in his proposals for promoting self-realization. He seems not to have questioned the trust in human nature which pervaded the nineteenth century, and assumes like Rousseau that the "self" which his educational efforts would bring to light would be essentially good.[31]

---

[30] S. J. Curtis, *An Introduction to the Philosophy of Education,* London: University Tutorial Press, 1958, pp. 192 and 211–213.

[31] This is a large generalization seemingly refuted by Nunn's direct comment on page 108 that "Man is not born good, as Monsieur Rousseau had maintained so eloquently in his *Emile,* nor is he born evil." It would seem to follow that Nunn therefore attributes all moral traits to environment, as most social scientists would claim to be doing also, and this proposition may be well documented from his book, though not from his model. For according to his model "the unperverted impulses of childhood . . . have a biological bias towards the good" (p. 109) and hence the aim of individual self-expression is the only tenable ideal (p. 13). He then becomes conscious that he may be charged with permitting no discrimination between "forms of individuality that ought to be encouraged and forms that ought to be suppressed" (p. 109), and proceeds to place the responsibility for the value judgments thus required upon parents and teachers. At the one moment he is following his model through with terms reminiscent of Rousseau: education for individuality is the "only education 'according to nature' " (p. 26), and discipline is best applied through natural consequences—"a teacher may justifiably tolerate much minor evil, waiting patiently for the spontaneous reaction that will generally come when experience reveals its unpleasant fruits" (p. 111). At the next he is invoking the shadowy sanctions of "school citizenship" and ultimately "Great Society"—a genuflection towards Mannheim in the

In view of the strictures maintained against Nunn here and by the other critics we have cited, it may be asked why Nunn's book has enjoyed such popularity. It is at least clear that it provided a useful introduction to the educational theory of the "new education" and, as such, had great value as a text for teacher training. It may not be unfair to suppose that most readers took the ideological speculations with a grain of salt, except that, before the Second World War, the democratic individualism that dominated Nunn's thought matched the mood of most Englishmen and was rather uncritically accepted for that reason.

later edition (p. 111) — to supply his norms. My quarrel is not with his views of self-development, morality, and citizenship, many of which I find most congenial, but with the unexplored tensions between them due to the lack of an articulated conceptual structure. In my view Nunn's vague, benevolent charter of human freedom leans too heavily on the shaky assumptions of natural decency and social stability. In his successor Sir Fred Clarke one detects a conscious reaction away from this climate of thought, most particularly in Clarke's "Note on Original Sin" at the end of *Freedom in the Educative Society* (London: University of London Press, 1948, pp. 97ff.), where he suggests that liberal optimism has failed to appreciate the moral perversity in human nature. By implication Clarke is saying that Nunn could only suppose he was espousing a view of "original a-morality" because he took liberalism's assumptions for granted.

KARL MANNHEIM

1893-1947

The task of interpreting Mannheim is far from complete, partly because he has been rather hastily pigeonholed by the first generation of his readers [1] and partly because some of his ideas changed during the time that he was in the public eye. We are therefore obliged to keep in view most of his major published writings, bearing in mind the differing environments out of which they successively emerged. Not the least remarkable of Mannheim's attributes were his literary candor and his desire to learn. He even tolerated contradictions in his writings if he thought that the frank admission of their opposition might prompt his readers to seek better solutions than his own.[2] Nor can one doubt the sincerity of his intentions when he says of himself that he is "a liberal . . . whose only capital is his learning and whose fundamental de-

---

[1] Thus he is recruited by pragmatists Bennis, Benne, and Chin to press their case; dismissed by Curtis and by Popper as a totalitarian thinker; and condemned by Bantock as an enemy of individuality. I hope to show such readings are premature. (Warren G. Bennis et al., eds., *The Planning of Change: Readings in the Applied Behavioral Sciences*, New York: Holt, Rinehart and Winston, 1961, pp. 34-38, 99-108, 132-140; Curtis, *Introduction to Philosophy of Education*, pp. 202-211; Popper, *Poverty of Historicism*, p. 67n; G. H. Bantock, *Freedom and Authority in Education*, London: Faber and Faber, 1952, pp. 34-36.)

[2] Thus: "Contradictions have not been corrected because it is the author's conviction that a given theoretical sketch may often have latent in it varied possibilities which must be permitted to come to expression in order that the scope of the exposition may be truly appreciated." (*Ideology and Utopia*, p. 47.)

mands on life are freedom of thought and free development of personality." [3]

Born [4] in Budapest and educated in the universities of Budapest, Berlin, Paris, and Freiburg, Mannheim was twenty-one when the First World War broke out, and saw Hungary at the end of that war pass through three revolutionary cycles. The irresistible social changes that were taking place in a formerly stable and stratified society fed the Marxist leanings which Mannheim had at this time. He settled in Germany, lecturing in sociology at the university of Heidelberg until 1930, when he moved to a chair at Frankfurt. Meanwhile Nazism had begun to conquer German life, and in 1933 Mannheim was one of those proscribed by Hitler. At once offered many posts, he lectured throughout the Netherlands before accepting in that same year a lectureship in sociology at the London School of Economics.

In his "German period" he combined a Kantian view of philosophy with a sociological discipleship under Marxist influence and developed "the sociology of knowledge" which insisted that "pure logical analysis has severed individual thought from its group situation" [5] and that "the ideological element in human thought . . . is always bound up with the existing life situation of the thinker." [6] Convinced that social change was inescapable, he pinned his hope for leadership on those who were most free of class ties, i.e., the "socially unattached intelligentsia" [7] in whom the insights of sociology might be expected to flower unhampered. However, the German tidiness of his vision was upset by the emergence of the Fascist schemers, whose skill in the use of social techniques was of a high order, and he arrived in England less assured about some of his premises. Writings that represent this period

[3] Karl Mannheim, *Essays on Sociology and Social Psychology*, ed. Paul Kecskemeti, London: Routledge and Kegan Paul, 1953, p. 255.

[4] Biographical details have been collated from various commentaries of which W. A. C. Stewart's "Karl Mannheim and the Sociology of Education" (*British Journal of Educational Studies*, vol. 1, May 1953, pp. 99–113) has the most information in one place.

[5] *Ideology and Utopia*, p. 3.

[6] *Ibid.*, p. 71.

[7] *Essays*, p. 88; and *Man and Society: In an Age of Reconstruction*, London: Kegan Paul, 1940, p. 100.

are his doctoral thesis "Structural Analysis of Epistemology" (1922) and *Ideology and Utopia* (1929), in which he expounds the sociology of knowledge. *Man and Society* also, though first published in England in 1935, was German in style and thought as well as language.

The last-named work, in English translation (1940), established his reputation anew, in England, and he founded the International Library of Sociology and Social Reconstruction. One of its first publications was the wartime essay *Diagnosis of Our Time* (1943), in which Mannheim spoke specifically to the British situation. In 1946 he was appointed to the newly created chair of sociology of education in the University of London. He died the following year. *Freedom, Power and Democratic Planning*, published posthumously in 1951, takes up themes in the *Diagnosis* and proclaims an intention to deal more systematically with them. It is clear in these works that Mannheim, like Marx, is convinced that the sociologist must serve in the marketplace and not remain in academic seclusion.

Mannheim's "English period" shows the influence of his new environment. At first it would seem that, like Hitler's advisers later, Mannheim underestimated the resilience of British democracy and saw through European eyes only a decadent liberalism resting on laissez-faire attitudes, typical of which was the individualism so well represented by Nunn. However, the effluxion of time brought Mannheim to a keener appreciation of the democratic checks and procedures which made Britain less susceptible to ideological take-over than the countries he had formerly known; and unlike that earlier refugee, Marx, Mannheim modified his views. Especially was this so in relation to religion. A generous footnote to the chapter subtitled "A Challenge to Christian Thinkers by a Sociologist" in *Diagnosis of Our Time*[8] acknowledges

[8] Page 100. Stewart identifies some of the thinkers referred to as J. H. Oldham, Middleton Murry, T. S. Eliot, and Lord Lindsay. Mannheim was also greatly interested in a religious community for personal renewal within Anglicanism, called St. Julian's, and Oldham suggests that this prompted him to recognize that institutional forms alone were inadequate to cope with social change. See J. H. Oldham, *Florence Allshorn: and the Story of St. Julian's*, London: SCM Press, 1959, p. 166.

the mutual stimulation provided by a group of Christians with whom he met frequently. Both in *Diagnosis* and (in germ) towards the end of *Freedom, Power and Democratic Planning* he indicates a shift in his views as to the part Christian leaders should play in planning, and as to the significance of long-enduring (he would not have said "absolute") values.

DEFINING "INDIVIDUAL"

Like Marx, Mannheim is concerned to champion the development of human personality and is convinced that it is lack of sociological sophistication which causes leaders to sponsor repressive social forms. However, he considers also that it is inadequate to locate the springs of human conduct only in economic relationships; he carries his analysis deep into epistemology, sociology, and psychology. He admits that he is attempting to unite speculative and empirical approaches, and the most impressive result is the "sociology of knowledge."

Wirth's introduction to *Ideology and Utopia* hails Mannheim as the pioneer of a study (sociology of knowledge) which puts values fairly in the center of social science. Its basic premise is that truth is not something absolute and objective, but a function of the relations that bind a particular society together at a particular point in time. As such, truth is not the disembodied ground of the epistemologies adopted by pure philosophy, nor is it the exclusive possession of the natural sciences as claimed by the Vienna circle of positivists. The quest for reality is not an attempt to avoid the problems of value in human affairs, nor is it merely the exposure of "ideologies"[9] (i.e., in Mannheim's sense, the normative rationalizations which unconsciously cloak the "real" interests of competing social groups). The quest goes further, into the social history of ideas and the psychosocial histories of human beings. Modes of thought "cannot be ade-

---

[9] To distinguish Mannheim's pejorative sense from the stipulative definition I am holding to in this study, I will place the word in quotes when Mannheim's meaning is intended.

quately understood as long as their social origins are obscured."[10] When we do understand them we shall then be more flexible and adaptable to encounters with reality, and therefore closer to "truth" than the epistemological absolutist. All knowledge arises from the structure of social relationships within which man acts, and all descriptions are perspectivistic.

> The problem is not how we might arrive at a non-perspectivistic picture but how, by juxtaposing the various points of view, each perspective may be recognised as such and thereby a new level of objectivity attained.[11]

Mannheim hastens to stress that this position is not relativistic.

> The result even here is not relativism in the sense of one assertion being as good as another. Relationism, as we use it, states that every assertion can only be relationally formulated.[12]

However, his critics generally agree, with Erös, that the philosophical implications of his sociology of knowledge are "in spite of all subtleties deterministic and relativistic."[13] Furthermore, it would seem apparent that Mannheim to the last believed that sociology held the key to human knowledge and that it could attain sufficient certainty to justify social planning on a large scale.[14] Inevitably therefore the nature and significance of the individual are situationally defined.

We understand man by proceeding from the initial behavioral premise that, as for any other organism, the key to his existence is adjustment. But unlike animals,

[10] *Ideology and Utopia*, p. 2.
[11] *Ibid.*, p. 266.
[12] *Ibid.*, p. 270.
[13] John Erös, "Book Review: Jacques J. Maquet, *The Sociology of Knowledge*," in *The British Journal of Sociology*, vol. 3, 1952, p. 185.
[14] Lord Lindsay, who knew Mannheim well in his later years, says: "Mannheim always resisted very strongly any suggestion that there was a limit to sociological knowledge.... One always felt that he had a sociological faith that all these blanks of ignorance about society could be overcome." (Reviewing *Freedom, Power and Democratic Planning* in *The British Journal of Sociology*, vol. 3, 1952, p. 90.)

> Man, besides adapting himself to his natural surroundings, adapts himself also to the psycho-social-institutional environment, . . . great variability of behaviour and adaptation to surroundings of a social character is typical for man.[15]

This means that traditional philosophical discussions about the nature of man couched in ontological terms are always victims of current social structures of thought which are already passing away. It is futile to seek for definitions that are permanently applicable or that suggest human nature is constant. These propositions are closely related to Pragmatism, but Mannheim claims to part company with the Pragmatists at the point where they equate successful personal adjustment with value judgments of right and wrong, and announce individual spontaneity as their ultimate goal. In Mannheim's eyes, the prior claim of social criteria refutes both of these.

This may also be shown by observing the operation of social factors on the rational and irrational elements in human behavior. Ideas are social products, and to know a man's life history is to know "the context from which novelty is produced in him."[16] Conversely it follows that we may determine the direction in which new ideas will be developed by the social milieu we fashion for the individual. Hence (anticipating later discussion), the ultimate educational unit is never the individual but the group. In the case of irrational elements, human behavior is considerably influenced by unconscious processes, and these are determined by the "collective unconscious" of social groups (using the term in a Jungian sense, for Mannheim is greatly indebted to psychoanalysis).

The problem of our age is control of collective unconsciousness, which is responsible for the "ideologies" that obscure "the real condition of society." The science that reveals the mechanics of rationalization and norm-formation is depth psychology, and Mannheim adopts its terminology in describing the structure of the individual. Man's psychic equipment,

---

[15] Karl Mannheim, *Systematic Sociology: An Introduction to the Study of Society*, ed. J. S. Erös and W. A. C. Stewart, London: Routledge and Kegan Paul, 1957, p. 8.

[16] *Ideology and Utopia*, p. 23.

then, comprises id, ego, and super-ego, subject to adjustment problems which may give rise to repressions, neuroses, sublimation, and so forth. Valuable insights are contributed to our understanding by behaviorism and Freudianism, but the special contribution of sociology to psychology has been to stress the importance of ideals and values in human behavior.[17] Whatever their origin, they do have what Allport calls a "functional autonomy" that requires enlargement of the psychoanalytic vocabulary, and they derive primarily from the group structure. Break down the cohesion of the groups to which a man belongs, as the Fascists did in Germany, and you find that "man left to himself cannot offer resistance."[18] Note that Mannheim's analysis is not purely academic, for it is his desire to recommend action, and therefore his evidence is presented with a view to supporting his call for social planning. Though he does refer rather tantalizingly in his last work to "certain unchanging aspects of the human mind,"[19] his general position is that personality is mutable and every social situation produces its corresponding personality type.

In his 1934 lectures Mannheim says: "It is competition and selection that decide which human types, which standards, which thought patterns will be dominant in a given society."[20] And again: "... behaviour depends more on social position than on inherent character."[21] The Marxist undertones of his analysis are muted but not lost in later discussions of the relation between the socioeconomic order and the individual. No economic order, he says in *Man and Society*, "can be brought into existence as long as the corresponding human type does

[17] *Systematic Sociology*, p. 16. I assume a working familiarity with this general approach. Mannheim does not add anything new to psychological theory, and is now somewhat dated, as Erös and Stewart suggest in their preface to this work. See also *Essays*, pp. 267–278.

[18] *Diagnosis*, p. 97. I take Mannheim to mean here not merely physical resistance but resistance to personality manipulation.

[19] Karl Mannheim, *Freedom, Power and Democratic Planning*, ed. Hans Gerth and Ernest K. Bramstedt, London: Routledge and Kegan Paul, 1951, p. 288.

[20] *Systematic Sociology*, p. 88.
[21] *Ibid.*, p. 49.

not also emerge," and he decrees in 1943 that education shall mold man in and for a democratic society.

One type now obsolete is the intellectual absolutist. Marx made this clear when he exposed the "ideological" element in the thought of all classed societies, and his debunking procedure is nowadays used by groups of every standpoint against the rest. This sophistication heralds "a new epoch in social and intellectual development." Another type now discredited is the authoritarian type, who presumes to be in possession of the truth for all time and therefore qualified to force conformity upon his inferiors.

The type which commends itself to Mannheim's judgment and feelings is the democratic type. In his earlier writings Mannheim considered that the individuals best qualified to represent the emerging type of the free individual were that small group without roots in any class, the European intelligentsia who had developed from German Protestant parsons' sons deprived of religious faith by rationalism.[22] Subsequently Mannheim observed that this very group succumbed to the Fascist lure and committed what Benda has called "la trahison des clercs." [23] He then observed British democracy in action and, while deploring the lack of planning, came to appreciate the part Christianity had played in its emergence and the driving power of a personal religious faith.

The pattern of the democratic personality which he describes in his last work is consequently an amalgam of relativistic and religious elements. He accepts the Pragmatist view that the "dynamic core of the Self is not pre-existent but evolves gradually out of the social process as an 'I,' " [24] and he says that "the democratic spirit is experimental: it does not even fix the reality levels as absolute, but considers life . . . as unceasingly dynamic." [25] However, he also considers that the conduct of the individual must be religiously

[22] *Essays*, p. 128. A prime example of course is Nietzsche.
[23] Quoted in Arnold S. Nash, *The University and the Modern World*, New York: Macmillan, 1944, p. 31.
[24] *Freedom, Power, . . .* , p. 241.
[25] *Ibid.*, p. 140.

based, partly because without religious fervor one cannot obtain that preparedness to serve the long-term ideals of society as opposed to immediate personal advantage, and partly because it is personality changes the planner is seeking to achieve, and only a "paradigmatic experience"—i.e., a religious conversion—will suffice to fix the new patterns.

Clearly then the individual as a person or self is entirely produced and conditioned by psychological and social factors, a late-arriving state within the organism. Even in history the private individual has been a recent development, owing much to the interlaced phenomena of Protestantism and bourgeois economics. In a strongly deterministic context Mannheim asserts rather wistfully that "the freedom for growth beyond the type is an essential," [20] but it is not till his English period that he provides any substantial grounds for believing that the individual has real freedom to become anything different. The enlargement of his definition of freedom is an interesting study and can only be summarized here, as follows.

His earliest writings discuss the issue within neo-Marxist class typologies. Awareness of freedom is related only to the private, subjective side of life. But a corner is turned in history by the rise of the socially unattached intelligentsia, who are free to cast in their lot with any prevailing "ideology," to stand aloof, or to become the sociologically aware ruling élite. In *Ideology and Utopia* Mannheim asserts that free conduct

> does not begin until we reach the area where rationalisation has not yet penetrated, and where we are forced to make decisions in situations which have as yet not been subjected to regulation.[27]

This seems to imply that the freedom to choose is a temporary phase belonging to our prescientific ways of living. However, Mannheim goes on to say that the sociology of knowledge makes us free by revealing the hidden determinants of our

[26] *Systematic Sociology*, p. 28.
[27] *Ideology and Utopia*, p. 102.

conduct, so that "whereas formerly we were the servants of necessity, we now find it possible to unite consciously with forces with which we are in thorough agreement."[28] But the question may be asked: Is it possible not to be in agreement?

The freedom here held out to us, shorn of Mannheim's liberal ardor, is a tenuous concept. Later he adopts the motto "Planning for Freedom" and observes rather negatively that "Freedom is expressed in the continual opportunity for resistance." Finally, his last work concedes much by asserting that "independent personality means some independent source of unpredictable change and creativeness in the individual" and that "freedom . . . means the right of the individual to develop within himself those resources which are the origin of change and creativeness."[29] It is in these later works, however, that Mannheim's liberal vision is most at odds with his sociological intuition, and such definitions as we have here quoted sit loose to his general theoretical view.

We see then that Mannheim declines to entertain the possibility that philosophy or theology as traditionally conceived can provide useful information about the nature of man's individuality. Whether through universals or eternal truths, both speak in absolutes which his sociology of knowledge has shown to be subject to prevailing "ideologies" and therefore relative. It is less profitable to speak of "human nature" than of "human behavior," for the latter opens the way for social science to solve the enigma. Individuality emerges from the interaction between a socially determined psyche and historically conditioned social groups, so that it may fairly be said that the ultimate scientific entity is the group, not the individual. Individuals invariably tend towards the personality type appropriate to the socioeconomic order in which they occur. Mannheim's wish is that the democratic personality type should win the day, and in the context of this wish he makes some brave statements about free and independent personality. One cannot but agree, however, with the many critics who have suggested that it is the wish which is father

[28] *Ibid.*, p. 169. The debt to Marx here is obvious.
[29] *Freedom, Power, . . .* , p. 240.

to this kind of thought and not the sociological model. This point receives fuller treatment in subsequent sections.

SANCTITY OF THE INDIVIDUAL

We must now discover on what normative grounds Mannheim urges respect for the individual. Since he considers that norms and ideals are the product of "ideologies" and "utopias," it is interesting to observe his preference for some norms above others, along with his efforts to prove that his selection is the obvious one from a sociological point of view.

He offers us historical sketches of the emergence of the ideal of individual freedom. In a passage reminiscent of Nietzsche and Comte he distinguishes three stages in the development of morals: the medieval man in horde solidarity, the post-Renaissance man in individual competition, and the presently emerging man in "super-individual group solidarity." The cumbersome third category applies equally to man in Communist, fascist and liberal-capitalist cultures, for the factor that unites them all is the phenomenon of Great Society which the industrial revolution has brought into being. The difference is not between cultures that exalt the state above the individual and those in which the individual comes first, but between well-planned and badly planned societies. The fate of the individual is in the hands of those who now consciously plan society.

Elsewhere he identifies the Protestant spirit as the spring of individualism, from which has developed liberalism, i.e., that "ideology" which has produced capitalism's free competition and political laissez faire. The emergence of Great Society prompts him to make two kinds of comment on liberalism. The first is typical of his German period.

> From the wreckage of liberalism nothing can be saved but its values, among others, the belief in a free personality. But its technique, which is based on the principle of laissez-faire, is gone for ever.[30]

[30] *Man and Society*, p. 364.

The second reflects lessons learnt later, after he had come to believe that "the British pattern comes closest to what we call 'planning for freedom'." [31]

> 'Planning for Freedom' is based upon a vision of society which in itself is not necessarily Christian but which creates the conditions under which Christian life is possible in modern society.[32]

It is therefore apparent that to his earlier conviction that the ideal had been born of a religious spirit was added the later conviction that it could only be preserved by the same agency.

Another of his sociological analyses, concerning the development of privacy, illustrates the same point and leads also to value judgments about the matter. At first Mannheim treats privacy as an escape mechanism, quoting Max Weber's thesis:

> The gradual *recession into privacy* of certain spheres previously public (the spheres of life in which personal and religious feelings prevail) is in the nature of a compensation for the increasing rationalisation of public life in general.[33]

He also says some harsh things about isolating practices such as monasticism and the Protestant stress on privacy. However, in *Diagnosis* we find him regretting the invasion of the privacy of the individual and even advocating monasticism for some because "modern society needs the counter-weight of solitude to the crowd experience." Stewart reminds us that Mannheim's comments on privacy and inwardness tend to be overlooked, yet Mannheim's attitude is that they are the strongest means of individualization and a great, "if not the greatest, asset in the growth of an independent personality." Consequently he makes prodigious efforts to ensure that his recommendations relating to planning include the guarantee of "free zones" and tolerance of deviators.

It is equally rare to find in Mannheim's critics an awareness of how much he stresses the primacy of personal relationships. In lectures at Oxford in 1938 he spoke of factors foster-

[31] *Freedom, Power,* . . . , p. 70.
[32] *Diagnosis*, p. 144.
[33] *Essays*, p. 88.

ing individualization, commending "the democratic organisation of small groups" and claiming that "It is in the long run not so much the freedom of the individual but the freedom of sects, cliques and other small groups which ensures free thought." [34] Subsequently he continued to stress the influence of primary groups like the family, albeit insisting that sociology and religion must study the behavior of large groups and relationships, in order to appreciate the effect they have on primary groups and relationships, and in *Diagnosis* he says emphatically that "we must create a society in which personal relationships carry weight." In *Freedom, Power and Democratic Planning* the final development of his thought is reflected in the fears he expresses about psychological manipulation, and in a danger warning:

> As usually happens with a type of experience that is about to be ruled out by social development, we have suddenly become aware of the significance of the person-to-person experience or, in Martin Buber's terms, the 'Thou experience.' [35]

Sociological determinism is here no longer in the saddle, for he counsels us to resist the trend to planned collectivism, insisting that person-to-person relationships and primary groups must be strengthened if we are to plan for freedom.

In his later works there is a modification of view which is probably the most marked of all: his view of the function and fruit of religion. His earlier comments on religion are skeptical, but he eventually comes to believe that religious agencies are the ones to whom the job of creating the desired personality type should be entrusted. This is because Christianity is the main source of the best human values (i.e., those that promote democratic personality) and because there is a need in a planned society for a unifying purpose, which "can be achieved either by the extermination or internment of those who do not agree, or by a spiritual integration of the members of society." [36]

---

[34] *Essays*, p. 283.
[35] *Freedom, Power, . . .* , p. 298.
[36] *Diagnosis*, p. 100. Contrast *Systematic Sociology*, pp. 58ff., 132; *Essays*, p. 287.

Christianity can serve this integrating function because its ideals promote a willingness to sacrifice personal comfort in order to plan for a democratic order of society and because by means of its symbols and ceremonies it provides paradigmatic experiences that fix the new standards of conduct and character in the individual's personality. Mannheim reiterates these views in *Freedom, Power and Democratic Planning*, which stops short just as he is beginning to develop a section concerning "dynamic religion." However, it is apparent here that his thought has progressed beyond *Diagnosis*, where he had treated religion as a useful sociological tool without any apparent appreciation of the basis of its adherents.[37] He now comments that "certain unchanging aspects of the human mind seem to indicate the need for a transcendental religious foundation in society," [38] and speaks of every individual's need to be assured "that there is a Purpose in what we are doing, and that there is a Personal Power to whom man can appeal." [39]

It is in this mellower mood that Mannheim couples with his consistent theme, the remaking of personality, reference to the uniqueness and nonconformity of each personality—a problem which has "puzzled our best philosophers." [40] Having quoted Hegel, Marx, and G. H. Mead on the social origin of the ego, he goes on to commend the achievement of liberal society in recognizing uniqueness and personal deviation, and refers with great warmth to the freedom, inde-

---

[37] Curtis observes that "Mannheim's point of view is that of an external observer who had never really understood the essential nature of the Christian religion" (Curtis, *Introduction to Philosophy of Education*, p. 207.) I cannot but agree. In particular it is diverting to find Mannheim saying in effect to avowed absolutists: "You realize of course that your norms and symbols are relative to the needs of men at different times. Learn from me the adjustment character of your values. However, I am happy to borrow from you the power to change personalities which social planning requires," as though Christians did not believe that Christianity's absolute values and its converting power were interdependent.

[38] *Freedom, Power, . . .* , p. 288.

[39] *Ibid.*, p. 289. In *Diagnosis*, it was only necessary to ensure an élite of converted persons.

[40] *Ibid.*, p. 239.

pendence, and creativity which belong to the individual. The most radical confession of this humane sociologist occurs when he says:

> Innovations come about mostly through a free integration of deviating types who remain as insignificant dissenters outside the established social structure, yet often contribute new ideas and possible solutions in crisis situations of social change.[41]

In summary, there is a clear evolution in Mannheim's thought regarding the sanctity of the individual, and the mutations are caused by the social crises that refuted some of his earlier sociological deductions and exiled him in England among religious friends of some intellectual vigor. Convinced to the end that social planning is inevitable, he expounds the desirability of democratic as opposed to totalitarian planning, the basic difference being the relative status given by each to the sanctity of the individual. In the search for sanctions of sufficient weight to shield this principle, he arrives by several routes at religious attitudes and finds in an alliance between Christian leaders and sociologists the surest formula for planning for freedom. In doing so, he is weaned away from purely sociological premises and indulges in speculative normative statements which compensate with ardor for what they lack in sociological testability. However, Mannheim's estimate of Christianity is made only in sociological terms, and his failure to take seriously its own vocabulary of meanings prevents him from employing it successfully as a safeguard within his plan for individualism.

SOCIETY AND THE INDIVIDUAL

As against those who impute to Mannheim a "totalitarian intuition" and dismiss his references to the sanctity of the individual as insubstantial concessions to sentiment, we have tried to sustain the view that these references represent his

[41] *Ibid.*, p. 190.

deepest concern.[42] How is it, then, that the general impression he has created is so contrary to this? The answer lies in his conviction of the inevitability of social planning and his faith in the social scientist's power to put planning on a scientific basis.

A constant refrain in his books is that planning is inevitable. "We are living in an age of transition from laissez faire to a planned society."[43] Like Marx he interprets the industrial revolution as heralding a new state of affairs in which mass society is the major phenomenon. This has given rise to an increasing "density of events" which makes regulation imperative, just as the traffic at a crossroads eventually requires a policeman to be stationed there.[44] As with morals, so with technology and politics, the dialectic of history has brought us to the point where casual invention and spontaneous consensus belong to the past and planning must come. We are in an age of crisis where industrial organization has outstripped social and moral controls and the Great Society has failed to

> re-establish on a larger scale the methods of value adjustment ... which were always active in small communities, and which, owing to the limited size of those communities, could do their work spontaneously.[45]

Not only are new methods of valuation needed, but values themselves need to be re-constituted. Once justified by Divine fiat, then by "ideology," they are now revealed by the sociology of knowledge to be culturally derived, and "the change to conscious value appreciation and acceptance is a Copernicus-like change."[46] We must now set up "a machinery

---

[42] I therefore dissent from Campbell's conclusion to an otherwise valuable study on "Tension in the Planners: Karl Mannheim" (*Australian Journal of Education*, vol. 2, July 1958) that "individual freedom is not the central consideration" (p. 114). Assuredly there was an unresolved tension, as I go on to show; but it was between the ideal of individual freedom and the assumptions and methods of sociology as Mannheim understood them.

[43] *Diagnosis*, p. 1.

[44] *Man and Society*, p. 157. The analogy is rather unfortunate, inviting extension of thought to the "police state"!

[45] *Diagnosis*, p. 104.

[46] *Ibid.*, p. 22.

pendence, and creativity which belong to the individual. The most radical confession of this humane sociologist occurs when he says:

> Innovations come about mostly through a free integration of deviating types who remain as insignificant dissenters outside the established social structure, yet often contribute new ideas and possible solutions in crisis situations of social change.[41]

In summary, there is a clear evolution in Mannheim's thought regarding the sanctity of the individual, and the mutations are caused by the social crises that refuted some of his earlier sociological deductions and exiled him in England among religious friends of some intellectual vigor. Convinced to the end that social planning is inevitable, he expounds the desirability of democratic as opposed to totalitarian planning, the basic difference being the relative status given by each to the sanctity of the individual. In the search for sanctions of sufficient weight to shield this principle, he arrives by several routes at religious attitudes and finds in an alliance between Christian leaders and sociologists the surest formula for planning for freedom. In doing so, he is weaned away from purely sociological premises and indulges in speculative normative statements which compensate with ardor for what they lack in sociological testability. However, Mannheim's estimate of Christianity is made only in sociological terms, and his failure to take seriously its own vocabulary of meanings prevents him from employing it successfully as a safeguard within his plan for individualism.

SOCIETY AND THE INDIVIDUAL

As against those who impute to Mannheim a "totalitarian intuition" and dismiss his references to the sanctity of the individual as insubstantial concessions to sentiment, we have tried to sustain the view that these references represent his

[41] *Ibid.*, p. 190.

deepest concern.⁴² How is it, then, that the general impression he has created is so contrary to this? The answer lies in his conviction of the inevitability of social planning and his faith in the social scientist's power to put planning on a scientific basis.

A constant refrain in his books is that planning is inevitable. "We are living in an age of transition from laissez faire to a planned society." ⁴³ Like Marx he interprets the industrial revolution as heralding a new state of affairs in which mass society is the major phenomenon. This has given rise to an increasing "density of events" which makes regulation imperative, just as the traffic at a crossroads eventually requires a policeman to be stationed there.⁴⁴ As with morals, so with technology and politics, the dialectic of history has brought us to the point where casual invention and spontaneous consensus belong to the past and planning must come. We are in an age of crisis where industrial organization has outstripped social and moral controls and the Great Society has failed to

> re-establish on a larger scale the methods of value adjustment . . . which were always active in small communities, and which, owing to the limited size of those communities, could do their work spontaneously.⁴⁵

Not only are new methods of valuation needed, but values themselves need to be re-constituted. Once justified by Divine fiat, then by "ideology," they are now revealed by the sociology of knowledge to be culturally derived, and "the change to conscious value appreciation and acceptance is a Copernicus-like change." ⁴⁶ We must now set up "a machinery

---

[42] I therefore dissent from Campbell's conclusion to an otherwise valuable study on "Tension in the Planners: Karl Mannheim" (*Australian Journal of Education*, vol. 2, July 1958) that "individual freedom is not the central consideration" (p. 114). Assuredly there was an unresolved tension, as I go on to show; but it was between the ideal of individual freedom and the assumptions and methods of sociology as Mannheim understood them.
[43] *Diagnosis*, p. 1.
[44] *Man and Society*, p. 157. The analogy is rather unfortunate, inviting extension of thought to the "police state"!
[45] *Diagnosis*, p. 104.
[46] *Ibid.*, p. 22.

of co-ordination and value mediation."[47] In short, every sign points to the inevitability of planning, and the examples of Russia and Germany show what happens when this planning is wrongly applied. Democracy is vulnerable until it takes heed of the weaknesses of liberalism and learns lessons from the social techniques employed in totalitarian states. "There is no longer any choice between planning and *laisser-faire*, but only between good planning and bad."[48]

The responses of critics to this conclusion have been varied, depending on how friendly they have been to the concept of planning in any form. For example, Bantock and Curtis tend to defend the free play of social political ideas and to abhor any suggestion of "planning" in those realms, whereas Popper, writing with more rigor, echoes Mannheim's respect for sociology and objects not to planning at many levels including these, but to holistic planning. Few would now dispute that social co-ordination is needed on a larger scale than hitherto, but the squeeze comes when it is claimed that social planning should be total, and that all areas of life including human values should be brought under the control of sociologically trained planners.

Mannheim's idea of planning, first developed in *Man and Society*, involves a total strategy in which society is controlled from "key positions, according to a definite plan." Individuals who object to this will require

> a thorough re-education to convince them that to combat the blindness of the social forces by the help of human regulation will make man freer than he has been before.[49]

The obvious problem of who is sufficient for these things, and competent to plan so boldly, is met in this work by Mannheim's "prodigious—one might, without disrespect, say . . . obsessional"[50] faith in the possibilities of applied sociology.

It is not necessary here to demonstrate the comprehensive-

[47] *Ibid.*, p. 6.
[48] *Man and Society*, p. 6.
[49] *Ibid.*, p. 376.
[50] Jean Floud, "Karl Mannheim," in *The Function of Teaching: Seven Approaches to Purpose, Tradition and Environment*, ed. A. V. Judges, London: Faber and Faber, 1959, pp. 45–47.

ness of Mannheim's vision as others have done so convincingly;[51] it will be enough to summarize the main features.

Society is to be planned in accordance with the insights of sociology, which is able to develop predictions of social change admittedly not having the standing of natural laws, but sufficiently definitive to warrant long-term plans being based on them.[52] Inevitably this will be a task undertaken by a small minority, whose "master control of the power process must necessarily be total."[53] This minority becomes in Mannheim's later thinking a body representing a consensus of those agencies in the community who are concerned with valuation, particularly the churches and politicians. It will be the planners' responsibility to know when to stop and where to draw the line between spheres in which planning must take place and those "in which individual freedom may be permitted without upsetting the whole plan,"[54] a line he says it is quite possible to draw.

The remodeling of society which Mannheim proposes is inseparable from a remodeling of personality. Education will be geared to change, recognizing the group as the ultimate unit and aiming, by a curriculum built around a social science core and by greater emphasis on boarding schools, to produce the right personality type. Our hope lies in youth, which is not yet trapped in traditional molds. Public information media will need to be controlled by responsible bodies.

The fixing and maintaining of patterns of conduct are the responsibilities of religion, which has already demonstrated, albeit in a relatively random way, its capacity to bring about personality change. Therefore religion must be planned in the sense that we foster the growth of the spiritual life and utilize the strength of its primordial symbols to organize conduct and collective action. A rebirth of genuine religion is

---

[51] E.g., by Campbell, "Tension in the Planners," and Popper, *Poverty of Historicism*. Popper calls *Man and Society* "the most elaborate exposition of a holistic and historicist programme known to me" (p. 67n) and criticizes it in detail.
[52] Mannheim calls them *principia media*.
[53] *Freedom, Power, . . .* , p. 54.
[54] *Man and Society*, p. 349.

Karl Mannheim

needed because men's values must change in a relatively short time. Clearly, psychological manipulation is involved here, but:

> Manipulation is democratic as long as it is based upon consent and carried out in a spirit that guarantees freedom among groups, even if the planning controls concern themselves with all the activities of the group.[55]

Contrasting such sentiments with those examined earlier in this chapter presents the problem Campbell calls "the tension among the planners" in its most acute form; for our reporting here is as faithful to the writings of Mannheim as our analysis of his views on the sanctity of the individual. Four major criticisms have been aimed at Mannheim's attempts to shield the individual by "planning for freedom."

The first is that he has misjudged the inner springs of human behavior. His lack of perception about Christianity is an instance of this, and so is the great trust he is prepared to repose in the hands of the planners. One is reminded of Acton's maxim that the tendency to corrupt behavior increases in proportion to the power a man is allowed to wield. Despite his increased respect for parliamentary procedures and the importance of the Opposition, Mannheim elsewhere speaks of placing restrictions on criticism so that it occurs within planned forums which avoid premature publication of their findings. The integrity required for this is of a higher order than most would consider possible, human nature being what it is.

The second is that though he speaks so much of change, Mannheim's heart is in stability. Floud points out that he develops no theory of social change, and thinks only of change at a global level. He is, she says, "haunted by a sense of social disorder and crisis" and by the very completeness of his planning is working for a utopia as fearsome as Plato's or Marx's.

Third, there is his confident eagerness to transform human personality. Floud speaks of his "planned attack on the Self,"

[55] *Freedom, Power,* . . . , p. 281.

and Campbell exposes the consistent strategy in all his writings on education, where the stress is on conformity, obedience, and "cohesion." He does make allowance for the gradual emergence at the upper educational levels of those qualities "which make for individualization and the creation of independent personalities," [56] but this provision appears to be restricted to the élite who get this far, and it further gratuitously presumes that education for individuality can emerge from a ground base of conformity and conditioning in the early years.

Fourth, there is the fundamental flaw in Mannheim's historicism which we have already criticized in Marx, aided by Popper's analysis. When he is challenged to justify his program for personality change, Mannheim's reply is that sociology provides both blueprint and techniques. Yet these depend on the ability of the sociologist to deal holistically with society (when in fact scientific method is unfitted to do so) and on the right of the sociologist to make the necessary value judgments (when in fact scientific theory is essentially descriptive). Bantock points out rather captiously that Mannheim favors scientific, mechanical, and military metaphors. These aid the rhetoric of the case but obscure the lack of a genuine scientific model or method, for holism provides neither. Campbell suggests that the dangerous ambiguities in Mannheim's writing stem in part from the fact that

> He sometimes argued his conclusions from purely sociological premises and sometimes from his total knowledge and beliefs without drawing the distinction between his views as a scientific sociologist and his views as a whole person.[57]

This comment stands if we accept the anti-historicist definition of sociology proposed by Popper, but if Mannheim's view of sociology is our guide, the distinction is well-nigh impossible to make.

[56] *Diagnosis*, p. 52.
[57] Campbell, "Tension in the Planners," p. 119.

COUNTERPOINT
NUNN : MANNHEIM

SOCIAL SCIENCE AND VALUES

In Nunn and Mannheim we have two social scientists at odds not only with each other but within themselves. The problem they both fail to resolve theoretically is that of normative theory in the social sciences: Nunn because his attack on the problem is superficial; Mannheim, though he makes this problem his central concern, because he finds the logic of his position conflicting with his personal sensibilities.

Nunn is a good example of the thesis put forward in Mannheim's sociology of knowledge, in that his philosophical and psychological views reflected the then prevailing pattern of British Liberalism. Yet his Realism has sturdier roots than capitalist "ideology," and it continues to be a position held by many in opposition to Pragmatism. His psychology, however, contains in germ that glorification of "self" which is a legacy of Freudian "id" and Nietzschean "will-to-power"; and had his logic been as inexorable as Nietzsche's, his biological model must have produced an equally bleak view of human relationships. There is undoubted evidence that Nunn did claim to be deducing his norms from the data of psychology [1] and that, having despaired of finding ideals of life

---

[1] For example: the ideal of individuality is inferred from the autonomy of organisms (*Education*, p. 22); the aim of education is an "Education according to nature" (p. 26); the artist "shows in the clearest and most definite

which would command general consent, he turned to his biological model for norms that would be indisputable because they were "scientific."

Mannheim's "relationism" is a far more subtle example of the same procedure. One might say that his model is a sociological "network."[2] He is impressed with the part played in human relationships by norms and value systems, and insists that they must constitute a major field of study, within sociology, to be defined as sociology of knowledge. As we have seen, this assumes that norms are products of the social network, and that study of social relationships at a particular time reveals the normative patterns most conducive to personal and social adjustment. Thus, planning is in the present day an unavoidable concomitant of the network of Great Society; and the alternative normative theories which may hold within this are "planning for dictatorship" and "planning for freedom" (in later writings, "democracy"). Sociologically speaking, democracy is a better form of adjustment, and therefore we ought to opt for the second alternative. The exercising of this option is what makes Mannheim's approach "relational" rather than "relativistic" in his own eyes. Even in his later sympathy for British democratic and Christian values, Mannheim describes his preferences as sociologically based, explaining for example that the success of Christianity resides in the social effectiveness of its archetypal symbols. The implication at all times in all his writings is that the value judgments he makes arise out of his sociological model.

One therefore finds that both thinkers, having accounted for the social facts within scientific models, proceed to prescribe valuations which they claim are thereby implied. But regardless of how effectively they do in fact cope with all

form what is fundamentally and ideally the way of all life" because he is self-expressive (p. 40); psychoanalysis vindicates autonomous development as an aim (p. 65); "play-way" allows expression of "the craving of the organism for free self-assertion" (p. 99); morality is the outcome of herd instinct (p. 193) as is all social life (p. 195); development of "will" requires free expression as this permits instinct tendencies to firm into sentiments (p. 217).

[2] I prefer this word to the less obvious "structure" used by Mannheim.

the social facts, they are guilty of a philosophical fallacy first identified by Hume and applied more particularly to the social sciences by many recent thinkers. Thus F. S. C. Northrop, discussing generalizations in the social sciences, suggests that they are of two kinds (*vide* Hume) — empirical and normative. Out of these come factual social theory and normative social theory. For example, democracies may be described factually, but "Democracy is a normative social theory"; [3] and as soon as one turns from analyzing it to commending it, without acknowledging a change in the sphere of discourse, one has committed what Northrop, adapting G. E. Moore, calls the "culturalistic fallacy." [4] Nunn does so by describing individuality as the key to organic life and then proceeding to set it up as an ideal and educational objective. Mannheim does so with respect to "democracy," "total planning," and Great Society. Even had they been correct in their method, the result would have been two "empirically verified" normative theories which were opposed to each other. Thus do psychology and sociology compete when they purport to pronounce on the nature of man.

Furthermore, even if we permit them to work within their models, we can gain little satisfaction in our quest for safeguards of the sanctity of the individual. Nunn's stress on free expression and self-assertion is only distinguishable from Nietzsche's because he goes elsewhere to invoke sanctions of the kind we need. Mannheim's objective of "total planning" is only different from totalitarian planning because of the emphasis he places on "liberal values" of which he evidently approves. Has the individual become — as Kierkegaard feared he must — the victim of scientific abstractions?

It is instructive to discover the kinship of Nunn and Mannheim with respect to the nature of the individual. In almost identical terms they speak of the "self" as a dynamic entity

[3] F. S. C. Northrop, *The Logic of the Sciences and the Humanities*, New York: Macmillan, 1949, p. 278.

[4] *Ibid.*, p. 279. I cannot discuss here how Northrop, having made this useful clarification, falls himself into the trap he has exposed, by endeavoring to take "our empirical philosophy of the natural sciences as the criterion of the correct normative philosophy of the social sciences" (p. 275).

subject to determining factors. When he is loyal to his model, Nunn speaks of engram-complexes or sentiments as present in the germ cell, but when resolved to say what he really believes, he asserts that

> The human organism, body and mind, is a centre of creative energy that uses endowment and environment as its working material; so that the elements it receives from nature and nurture do not make it what it becomes, except insofar as they are the bases of the free activity that is the essential fact of its existence.[5]

Likewise, Mannheim speaks of the "most elementary processes which integrate, dissolve, reintegrate, fix and shift the libidinous psychic energy" and opines that "very likely . . . behaviour depends more on social position than on inherent character," [6] thereby making it seem natural to speak as he does of changing human personality in line with predetermined stereotypes; yet he comes out in defense of the deviant, attributing to him, as does Nunn, again in almost identical words, the most significant advances in human life. Of course they differ fundamentally on some points. Nunn seems unaware of the magnitude of social changes, whereas Mannheim is so obsessed by them that he prompts Nunn specifically to comment that Mannheim is pessimistic about human progress; politically they are poles apart; and educationally their proposals are quite dissimilar. However, the fact remains that as whole persons they both find it necessary to forsake the strict canons of scientific method in order to acclaim the sanctity of the individual.

In short, though neither Nunn nor Mannheim was a stranger to philosophical discourse, whether of Hume and Kant or of contemporary positivism and naturalism, yet they both exhibited philosophical naiveté in their approach as social scientists to normative theory. Even Mannheim, whose descriptive analysis of norms and ideologies is profound and important, is ingenuous when he becomes a commender. As

[5] *Education*, p. 118.
[6] *Systematic Sociology*, pp. 33 and 49.

regards the sanctity of the individual, Nunn offers the firmest reassurances, but they tend to be dogmas rather than rigorous concepts. Mannheim's liberal views are so clearly at odds with his model of social interaction that we fear to let the social scientists loose. Is our need, then, for a more sophisticated social scientist who can maintain theoretical consistency in his handling of normative data (like Dewey), or for someone who will rephrase the problem at Kierkegaard's ethical level (like Buber), or for a synthesis different from both? Our succeeding chapters are, in part, a quest for that synthesis.

EDUCATIONAL THEORY

The sanctity of the individual matters to educationists both as a value to be inculcated and as a guiding principle for curriculum planning and teaching methods. Since Nunn and Mannheim both write specifically about education, it is necessary to see how they handle this issue.

Nunn maintains that "individuality is the ideal of life," and that therefore "the primary aim of all educational effort should be to help boys and girls to achieve the highest degree of individual development of which they are capable." Individuality is also the way to satisfy the claims of society, for "the most clearly 'social' conduct always implies a strong self behind it." In school organization "the individual pupil is the unit" and the teacher an idea-carrier, observer, and prompter utilizing the psychological tool of suggestion as opposed to coercion. Hence one may say that "the proper aim of education is positive, to encourage free activity."

The methods of teaching and control used in the school will, it follows, be "progressive." Social interactions and sanctions will develop out of the gregarious instinct which prompts individuals. One will be especially respectful of individual differences, utilizing mental tests and other psychological measures. The training of the will is dependent upon "the activity of the self-regarding sentiment" and therefore takes place not by dictation but through self-expression, as in the Montessori method. In our ideal school the ultimate veto lies with the pupil," but we need not fear anarchy if we provide a suitable educational medium and rely upon opportunity for play, socialization, and imitation. Naturally the curriculum will be geared to the needs of the pupil and his own rate of learning will govern the timetable. This will probably require that separate types of schools be available to provide varied media. Practical experiments in education that can guide us toward freedom in education are Montessori's "playway" with younger children, Parkhurst's "Dalton Plan" for guiding the learning of older children, and Homer Lane's "Little Commonwealth"—a reform school in which great gains have been made by such enlightened procedures as giving students a high degree of self-government. These examples quoted by Nunn illustrate the position he occupied as a popularizer of the "new education" in Britain.

Nunn's educational theory seems guaranteed at first glance to do justice at many levels to the principle of individual autonomy. However, the treatment of social factors is weak, as in the case of Kierkegaard. It is not clear how the interplay between individual and society is to be governed, partly because Nunn goes beyond his model when talking about moral and social factors, and partly because he leaves us with a vague feeling of some substantial but undiscussed authority hovering at the verge of his proposals. He touches on the teacher's use of such manipulative tools as sublimation, rituals, and suggestion; refers in passing to certain moral standards of "proven worth" and "permanent validity"; and speaks of the significance to the student of religious confirmation, without explaining what this is. Nowhere does Nunn come forth and declare his world-view as such, apparently assuming that we understand and accept British society as it was when he wrote, as he evidently did. Insofar as this was even then in transition, his educational theory was built on sand soon to be disturbed, as Mannheim foresaw, by advancing tides of social change.

If Nunn's was in some ways American "progressivism" in more sober British dress, then Mannheim's educational theory was a foretaste of what is being popularized in the United

States by Theodore Brameld as "reconstructionism," a view of the school which places it in the vanguard of social change and reconstruction. Education is considered to be one of the most powerful tools of the planners, and its aim is to "mould man . . . in and for a given society." To explain why education's role is so significant, Mannheim points out that in an era when social change is the order of the day, only an education for change will do. Furthermore, the "sociological function of youth in society" is that they are malleable, not yet wedded to the status quo, and therefore ideal subjects for social planning and innovation. The ultimate unit in education is the group, and our initial educational strategy will aim to produce

on the lower levels basic conformity, cohesion, habit-making, emotional training, obedience . . . and on the higher levels a gradual emergence of those qualities . . . which make for individualisation and the creation of independent personalities.[7]

Such objectives clearly affect policies relating to teachers and curricula. The teacher now becomes the handmaid of the planners, with the responsibility of fashioning the desired personality types. And not alone.

Functions formerly fulfilled by the priesthood alone are now shared by the educator, administrator, political propagandist, journalist, and public-relations counsellor.[8]

These are strange bedfellows for an occupational group noted for the catch-cry of "academic freedom." The school now becomes a planned society intermediary between the family and the state, and it has no choice but to "intensify and broaden its contacts with other areas of life and social institutions; it will have to give up its older, purely scholastic character."[9] The teacher's greatest aid will be sociology, and the core of "a curriculum destined to integrate a new ruling élite" may well be "social science instruction." Mannheim throws out the hint

[7] *Diagnosis*, p. 52.
[8] *Freedom, Power*, p. 53.
[9] *Ibid.*, p. 249.

that more use could be made of the socialization opportunities provided through boarding schools and camps.

This brief summary of Mannheim's educational theory must suffice as evidence that whereas Mannheim's concern for the sanctity of the individual is frequently stated in general terms, his advice concerning planning procedures and social integration is buttressed by suggestions for practical implementation which point all too clearly in the opposite direction. It is possible to claim that the indoctrinative function he prescribes for education is only a realistic recognition of the function all teachers consciously or unconsciously perform, but the difference lies in whether the good of the group or the individual is the ultimate criterion. The distinction here drawn will become clearer when we discuss the educational theory of John Dewey. Dewey's vision is for what may be described as a "planning society" as opposed to Mannheim's "planned society."

PART FOUR:

SCIENTIFIC

WORLD-VIEWS

In Part Four we compare the views of Dewey and Whitehead. Both are professional philosophers for whom the problem of constructing a system of thought adequate to the demands of the age of science is of major concern. Dewey is not only indebted to biological and social science but makes an original contribution to the latter. Whitehead turns to pursue the philosophical quest after a distinguished first career in mathematical science. Both in their own way develop scientific world-views of considerable sophistication, in order to travel on to moral and social issues. That is, their goal is to lay down principles that will guide human endeavor. Inevitably, therefore, the human individual comes under the scrutiny of both, with outcomes significant for this study.

JOHN DEWEY

1859-1952

Dewey has been acknowledged a leading thinker in two fields: philosophy and education. He has been acclaimed America's greatest philosopher not only by former students but also by less sympathetic observers such as Bertrand Russell. And most modern theorists of education find it necessary to do battle with Dewey's Experimentalism in order to clarify their own positions.[1] His biography is the story of the U.S.A. in little, as he moves away from the diluted Protestant heritage of his parents, and from the Hegelian Idealism of the Old World, into views that are fresh, bold, and experimental. His literary output, extending over at least seventy years, is voluminous and, because of his practice of publishing lecture series given by invitation in various places, repetitive to a fault. The student might well despair, were it not for the general consistency of Dewey's views after his repudiation of Idealism in the late 1880s, making it possible for us to regard certain works as usefully representative of his position. What makes this easier to do is that Dewey lived long enough to hear criticisms and periodically review his main themes in the light of them.

---

[1] Apposite to this is a shrewd remark made by Dewey when challenged to discuss the relation of his position to Progressivism: "In spite of itself, any movement that thinks and acts in terms of an 'ism becomes so involved in reaction against other 'isms that it is unwittingly controlled by them." (*Experience and Education*, New York: Macmillan, reprinted 1955, p. vii.)

Born [2] in 1859 to parents of pioneering stock and latitudinarian beliefs, John Dewey attended state school in Vermont, finding it dreary in comparison to the informal education and rich friendships provided by the close-knit rural community in which he lived. At the University of Vermont he discovered both aptitude and penchant for philosophy, meanwhile experiencing a considerable shift of view through studies in evolution guided by a T. H. Huxley textbook and readings in Auguste Comte. The first prepared the ground for his denial of a unique mind or spirit in man, and the second assisted him, according to his own report, to see the "disorganization of existing social life and the necessity of finding a social function for science." After graduating in philosophy he taught in high schools for three years and then, encouraged by W. T. Harris's interest in some philosophical articles he had written, borrowed money to enter the Johns Hopkins University as a graduate student in 1882. Encountering well-taught Hegelianism, he became a disciple, and when his professor moved to Michigan, he was invited along as an instructor in philosophy. He was still at this stage a religious idealist; in his early years at Michigan he conducted Bible classes for the Student Christian Association.[3] Meanwhile he was impressed by the democratic climate of President Angell's staff room, and profoundly influenced by William James's *Principles of Psychology* — according to Jane Dewey "much the greatest single influence in changing the direction of Dewey's philosophical thinking." He also met and married Alice Chipman, an intelligent and individualistic student.

After a year as professor at Minnesota, Dewey returned to Michigan to occupy the chair rendered vacant by his former teacher's death, and became a close friend and colleague of George Herbert Mead, whose social psychology, built around

---

[2] My chief biographical source is the résumé edited by Jane Dewey in *The Philosophy of John Dewey,* ed. Paul Arthur Schilpp, The Library of Living Philosophers, vol. I, Evanston and Chicago: Northwestern University, 1939, pp. 6–45, with later details gleaned from other sundry sources.

[3] See Arthur G. Wirth, "John Dewey in Transition from Religious Idealism to the Social Ethic of Democracy," in *History of Education Quarterly,* vol. 5, Dec. 1965, p. 264.

the notion of organisms acting and reacting in their environment, was exactly to his liking. Dewey's other great interest, education, was strengthened by the arrival of three children, and he accepted an invitation to become professor and head of the department of philosophy and psychology at Chicago on condition that the department be reorganized to include "pedagogy." In the same period he became a distinguished member of the National Herbart Society.

By now his passage from absolutist philosophy to Experimentalism was complete,[4] and in retrospect he saw his affinity with the logic lecturer he had rather discounted as a student at Johns Hopkins, C. S. Peirce. For Peirce had said:

> To determine the meaning of any idea, put it into practice in the objective world of actualities and whatever its consequences prove to be, these constitute the meaning of the idea.[5]

What was for Peirce a maxim about meaning became for Dewey the keystone of truth, leading on to his logic of enquiry, sociological relativism, and educational progressivism. Publications began to appear which corresponded to the temper of the times and were widely acclaimed. In particular, *School and Society* foreshadowed themes that later works would expand, being composed of lectures given to raise money for the Laboratory School which Dewey established in association with his department, in order to test group work and activity methods.

Friction with the president over the administrative control of his school led Dewey to resign in 1904. Through the efforts of J. McKeen Cattell he obtained a position at Columbia University, supported by some lecture commitments at the adjacent famous teachers' college. Here he remained till retirement in the early thirties, earning international recognition and writing copiously (and this he continued through-

---

[4] See his "From Absolutism to Experimentalism," in *Contemporary American Philosophy*, vol. 2, ed. G. P. Adams and W. P. Montague, New York: Macmillan, 1930, pp. 13-27.
[5] Quoted in Butler, *Four Philosophies*, p. 412.

out the twenty years of his retirement). He traveled widely by invitation, accumulating disciples in such countries as Russia, Turkey, Japan, China, India, and Mexico. Life in New York quickened his interest in political problems and prompted works on sociological themes. It has been suggested that his views underwent some modification around 1930, veering away from radical Pragmatism to a greater insistence on the long-term goals of democracy and the need for proper and planned social relationships.[6] I consider that what accounts for this interpretation is not a shift in Dewey's basic stance but a consequence of the fact that Dewey had won so decisively his battle against the speculative metaphysicians in philosophy and the traditionalists in education that he was in jeopardy from the extremism of some of his own disciples and needed to stress neglected elements in his already declared position. A review of the books to which we shall chiefly refer supports this view.

In 1916 Dewey published *Democracy and Education*, in which he brought philosophy to the service of education and presented an ideal of education in and for a secular, scientific democracy — an ideal from which he subsequently never wavered. In 1919, *Reconstruction in Philosophy* appeared, after a lecture tour in Japan which forced him to clarify and summarize the thinking of three decades as an Experimentalist in philosophy; and shortly thereafter, a winter course in ethics on home soil prompted him to publish *Human Nature and Conduct: An Introduction to Social Psychology* (1921), which in retrospect illuminated *How We Think* (1910). Acknowledging the presence in human nature of a religious urge, Dewey

[6] Thus Robert Ulich, *History of Educational Thought* (New York: American Book Company, 1945, p. 322), and Clyde V. Martin, "The Metaphysical Development of John Dewey" (*Educational Theory*, vol. 8, Jan. 1958, pp. 55–58). But see also Dorothy J. Newbury's Note on Martin's article in *Educational Theory* (vol. 8, July 1958, pp. 183ff.); it casts doubt on the evidence Martin invokes to prove his point. And John Paul Strain proposes a different kind of mutation, from an emphasis on Pragmatism to a devotion to scientific method ("An Answer to the Misconceptions of John Dewey's Philosophy of Education," in *Educational Theory*, vol. 8, Oct. 1958, p. 273), which is an equally tenuous change within the ideology rather than an alteration of it.

believed that its fulfillment lay in recognition of the reconstructive and democratic function of naturalized intelligence. This he sought to show in *The Quest for Certainty: A Study of the Relation of Knowledge and Action* (1930), *Individualism, Old and New* (1930), and *A Common Faith* (1934, after his retirement). In the face of mounting criticism of the Progressive movement in education, Dewey was invited to deliver lectures discussing the controversies between traditionalists and progressives; and the result firmly preserved him from either label. The lectures were published as *Experience and Education* (1938), reaffirming the views of *Democracy and Education*. In 1946, *Problems of Men* brought together essays written since his seventy-fifth birthday; the last of these included a discerning tribute to William James. And again the main lines of Dewey's thought were congruent with his themes of thirty and forty years earlier. Hence, although the bibliography of Dewey's writings up to 1939 occupies 58 pages in Schilpp's volume, it may be claimed that our sample is representative of his views, especially as they relate to the theme of this study.

At the age of eighty-seven, Dewey remarried and founded a second family; and he continued writing till his death from pneumonia in 1952. During his life, ardent but extreme followers discredited the Progressivist movement, but more discriminating disciples continue to uphold the sophisticated ideology of his Experimentalism, which is sometimes still referred to as Pragmatism or Instrumentalism. "Experimentalism" will be used here to refer to the total ideology of John Dewey. In this usage we are dealing with a complex position ramified in many directions and not always easy to pin down. It is a matter of observation that both followers and foes of Dewey are invariably selective in their interpretations and simpler and more dogmatic in their findings than he; and one must endeavor to rescue Dewey from both parties. Nevertheless it is a legitimate criticism of Dewey that he has written diffusely and is in very much need of the ministrations of those British and other Analysts of whom he sometimes speaks in a derogatory manner.

DEFINING "INDIVIDUAL"

Basic to Dewey's thinking are the metaphysical categories of change and process, and the pattern according to which they operate in living things is, he believes, organic evolution. The individual is therefore an emergent entity, whose identity depends on the degree to which he exercises control over the process of which he is a part.

In a tribute to Darwin, Dewey insists that "the influence of Darwin upon philosophy resides in his having conquered the phenomena of life for the principle of transition."[7] The result has been the overthrow of all absolutist approaches to the study of reality, and by surrendering its "somewhat barren monopoly of dealings with Ultimate and Absolute Reality" philosophy has taken on a constructive role in actual human affairs—that of performing the "act of midwifery"[8] whereby a culture reconciled to evolutionary change in all aspects of life may be born.

It is now apparent that man's home is nature; "the doctrine of biological development . . . shows that man is continuous with nature, not an alien entering her processes from without."[9] Essentially he is a complex animal interacting with the natural environment. Insofar as he is different from lower animals, the difference is one of degree only, in that man preserves his past experiences in memory, the basis of which is largely emotional. Dewey puts this another way when, talking about art in experience, he says:

> Interaction of a living being with an environment is found in vegetative and animal life. But the experience enacted is human and conscious only as that which is given here and now is extended by meanings, and values drawn from what is absent in fact and present only imaginatively.[10]

[7] John Dewey, *The Influence of Darwin on Philosophy and Other Essays in Contemporary Thought,* London: Bell and Sons, 1910, p. 8.
[8] John Dewey, *Problems of Men,* New York: Philosophical Library, 1946, p. 20. Inevitably many writers have drawn the comparison with Marx.
[9] *Democracy and Education,* p. 333; see also 392f.
[10] Joseph Ratner, ed., *Intelligence in the Modern World: John Dewey's Philosophy,* New York: Random House Inc., 1939, p. 993.

In saying this, Dewey resolutely denies that he has established "mind" or "soul" as an entity over against the body. Man is a unity; "mind" is simply one of the functions of this unity, and the popular distinction between higher (i.e., spiritual) and lower (i.e., physical) functions is merely due to the interplay of internal physiological and external social processes.

It follows that in defining the individual one must take stock of him not as an isolated being, but as a creature with "an inherent tendency to action" defining himself by the way he acts and the habits he acquires. "All habits are demands for certain kinds of activity; and they constitute the self. In any intelligible sense of the word will, they *are* will." [11] Similarly reason or "thought," pictured by prescientific philosophers as some mysterious entity, is merely one response to environmental obstacles — and not always the main one.

> Thought is born as the twin of impulse in every moment of impeded habit. But unless it is nurtured, it speedily dies, and habit and instinct continue their civil warfare.[12]

Yet even if thought is an emergent late-comer, it holds the key to the distinctively human reaction to evolution, for by it man learns to exercise control over himself and his environment. He is by nature a problem-solver as opposed to an abstract thinker. "One is mentally an individual only as he has his own purpose and problem."

In one of his tributes to William James, Dewey commends the insight that "mind" is not some static or permanent entity within a man but a function of reflective behavior. Determined as he is to banish all philosophical dualisms with his own post-Hegelian "mediation," Dewey insists that mind can only be known by inference from the behavior that results. Insofar as that behavior is intelligent and purposeful, the individual is displaying or achieving mind. "Mind as a concrete thing is precisely the power to understand things in terms of the use made of them." Dewey thus helps to confirm

---

[11] John Dewey, *Human Nature and Conduct: An Introduction to Social Psychology*, London: George Allen and Unwin, 1921, p. 25.

[12] *Ibid.*, p. 171.

both the anti-mentalist orientation of most American psychology and the debunking of philosophical dualism by Gilbert Ryle.

A special slant is thereby given to Dewey's discussion of human thinking and its relation to acting. Thinking is "instrumental"; that is, it is prompted by a problem which arises in the on-going activity of living, and it is directed toward a practical outcome, the solving of a problem. Some have inferred from selected writings that Dewey belittles reflective and abstract thought with his stress on the pragmatic utility of thinking; certainly many of his disciples have followed this line. But Dewey also says that "Ideas are our rulers — for better or for worse" [13] and that the direction in which education should move is toward "an interest in intellectual matters for their own sake." [14] He just manages not to be inconsistent. He places stress on abstract thought because it enlarges the capacity to rehearse possible solutions to practical problems, and in an adaptation of Peirce he defines an idea instrumentally, as "a meaning that is tentatively entertained ... with reference to its fitness to decide a perplexing situation." [15] Thus a firm anchorage is found for thinking in acting, to discourage that divorce between aristocratic, contemplative man and plebeian, practical man which Dewey constantly blames on the Greeks.[16]

Dewey's view of "mind" has further implications for "knowledge." Having rejected Herbart's description of the mind as a repository of accumulated ideas, he insists that true knowledge is based on ideas which are problem-solving hypotheses, that is, on ideas which have meaning and relevance for the knower. Inherited information is only significant if it

[13] John Dewey, *How We Think*, Boston: Heath and Co., 1910, p. 19.
[14] *Ibid.*, p. 141.
[15] Dewey, *Human Nature and Conduct*, p. 108.
[16] E.g. *Democracy and Education*, p. 306, and *Reconstruction in Philosophy*, New York: Mentor, 1950, p. 42. Note that despite my care not to equate Dewey with cruder forms of Pragmatism, I find that his mediation between theoretical and practical is weighted towards the practical, as is his interpretation of the scientific method as reaching fulfillment in the laboratory rather than the armchair. A similar conclusion is reached by Savery in "The Significance of Dewey's Philosophy," in Schilpp, *John Dewey*, p. 512.

continues to have instrumental value for the individual. Thus Dewey does not discount it—"knowledge of the past is the key to understanding the present"—but he does warn us against "knowledge which is mainly secondhand, other men's knowledge."[17] Hence present experience takes precedence over the cultural inheritance, because the individual's role is to re-employ or reconstruct inherited knowledge for himself, without which activity it ceases to be "known." Individuals work at different rates, but all are indispensable; it is misleading to discount some as "dull,"[18] or to subordinate any to the immutable authority of an idea or system of values, for it is in the uninhibited interaction of individuals reconstructing their environment that human evolution best proceeds. Therefore there is nothing socially immutable about human nature; its fixed physiological constituents find different expressions under different conditions, so that we cannot assume we possess authoritative knowledge in advance about what individuals in society ought to be and do.

From our exposition it will be seen that there are grounds for comparing Dewey's view of human nature and individuality, in relation to the organic process, with white spume forming transiently on the crest of a wave as it rises for a moment from the sea. The case is strengthened by his observation that the intellectual life is "a comparatively late achievement" very limited in its influence compared with physiological factors. "Self"-consciousness has already been ruled out (*vide* James),[19] but even consciousness is to be divested of its metaphysical roles and recognized, "whether as a stream or as special sensations and images, [as expressing] functions of habits."

If the individual defines himself by what he does, if what he

[17] *Democracy and Education*, p. 220. In Randall's view Dewey does not preserve a balance but loads emotionally liberation from past knowledge. (See John Herman Randall, Jr., "Dewey's Interpretation of the History of Philosophy," in Schilpp, *John Dewey*, p. 100.)

[18] *How We Think*, p. 29. Gordon Allport notes Dewey's disinterest in rigid test scores and I.Q. concepts, in "Dewey's Individual and Social Psychology." (See Schilpp, *John Dewey*, pp. 275 and 280.)

[19] "My thinking is first and last and always for the sake of doing," said James. Quoted by Dewey in *Problems of Men*, p. 401.

does is contingent on interaction with a changing environment which includes other self-defining individuals, and if the authority of knowledge resides ultimately in its instrumental value to him, then one can understand why Dewey asserts that successful growth is the only legitimate aim. Wynne considers this so central to Dewey's educational theory that he labels it the Universal Growth Theory and points out how Dewey meets the objection "Growth to what end?" by stressing the growth and enlargement of the whole individual. If one objects that growth might be referred to an ability to burgle better, the reply would be that the burglar's total or general growth would be retarded by his clandestine skill, particularly since man is a social being.[20] Elsewhere Dewey specifies for education process aims like "natural development" and "social efficiency," which are clearly regarded as phases of universal growth. Even his liberal advocacy of democracy not only as a technique of government but as a way of life is consistent with this, in that he does not see democratic organization as static but as a dynamic process in which the growth of individuals is least impeded and restrictions are minimal. The status of various human values is contingent on the contribution they each make to universal growth at any given time.

It is easy to interpret this as meaning that individuals are opportunists living for the moment without deep convictions or distant goals, and some disciples did take Dewey this way. Hence Dewey had to remind them that the relativism of values does not necessarily imply that they have short lives, and he takes pains to defend the long-standing validity of such ideals as justice, affection, and truth.[21] He also insists that social life does require planning ahead, and that scientific knowledge accumulates through purposive research, though of course always based not on certainty but probability. Growth in man is subject not only to impulse and habit but to the in-

---

[20] John P. Wynne, *Theories of Education*, New York: Harper and Row, 1963, p. 190.

[21] John Dewey, *A Common Faith*, New Haven: Yale University Press, 1934, p. 44. This is one of the evidences that Martin cites for Dewey's shift of view, but I contend here that Dewey remains consistent. Such values are still not absolute. (See Martin, "The Metaphysical Development of John Dewey," p. 57.)

creasing employment of both by a wide-ranging intelligence. But it is important that we interpret "intelligence" in the light of the experimental method, not as traditionally related to abstract contemplation.

The great fact of the present era has been the rise of science and the resultant industrial society. A method of knowing has evolved which provides us with the clue whereby all of human experience may be integrated and unified, and growth promoted. Dewey's logic stresses not the attainment of truth but the successful completion of enquiry, whereby certain proposed acts prove effective in solving the problem which initiated the enquiry. "The true means the verified and means nothing else." In social affairs moral validation works the same way, for the method is universal.

Thus, individuality appears in the man with a problem; the traits of individual method are problem, collection of data, hypothesis, experimental test, assessment of results; an act of thought proceeds along the same route; scientific method is the ideal for experience; and value judgments are verified by social experiment. It is the nature of man as a biological entity to seek harmony and continuity with his environment, and when it presents him with an obstacle he seeks to overcome it. It is his glory that he has emerged from the times of superstition, contemplation, and deification of obstacles and has developed that systematic use of naturalized intelligence which is Experimentalism or the scientific method.

In this context it is appropriate to stress that man is a social being. The society of other men is part of that environment which we have said defines him and from which he arises to individuality. Men "are chiefly interested upon the whole, in entering into the activities of others and taking part in conjoint and co-operative doings."[22] Most of the problems with which they are concerned, and derivatively with which education is concerned, are social. Indeed Dewey equates moral and social categories constantly and explicitly.[23] Ability to adjust to society and make one's individual contribu-

[22] *Democracy and Education*, p. 38.
[23] E.g., *Human Nature and Conduct*, pp. 15-85, and *Problems of Men*, p. 281.

tion is the scientific method or the method of organized intelligence. Collective intelligence used as in the natural sciences has already achieved authoritative status because it is experimental, self-adjusting, and democratic in its membership. "The postulate of moral science is the continuity of scientific judgment." [24]

While I shall as usual take up the evaluative task in a later section, it is helpful at this point to illumine the analysis of Dewey's definition by noting some of the comments of others on his attempt. Holmes points out that the individual is environmentally defined and has no separate existence except in a limited physical sense.[25] Butler takes the point further by claiming to see in particular two metaphysical assumptions behind Dewey's view: "Man is continuous with the world" and "Man is not an active cause in the world." [26] Citing the second, he suggests that Dewey seeks to resolve the old determinism-or-free-will argument by a pragmatic merger, but ultimately loads social determinism. Santayana lays a charge subsequently quoted by many: that in Dewey "there is a pervasive quasi-Hegelian tendency to dissolve the individual into his social functions." [27] Allport, speaking of Dewey's psychology, suggests that Dewey has failed to provide a personality theory adequate to contain the whole individual, especially in view of the diverse sub-publics of which modern society is composed.[28] These comments would seem to hold good in spite of the liberal individualism which is so marked in Dewey and which opposes so strongly ideological and other threats to individual freedom. It is as though Dewey defines society in such a way as to release the full powers of an in-

[24] *Problems of Men*, p. 244.

[25] Brian Holmes, "The Reflective Man: Dewey," in Nash et al., *The Educated Man*, p. 310.

[26] Butler, *Four Philosophies*, pp. 434–435. The second is hardly just in view of Dewey's praises of organized intelligence. But the sole individual does not fare too well.

[27] George Santayana, "Dewey's Naturalistic Metaphysics," in Schilpp, *John Dewey*, p. 247.

[28] Gordon W. Allport, in Schilpp, *John Dewey*, p. 287. Dewey admits the charge but retorts that neither has anyone else (*ibid.*, p. 556).

dividual who is only defined as a social function. Mediation has obscured a vital dichotomy.

SANCTITY OF THE INDIVIDUAL

The grounds upon which Dewey champions the sanctity of the individual have already been implied above to some extent, inevitably because Dewey's definition of individuality is polemical in the sense that it incorporates the values that he wishes us to associate with it. For Dewey seeks constantly to dissolve traditional dualism, such as pragmatic is and moral ought, natural and moral, individual and social, intellectual and practical; and the mergers are thorough.[29] However, we must try to marshal his views under this heading because some things remain to be said. The leading idea in his normative theory is "democracy." [30]

Several points have already been made: life is governed by the evolutionary principle, which elevates the categories of process and change, novelty and chance; human life is not only biological but social, and the social milieu emphasizes the importance of co-operation; social efficiency hinges on collective intelligence. Only in recent years, so the story runs, has submission to traditional systems of authority been superseded by recognition of Bacon's aphorism that "knowledge is power"; and the scientific method has come to maturity as the greatest tool yet devised by the human species. Just as in the natural sciences research advances through experiment and publication of results, so in social life progress

---

[29] One of his more irascible critics has claimed that he does not resolve the problems represented by such dualisms but dissolves the realities at which they hint, so that in explaining he explains away, and leaves us in the slough of nihilism. (See Paul K. Crosser, *The Nihilism of John Dewey*, New York: Philosophical Library, 1955.) This exaggerates the defect I have been discussing, for though Dewey does leave us in many conceptual tangles because of this approach to explanation, there is a great deal which comes through very clearly to produce a characteristic ideology.

[30] In order to distinguish the programmatic meaning that Dewey gives to this word from a merely descriptive usage, I will enclose the word in quotes for the former purpose.

occurs through Experimentalism in values and the open forum of a "democratic" society. Hence Dewey's main justification for recognizing the worth of the individual is that social efficiency depends on it.[31]

A second line of argument is also typically Pragmatic. In the "foreground" (in Santayana's sense) of modern life is the general respect accorded to the individual in advanced societies. While agreeing that, historically, it was religious individualism that first produced "belief in the sacredness of individual conscience and in the right to freedom of opinion, belief and worship," Dewey views this valuation of the individual as a "given" in our time, honored by people of diverse persuasions and needing no metaphysical scaffolding to form the basis of social action (though of course the scientist is more faithful in putting it into practice than anyone else, because the nature of his task requires him to be).

Another line of argument is the plea of historical necessity. In company with Marx, whom he admires on this point, and with Mannheim, Dewey regards the present age as a radical departure from all previous ages, due to industrialization. "For better or worse, we are living in a corporate age." We are also living at a time when former authorities such as custom, organized religion, and absolutist philosophy have lost their hold on men to the new, flexible authority of "organized intelligence"; and it is imperative that we oppose modern dogmatisms, such as Marxism and Fascism, that are recrudescent anachronisms.

In such a social context older individualisms are inadequate; a new individualism is called for, by sheer historical development, based on a democracy secularized through systematic extension of the scientific method into every depart-

---

[31] The ideological character of this assumption needs to be recognized. Both Dewey and Nietzsche take their cue from the evolutionary analogy. But whereas Nietzsche stresses competition for survival, Dewey lays emphasis on co-operation. Not logic or evidence decides this ultimately, but emotional preference. It is a tenable alternative to Dewey's polemical account of history to suggest that competition for survival accounts for the phenomenal rise in the prestige and power over human affairs of science and its exploiters.

ment of life. Those who base their hopes on moral revival forget that the old institutions must go and morality be remade for this new age.

The new morality is instrumental, and may be discerned already in scientific endeavor. Characteristic of this are traits of directness, open-mindedness, single-mindedness, and a sense of responsibility. Exactly similar are the attitudes most conducive to social life:

> Open-mindedness, single-mindedness, sincerity, breadth of outlook, thoroughness, assumption of responsibility for developing the consequences of ideas which are accepted, are moral traits.[32]

The new morality also affects the traditional dichotomy between labor and leisure, inherited from Greek philosophy and hierarchically organized societies. In technological society, work is properly part of every man's fulfilling experiences, and leisure pursuits are no longer the privileged preserve of the élite. In a balanced life they will indeed shade into each other.

Furthermore the new morality is social, as against the abstract, personal morality of former times. This does not mean that morality has become impersonal and collective, for "it remains and must remain personal in that social problems have to be faced by individuals."

> The virtues of the individual in a progressive society are more reflective, more critical, involve more exercise of comparison and selection, than in customary society. But they are just as socially conditioned in their origin and as socially directed in their manifestation.[33]

And again:

> Full education comes only when there is a responsible share on the part of each person, in proportion to capacity, in shaping

[32] *Democracy and Education*, p. 413, and compare pp. 204f.
[33] John Dewey and James H. Tufts, *Ethics*, New York: Henry Holt, 1908, pp. 434f.

the aims of policies of the social groups to which he belongs. This fact fixes the significance of democracy.[34]

SOCIETY AND THE INDIVIDUAL

It is clear that Dewey is at pains to remove the dichotomy of individual versus society; as a result one tends to find that his definition of "individual" is based on social functions and that, conversely, his definition of society leans to political individualism. In asking whether he preserves the sanctity of the individual by so doing, we are better employed not in a technical study of the logical web which holds his system together but in an examination of some concepts which are crucial to the maintenance of the whole.

The first of these is the view he takes of the scientific method. Randall makes the point that

> Dewey's experimentalism is not primarily based on the methods of the laboratory . . . in the broadest sense, it is the experimentalism of the anthropologist, of the student of human institutions and cultures. . . . It is essentially a social method of doing and changing things.[35]

Hence Dewey stresses problem-solving as the keystone of the scientific method, but usually with social problems in view. Hence also he emphasizes the particular rather than the general, even to the extent, in Ratner's view, of virtually denying the "need for any general theory of society, of the state, of the individual, etc."[36] A similar criticism is leveled by Rusk when he observes that of three examples of problem-inspired thinking cited by Dewey in *How We Think*, two in fact originate in theoretical curiosity and only one from practical needs.[37]

Each of these critics for various reasons is objecting to the interpretation of scientific method as a primarily practical ac-

[34] *Reconstruction in Philosophy*, p. 162.
[35] Randall, "Dewey's Interpretation of the History of Philosophy," p. 82.
[36] Joseph Ratner, "Dewey's Conception of Philosophy," in Schilpp, *John Dewey*, p. 63.
[37] Rusk, *Doctrines of Great Educators*, p. 299.

tivity, in which the theory-building aspect is kept as minimal and functional as possible. From this derives the jibe directed at Pragmatism that it sees no use for the armchair scientist. But we have seen that Dewey is not to be so easily dismissed, for he explicitly commends the theoretical element in thought. Even so he cannot altogether escape the charge, as Northrop shows in his analysis of the logic of scientific method. It is Northrop's contention that Dewey makes too much of what is basically a tautology when he stresses that enquiry is initiated by a problem; and he goes on to propound the view that, contrary to the views of Dewey and earlier nineteenth-century philosophers, the essence of science resides in the formation of deductively obtained theory. In an age when mathematical models have outflanked mechanical and organic models in scientific investigation, Northrop's point is well taken, and it becomes apparent that Dewey's view is ideologically loaded and subverts the objective pursuit of the scientist to the instrumental goals of Dewey and his followers.

This outcome is best observed in the instrumental view of "truth" for which Russell and many Realists have consistently berated Dewey. This shifts the locus of human awe from the objective world to the communal human being, by making truth a function of social interaction rather than of autonomous pursuit. Inherent in Dewey's view, in spite of his championing of intelligence, is a debasement of reason as the objectifying power traditionally described by philosophers, a debasement leading eventually to a disproportionate reliance being placed on the group by the enquiring individual; for what legitimate ground remains for nonconformism?

But another strand in Dewey's account of the scientific method works in the opposite direction. The same relativism which evaporates "truth" also prevents one from ever claiming to have the final answer. Therefore social blueprints are out of order, and only a continually reconstructing society is admissible.

> What *claims* to be social planning is now found in Communist and Fascist countries. The *social* consequence is complete suppression of freedom of enquiry, communication and voluntary

association . . . . The results are such that in the minds of many persons the very idea of social planning and of violation of the integrity of the individual are becoming intimately bound together. But an immense difference divides the *planned* society from a *continuously planning* society. The former requires fixed blueprints imposed from above and therefore involving reliance upon physical and psychological force to secure conformity to them. The latter means the release of intelligence through the widest form of coöperative give and take.[38]

It is this which leads Dewey to favor political individualism [39] and preach the form of "democracy" analyzed above.

This manifest tension within Dewey's thought evoked controversy in the post-Depression years. One party followed George S. Counts into socialistic programming in the name of Pragmatism, while others repudiated it in the same name, remaining loyal to Dewey's own stance. Since the Second World War, Theodore Brameld has avowed his direct line of descent from Experimentalism while using language that recalls Mannheim's "sociology of knowledge" to promote "reconstructionism."[40] However, the general run of Experimentalists continues to adhere to the flexible and open-ended individualism which is truer of the political Dewey, of whom Curtis and Boultwood observe that he always avoided conclusive political allegiances.[41]

Something of the same systematic ambivalence may be seen in Dewey's specification for the school in society. We have already seen how he declared that education has no aims be-

[38] Written specially for Ratner's volume. (See Ratner, *Intelligence and the Modern World*, pp. 431f.)

[39] Broudy commends Berkson for having in his analysis of Experimentalism charged that Dewey and Kilpatrick had both been unable "to shake off their allegiance to 19th century individualism" and notes the "furious back-pedalling into a more collective stance by the Progressives during the 'Thirties' in the era of New Deal social planning." (See Harry S. Broudy, book review of I. B. Berkson, *The Ideal and the Community*, in *Educational Theory*, vol. 9, Jan. 1959, p. 62.)

[40] Theodore Brameld, *Toward a Reconstructed Philosophy of Education*, New York: Holt, Rinehart and Winston, 1956. See his explicit acknowledgement of Mannheim on p. 91.

[41] Curtis and Boultwood, *Short History of Educational Ideas*, p. 473.

yond the fostering of growth, or, in its collective dimension, social efficiency. Education is "that reconstruction or reorganization of experience which adds to the meaning of experience, and which increases the ability to direct the course of subsequent experience." [42] However, he also speaks of the school as a "purified medium of action . . . such as makes for a better future society" and, again, of the fact that the school "must extract desirable traits of forms of community life." Now it should be clearly recognized that the school can never be neutral — and these very comments imply that it *should* not be neutral — in relation to ideologies current in the culture; yet much has been written by Dewey and his disciples about the school as a neutral agency for the training of critical and evaluative skills. In fact, however, in insisting that such aims as these are the only allowable objectives, they are preaching a dogmatic world-view. The voice is the voice of "organized intelligence" but the hand is the hand of Experimentalism, an approach with a very distinctive value theory.

It is therefore appropriate to look critically at the human values of this ideology. Earlier we noted the traits which Dewey infers from scientific method it is desirable to cultivate, and the dignity with which he invests labor. The question of value judgments must be taken further back, however, and critics have noted that Experimentalism gives rise to certain distinctive norms. Rusk, for example, fastens on the point that motives are disregarded in favor of consequences so that the stress is placed on the external life of man.[43] Similarly, Lilge detects in Experimentalism a defective grasp of the nature and significance of the intellectual and creative life of the individual: "Spiritual culture in the quietistic sense he condemned as futile and as having 'something rotten about it'."[44] Mumford believes that Dewey has surrendered to "industrial utilitarianism,"[45] and Russell argues the same point

[42] *Democracy and Education*, p. 89.
[43] Rusk, *Doctrines of Great Educators*, p. 294.
[44] Frederic Lilge, "John Dewey in Retrospect: An American Reconsideration," *British Journal of Educational Studies*, vol. 8, May 1960, p. 109.
[45] Quoted by Holmes, in "The Reflective Man: Dewey," p. 311.

even after explicit disavowal by Dewey.[46] Ulich protests Dewey's allegedly persistent denial of spiritual values,[47] albeit *A Common Faith* and *Quest for Certainty* do suggest respect for a religious dimension in life. Analyzing this point, Lilge suggests that Dewey's gesture to religious sentiment results from a longing for unity of thought and belief—a longing which, "denied satisfaction by such diverse systems as economic liberalism on the one hand and by dogmatic religion on the other," infuses science with a "quasi-religious significance."[48]

While the derivation of value theory from behavioral and scientific sources is probably a matter of preference and no more refutable than any other procedure, in the context of our study it is a matter for concern that Dewey's approach should have led to the identification of social efficiency with personal culture, and of "moral" with "social"; for one result is the evaporation of many "personal" values.

In conclusion, it is true to say that Dewey is a champion of the individual against moral, political, and ideological oppression and has done much in a practical sense to preserve the sanctity of the individual in a technological society. He does this, however, at the expense of values which invest the individual with a significance beyond the social and the scientific. Perhaps such values are in fact chimerical; but they may well be our only protection against the absorption of the individual by mass society and objective science (the absorption that Kierkegaard prophesied), in which case they must become substantial. It is little wonder that modern religious thinkers have objected to the Experimentalist view, but it is perhaps surprising at first glance that Whitehead also parts company with Dewey at this point, as we shall next discover.

[46] Russell, *History of Western Philosophy*, p. 855.
[47] Ulich, *History of Educational Thought*, p. 330.
[48] Lilge, "John Dewey in Retrospect," p. 100. It is interesting to note that in the transition years when Dewey was shedding his religious Idealism, he spoke often of democracy as having a religious or spiritual meaning, in "Christianity and Democracy" (1893) and "The Ethics of Democracy" (1888) (cited by Wirth, "John Dewey in Transition . . .", pp. 264–268). Later his vocabulary changed, though not the sentiment.

ALFRED NORTH WHITEHEAD

1861-1947

By an extraordinary combination of talents, upbringing, and scholarship, Whitehead has achieved a synthesis of thought which gives to the humanities and the sciences more equal treatment than almost any of his contemporaries have managed, Dewey included. In his lifetime he gained high renown in three successive careers of scholarship, each contributing to his "philosophy of organism," which is even now gaining ground as a world-view for this modern age.

Born in a rectory in Kent,[1] he received a strict classical education at Sherborne in Dorsetshire. A home weighty with tradition, a school older than a millennium, and a classical curriculum—all this combined to make him very sensitive to historical perspective, despite the channeling of his talents into modern mathematics when he went up to Trinity College at Cambridge. This venerable institution and the endless informal discussion that raged between staff and students within it served to offset the narrow concentration of his formal studies. In 1885, Whitehead became a Fellow of the college and entered on his first career, as a mathematician. He testifies in many places to the magnitude of the shock he ex-

[1] Biographical details are drawn mainly from Whitehead's own notes in *The Philosophy of Alfred North Whitehead*, ed. Paul Arthur Schilpp (The Library of Living Philosophers, vol. 3, Evanston: Northwestern University, 1941, pp. 1-14), and *Essays in Science and Philosophy* (New York: Philosophical Library, 1948, pp. 7-59), together with Lucien Price's prologue to *Dialogues of Alfred North Whitehead* (New York: Mentor Books, 1954).

perienced when he became aware of the new mathematics that was then making its appearance, whereby the discoveries of geometries alternative to Euclid, and of relativity concepts which shattered the absolute time-space of the Newtonian universe, implied the loss of all the old certainties. He is reported to have said to Richard Livingstone, near the end of his life:

> Still speaking personally, it had a profound effect on me; I have been fooled once, and I'll be damned if I'll be fooled again! . . . The danger is dogmatic thought; it plays the devil with religion, and science is not immune from it. I am, as you see, a thoroughgoing evolutionist.[2]

At Cambridge he ascended steadily to eminence as a mathematician (while also reading deeply in theology), and his *Treatise on Universal Algebra* (1898) secured his election to the Royal Society. A second projected volume of his treatise was passed over in favor of a collaborative work by himself and former pupil Bertrand Russell—the remarkable *Principia Mathematica*, which emerged in three volumes from 1910 to 1913. The *Principia* marked the transition in his interest from mathematics as such to logic, and a shift of venue emphasized the change. In 1910 he moved with his family (wife and three children) to London University. Here recognition was rapid, and he found himself assuming heavy administrative responsibilities, speaking at the opening of technical institutions, and engaging in mild political skirmishes as a Liberal party supporter. Those experiences, he said, "transformed" his views as to "the problem of higher education in a modern industrial civilization."[3]

The First World War was another signpost, ending the brash optimism of the nineteenth century with a jolt, and bringing personal tragedy to the Whiteheads through the death of a son. Whitehead's interest was now turning more to philosophy, and in his participation in meetings of the Aristotelian So-

[2] Price, *Dialogues*, p. 277.
[3] Schilpp, *Whitehead*, p. 12.

ciety he showed sympathy with the Realism of Nunn and Russell, though never, in Lowe's view, as more than a spectator.[4] His main concern at this time was to develop a philosophy of natural science, as in *An Enquiry Concerning the Principles of Natural Knowledge* (1919), *The Concept of Nature* (1920), and *The Principle of Relativity* (1922). His encounters with educational problems gave rise to several addresses[5] and the widely acclaimed *Aims of Education and Other Essays* (1929).

Whitehead's third career began when, at the age of sixty-three, he accepted an invitation from Harvard to become professor of philosophy. There for thirteen years he lectured and wrote in the area of, as he called it, speculative philosophy, and secured his position as one of the leading ideologists of his day. The accumulated insights and themes of previous years were drawn together in the trilogy of famous works upon which we will chiefly draw. As he said in the preface to one of them:

> The three books—*Science and the Modern World, Process and Reality, Adventures of Ideas*—are an endeavour to express a way of understanding the nature of things, and to point out how that way of understanding is illustrated by a survey of the mutations of human experience.[6]

Process and Reality (1929) in particular is a study in speculative philosophy, developing the viewpoint Whitehead calls "philosophy of organism." In a later work, *Modes of Thought* (1938), he observes that philosophy must indulge the imaginative as well as the critical sense; and he distinguishes between the "critical school" and the "speculative school" by noting

---

[4] Victor Lowe, "The Development of Whitehead's Philosophy," in Schilpp, *Whitehead*, p. 79. Curtis imputes to Whitehead a more active involvement, and contributions to the Aristotelian Society lend support to this view, except that, with the full sweep of the philosophy of organism before us, I am inclined to consider that Whitehead's Realism was of a very special kind and that his support of the New Realists was mostly owing to his and their common distaste for certain elements in Pragmatism.

[5] See especially pp. 119-147 in Whitehead, *Essays*.

[6] Alfred North Whitehead, *Adventures of Ideas*, Penguin, 1948.

that the "divergence between the schools is the quarrel between safety and adventure"—a sentiment reminiscent of Nietzsche's attack on thinkers who "sit in the cool shade." Whitehead died at eighty-seven, laden with honors, in the Cambridge of the New World.

In the post-war period it would appear that some American philosophers are turning from Dewey to Whitehead because, while the cultural relativism currently espoused is in both, the breadth of sympathy and awareness of the humanities that characterize Whitehead offer a more harmonious synthesis. In the educational sphere Frank C. Wegener has presented an "Organic theory of education"[7] purporting to be derived from Whitehead's "organic philosophy," and the October 1961 issue of *Educational Theory* is devoted to Whitehead's significance for education, drawing deliberately on his philosophical writings in preference to his directly educational essays.

DEFINING "INDIVIDUAL"

In Whitehead's philosophy of organism the realm of actuality is inhabited by unique individual occasions, all possessed of a life and history of their own, so there is every reason to suppose that the individual will be defined in considerable detail. However, the very pervasiveness of the concept of individuality may lead to difficulty in differentiating the human person from other entities. We shall try to show that both these expectations are justified. Our analysis must begin with the "categoreal scheme" of *Process and Reality*.

The ultimately real things are held to be "actual entities" or "actual occasions," that is, moments or events occurring within the web of reality. The old battle between Idealists and Realists as to whether the ultimate constituent of reality was mental idea or material atom has been displaced by the new scientific cosmology. We owed this warfare to the division driven between matter and mind by seventeenth-century

[7] Beginning with "The Ten Basic Functions of Man," *Educational Theory*, vol. 5, Apr. 1955, pp. 110–117.

thinkers. The viewpoint was fruitful but mistaken, for the dualism excluded concepts that lie in between the two realms, such as "life, organism, function, instantaneous reality, interaction, order of nature, which collectively form the Achilles' heel of the whole system." [8] The categories of existence and value had been squeezed out, and it was not until the foundations of physics were broken up by relativity and quantum theory that the way to readmit them was made apparent. Relativity notions suggest that time as well as space is relative to the actual occasion, so it may be said that not only does an entity have a unique location in three-dimensional space, but it is an event having a linear time pattern, requiring a duration to be actualized. Furthermore, quantum theory has replaced our atomic model of matter with the concept of quanta or primary energy space-time patterns; it is no longer sufficient to speak of inert particles of matter combining according to mechanically determined laws. Our new starting point is from "the analysis of process as the realisation of events disposed in an interlocked community"; and the event is "the unit of things real." [9] Reality is a process, in which multitudes of occasions are becoming and perishing, influencing and being influenced by other occasions adjacent in time and space, but unique in two vital respects: as enduring societies of occasions they have their own histories, and each occasion achieves concretion in a manner causally independent of other contemporary occasions. Insofar as a sequence of actual occasions is predictable, it is not because it is rigidly determined by external laws, but because some occasions display considerable endurance. "The evolution of laws of nature is concurrent with the evolution of enduring pattern."

Actual occasions do not have histories; they only become and perish. But whereas some only occur once, others recur, and the most important endure. The togetherness of actual entities establishes a "nexus," but when a nexus begins to exhibit a common element of form, it becomes a "society,"

[8] Whitehead, *Science and the Modern World*, New York: Mentor, 1958, p. 58.
[9] *Ibid.*, p. 152.

or social order. "A society must exhibit the peculiar quality of endurance. The real actual things that endure are all societies. They are not actual occasions." Societies are continually defining themselves; for example, until death the society "man" has no determinate nexus. Some societies exhibit great permanence over long periods of time, and it is these we have in the past regarded as inert matter to be studied by physicists. Now, however, the physicist has penetrated this relatively stable organization of occasions and has become the student of organisms. All science is turning out to be the study of organisms. "Biology is the study of the larger organisms; whereas physics is the study of the smaller organisms." Therefore the supposed boundary between living and inert matter is obliterated. "Life" is to be taken as referring to the measure of novelty which enters into the becoming of an entity. In this sense there is life, or, as the physicist calls it, energy, in the electron as well as in biological organisms; indeed, a society is properly termed "living" only in a derivative sense. Evolutionary theory has been one-sided through neglect of this distinction and, leaning on mechanistic determinism, has stressed the effect of environment and neglected the organism's *creativeness*. "The organisms can create their own environment. . . . the environment has a plasticity which alters the whole ethical aspect of evolution."

Supposedly inert matter has enduring social order through both time and space. But a social order whose enduring form is "purely temporal and continuous" is to be termed a "personal order." Animal bodies exhibit this—they retain a temporal identity despite the material or spatial changes we term "growth." However, "personal order" is not the same as growth pattern, for it is to be taken as referring to some degree of hierarchical organization of subordinate societies within the organism. Thus lower forms of life, such as vegetation, are not personal—"a tree is a democracy"—whereas most animal forms appear to have their social system dominated by a subordinate society which is personal. In the case of man, Whitehead makes the intriguing suggestion that the route of presiding occasions probably wanders from part to part of the brain, dissociated from the physical and material atoms. But central personal dominance is only partial, and in pathological cases is apt to vanish.[10]

So far, in defining the terms basic to Whitehead's speculative philosophy, we have not invoked the term "consciousness." This is deliberate, for whereas in common speech we associate "personal" and "conscious," in this schema "personal" has a more general application, and "consciousness" is a late-emerging capacity of *some* personal orders. Mentality is to be understood as the appearance of teleological purpose in the succession of occasions. It is the beginning of a sense of past, present, and future, which gradually rises to the level of cognition.

> Cognition is the emergence, into some measure of individualised reality, of the general substratum of activity, poising before itself possibility, actuality and purpose.[11]

From this it is apparent why Whitehead claims that William James, while justified in debunking the Cartesian mind or consciousness as an entity, failed to account for "this undoubted personal unity, maintaining itself amidst the welter of circumstance" because his metaphysical categories of reality were inadequate.

When mental life emerges, it does not tread in ghostly two-step with physical occasions, to the music of Leibniz's pre-established harmony, but derives from previous physical occasions and enters into the environment of future physical occasions. "We awake to find ourselves in process" and begin to be susceptible to the influence of ideas as well as instinct and appetite. Even now men "are only intermittently rational — merely liable to rationality." Yet a vital dualism has come into being: between physical and mental occasions. Interaction continues to occur because

[10] *Process and Reality*, p. 153.
[11] *Science and the Modern World*, p. 153.

There are two routes of creative passage from a physical occasion. One is towards another physical occasion, and the other is towards the derivative reflective occasion.[12]

To characterize the personal order of mental occasions Whitehead boldly employs the word "soul," though stressing its fusion with "body" in actual events.[13]

We may therefore infer that human personality is the enduring high-grade experience of some personal orders. The conscious soul experiences events in two ways: physical and mental. The particular function of mentality is "to modify the physical participation of eternal objects."

To man belongs the capacity of recognizing beyond the apparently universal flux the reality of the "eternal objects" which constantly await actualization in it. His dual nature intuits the bipolarity of flux and permanence which characterizes the world. Whitehead's eternal objects have been much debated, but they appear to be the Platonic Forms or Ideas, deprived however of that substantive independence which Plato postulated. They are "devoid of intrinsic value, but are valuable as elements in purpose." They are therefore not possessed of that power over particular events that Hegel gave to ideas but reach maximum fulfillment through their creative employment by individuals. "Enduring Individuality in the details is the backbone of strong experience." The evolution of man is a progress toward greater rationality, and the adventure of ideas is the story of the progressive realization over centuries of those eternal values which best contribute to the health of societies of human individuals. "The topic of religion is individuality in community," and what is called for today is rational religion.

It is apparent that individuality for Whitehead is not merely a "sop thrown here to man's natural inclination to look for

---

[12] *Religion in the Making*, Cambridge: Cambridge University Press, 1927, p. 89.

[13] *Adventures of Ideas*, pp. 218–222. It is not completely clear whether Whitehead confines this dichotomy to the experience of man. Compare his unexpanded reference to "the personal succession of occasions which is the soul of the animal." *Ibid.*, p. 249.

Alfred North Whitehead

such 'general principles'" but a "metaphysical principle."[14] Human individuality and the datum of free will are not suspect intrusions into a mechanistic world, but special cases of the entities that constitute the whole universe as understood by modern science. Whitehead declares that this insight was not possible until religious intuition had fastened on the unique importance of the human individual and created the climate of thought which led eventually to the rise of democracy and the advance of science. What we call "individuals" are in fact societies of societies, and effective individuality depends on the harmony established between the co-operating parts. In his metaphysical exposition Whitehead speaks more to the general case than to that particular exemplification of it, human personality. This is why on philosophical grounds Morris questions whether the existence of individual man has been adequately established[15] and Sellars asserts flatly that "Whitehead hardly does full justice to an enduring self."[16] We would concur with the nub of these criticisms to the extent of suggesting that in urging the continuity of man with lower organisms, Whitehead glosses over some of the distinctive features of human intercourse and community; that is, his "individuality" remains at a high level of abstraction, as befits a mathematical mind, notwithstanding his generous overview of the human pageant in other writings such as *Adventures of Ideas*.

To sum up, the new scientific cosmology requires that we adopt a philosophy of organism. This has the advantage of bringing life, existence, and value back into reality descriptions. The ultimate units are individual events or actual occasions, and out of these arise social orders which acquire marked individuality when they are hierarchically organized,

---

[14] Paul Arthur Schilpp, "Whitehead's Moral Philosophy," in Schilpp, *Whitehead*, p. 603.

[15] Bertram Morris, "The Art-Process and the Aesthetic Fact in Whitehead's Philosophy," in Schilpp, *Whitehead*, p. 481.

[16] Roy Wood Sellars, "Philosophy of Organism and Physical Realism," in Schilpp, *Whitehead*, p. 418. My agreement with Sellars' point does not extend to his reasons for making it, since he seems not to have grasped the implications of the new scientific cosmology.

or "personal." The mark of individuality at all levels is creativity, but with the emergence of consciousness in man this takes on the new dimension of mental cognition. By its capacity to seek out the permanences or "eternal objects" inherent in events, the soul of man imparts reality to the world, and learns to modify the physical world in the direction of the greater actualization of value.

SANCTITY OF THE INDIVIDUAL

While it was to Whitehead's metaphysics that we turned to define the individual, it is to his cultural analysis that we must go for a demonstration of how he sees the worth of the human individual, for it is here that his value theory is worked out with specific reference to the human condition, especially in the part of *Adventures of Ideas* labeled "sociological." He traces the emergence of certain fundamental ideas that would undoubtedly qualify as "eternal objects" in his metaphysics, to wit: the human soul, the humanitarian ideal, individual freedom, and persuasion as the mode of social influence—all of which are germane to this study.

Whitehead's thesis is that "human life is driven forward by its dim apprehension of notions too general for its existing language." Thus the notion of the human soul, stated by the Greeks, assimilated and endowed with ethical stature by the early Christians, and secularized by the Enlightenment, became the lever with which Methodist enthusiasm ousted the age-old institution of slavery. This ideological step forward came only just in time to mitigate some of the excesses of industrial oppression and the implications of the selection theory of Darwin and Malthus, and it now requires more sophisticated definition in the present day.

Whitehead is therefore implying that the sanctity of the individual is a great idea which only began to permeate society as a whole, as distinguished from a small coterie of advanced thinkers, in the eighteenth century; and he affirms that it found expression then in the Constitution of the United States of America and became the basic, unifying idea of that

Alfred North Whitehead

nation.[17] By the nineteenth century the religious rationale which had given birth to the idea was being rejected by the utilitarians, who considered that such generalized concepts as this were

> ultimate moral intuitions, clear matter of fact, requiring no justification, and requiring no ultimate understanding of their relations to the rest of things.[18]

However, Whitehead continues, this pragmatic basis for value, though it facilitated reform then, is not devoid of the weaknesses of more overtly metaphysical rationales, and it suffers the particular weakness that assessment of happiness of the greatest number is an impossible addition sum and therefore no guide to practical action! Furthermore, in the present day the political individualism of the liberal era is inadequate to cope with social stresses and economic complexity.

As might be expected, Whitehead believes that the idea needs the support of an ideology which defines it in relation to all the major concerns of life, and these concerns he lists as technology, science, art, and religion. We have already spoken of his scientific cosmology, but must now look at the comments he makes about the other three domains.

Whitehead's encounter with technical and working-class education in London gave rise to comments on the honorable standing that labor should enjoy, comments we shall amplify in discussing his educational theory. In addition, his remarks on the economics of modern business are relevant. He observes that "today private property is mainly a legal fiction," so that in practical terms it is nearly certain that there was more individual freedom in the London of 1633 than in a modern industrial society. We have reached the end of the epoch in which "free, unfettered, individual activity in craftsmanship, in agriculture, and in all mercantile transactions" could go on. At the present time our economic system produces "a starvation of human impulses, a denial of oppor-

---

[17] Price, *Dialogues*, p. 126.
[18] *Adventures of Ideas*, p. 50.

tunity, a limitation of beneficial activity—in short, a lack of freedom." This observation was made in 1933, but its relevance is not blunted by the passage of time. Consequently Whitehead considers that business executives should receive training not only in business routines but in philosophical understanding of the flux of human societies and the worth of human life. He argues for the pragmatic relevance of such understanding by saying that "The task of democracy is to relieve mass misery and yet preserve the freedom of the individual."

Whitehead's views on religion include a commentary, at once critical and deeply appreciative, on the role of Christianity in the history of ideas. It arose, he says with an "unrivalled programme for reform" focused on a deep conviction concerning the brotherhood of man. In *Religion in the Making* he commends the encouragement that Christianity gives, in contrast with Buddhism, to the sense of active personality. However, he makes two severe criticisms. The first is that the retention of a God with the attributes of an oriental despot, especially as by the apostle Paul, preserves a barbaric element that prevents acceptance of Christianity by rational man. The second is that Christianity has fallen victim to the dogmatic fallacy and thereby become rigid and conservative in a day when change is quickening on all sides. He therefore abandons dogmatic religion and calls for rational religion, wherein the main plank is "that we know more than can be formulated in one finite systematized scheme of abstractions."

This rational religion has a God, who presides at the marriage of religious awe and science by meeting the demands of the philosophy of organism, in which many of the propositions require the premise of God for their coherence. Since "religion is what the individual does with his solitariness," rational religion will enable man to come to terms with his fluctuating environment by submission to a God who is both primordial and consequent, eternal and creative. Religion must learn to welcome change as readily as science does if it is to survive, for "the worship of God is not a rule of safety— it is an adventure of the spirit."

We have left the discussion of art till the last, because it is here that the values Whitehead commends derive most directly from his speculative philosophy. In *Adventures of Ideas* he gives headings to truth and beauty, but ostentatiously deranks goodness in order to emphasize that it is in his view subordinate and derivative. Indeed he does not explicitly discuss ethics as such, though high values that would normally be considered ethical in kind infuse his writings. The reason is that he believes ethical judgments are a special case of the value judgments on which not only ethics and aesthetics are based, but even science. In the *Essays,* pointing out that philosophy has to start from some abstracted standpoint, he expresses his preference for aesthetics. This is no idle choice but reflects the essence of his philosophy and his insistence that the scientific divorce of fact and value in the seventeenth century must be redressed. His solution is to assert that value is related to the degree of creativity displayed by an actual occasion. On this basis, "Personality is the extreme example of the sustained realization of a type of Value." The measure of value is therefore the satisfaction or aesthetic harmony provided by a becoming, and the motive power is feeling. "There is nothing in the real world which is merely an inert fact. Every reality is there for feeling: it promotes feeling; and it is felt." [19] On this view, the aesthetic base of value is continuous from the electron to the human spirit, with ethics a derivative at the upper end. It is no wonder that, as Morris reports, some commentators have called Whitehead's philosophy an aestheticism.[20]

Whitehead applies his own criterion consistently. He speaks of "style" as the "ultimate morality of the mind," he claims that "the real world is good when it is beautiful," and he suggests that the primary function of cognitive theories and propositions is to be a "lure for feeling, thereby providing immediacy of enjoyment and purpose." It is the aesthetic phases of education which most contribute to satisfactory living,

[19] *Process and Reality,* p. 439.
[20] Bertram Morris, "The Art-Process and the Aesthetic Fact in Whitehead's Philosophy, p. 463.

since what is wanted is "an appreciation of the infinite variety of vivid values achieved by an organism in its proper environment." Whitehead has often been quoted as saying that "moral education is impossible apart from the habitual vision of greatness"; but admirers of this aphorism are not always aware that he is prescribing vision not merely of great virtue, as realized in classical civilization, but also of its obverse, great evil. It is the aesthete's demand for vivid experience, not the moralist's demand for edifying experience. Hence it is not surprising that Whitehead approves the Aristotelian concept of the "golden mean," of the rhythm that underlies opposites in conflict and is the significance of the Greek interest in harmony. That is, he resolves clashing ideas in terms of an aesthetic pendulum swinging between them:

> In our cosmological construction we are, therefore, left with the final opposites, joy and sorrow, good and evil, disjunction and conjunction—that is to say, the many in one—flux and permanence, greatness and triviality, freedom and necessity, God and the World.[21]

There is no room here for the more familiar linear ethical model of gain in goodness, but Whitehead secures this advantage by emphasizing the role of creativity in evolution and by claiming that "the history of ideas is . . . the history of the gradual purification of conduct." It is significant that his proof is found in his interpretation of history, not in his metaphysics, and it assumes gratuitously that goodness is synonymous with progress. Were this not so, it would be trivial to equate evolution with progress, as he does. As Urban insists, for all that he speaks of God, of ideas and religion, Whitehead is a naturalist,[22] and his ethical value theory is a reversion to the "golden mean" which substitutes aesthetic harmony for moral imperative.

[21] *Process and Reality*, p. 482.
[22] Wilbur Urban, "Whitehead's Philosophy of Language and Its Relation to His Metaphysics," in Schilpp, *Whitehead*, p. 324.

SOCIETY AND THE INDIVIDUAL

Whitehead's initial impact as an ideologist was through his more general discourses and sparkling aphorisms about life and education, but subsequently some have probed behind these into his speculative metaphysics [23] to look for assistance at a more basic level in the systematization of values. Although there is more unity between these two aspects of Whitehead's thought than may be at first apparent, it is useful to pursue this part of our enquiry in two stages.

The first stage concerns that part of his writing which deals with cultural description. There can be no doubt that *Adventures of Ideas* and *Religion in the Making* in particular are treatises in defense of the autonomous human spirit. They seek to show how the free individual is the pivot of progress and the safeguard against a relapse into barbarism. They draw the reader himself out into the adventure of creativity, commending the "power of wandering" which has given rise to "the Odyssey of the human spirit." As Whitehead once observed in conversation:

> Very few people are adequately drawn out. . . . the waste of undeveloped faculties must be tremendous. For the powers of the individual are unique and unpredictable. This has been one of the great discoveries of the human race and it is still proceeding very slowly.[24]

However, this does not mean that Whitehead is blind to the social dimension, and in fact he rejects several kinds of individualism which have found recent expression. There is for example moral individualism, which he describes as the view inherited from Cartesian dualism that morals are a private realm of experience divorced from communal life. Economic individualism and what is now the legal fiction of private

---

[23] Which I am calling, undeterred by his mode of justification for this as a discipline, his ideology proper. William Oliver Martin supports my action in "Whitehead's Philosophy as the Ideology of Consensus Theory," *Educational Theory*, vol. 8, Jan. 1958, pp. 1–7.

[24] Price, *Dialogues*, p. 126.

property are repudiated; so is the political, liberal faith of the nineteenth century with its policies of laissez faire. It is not easy to establish what Whitehead would substitute for these, and Needham claims with some justice that "Whitehead has not been sufficiently outspoken in leading along the sociological and political directions in which his philosophy clearly points."[25] Wegener describes his position as "qualified individualism" and discusses "the Organic society," balancing competition and co-operation, which he infers from Whitehead's works.[26] Whitehead's political leanings were toward the English Liberal party, and he is reported by Price as stating that

> inside the state men pursue numerous corporate enterprises which do express other aspects of their natures: educational, charitable, creative, artistic, social; . . . perhaps the function of the state thus far is to provide conditions of sufficient tranquility within which those more varied forms of activity can proceed. Already many of them, such as science and education, are international, and supervene the state boundaries.[27]

Recognizing that the individual is powerless without institutional backing, Whitehead develops the story of the growth of freedom in terms not only of individuals like Akhnaton, the Hebrew prophets, and Pericles, but of institutions which stood over against the state, like the medieval church, scientific bodies, and universities. He concedes that such agencies exercise powers of censure over individuals, but stresses that the basis of this is not personal opinions but ability and competence.

Linked with the operation of such bodies is the principle of persuasion as opposed to coercion or force. "The worth of men consists in their liability to persuasion," he says, and adds that the use of force is a failure of civilization. This does

[25] Joseph Needham, "A Biologist's View of Whitehead's Philosophy," in Schilpp, *Whitehead*, p. 267.
[26] Frank C. Wegener, "Alfred North Whitehead: An Implied Philosophy of School and Society," *Educational Theory*, vol. 11, Oct. 1961, pp. 195–201.
[27] Price, *Dialogues*, p. 97.

not lead him into the individualistic excess of pacifism, for he regards "the absolute pacifist [as] a bad citizen; times come when force must be used to uphold right, justice and ideals"; [28] but he does insist in the *Essays* that war is a last resort because it is intrinsically anti-creative.

Our last observation on his cultural description relates to the picture he paints of communal life. It is a canvas of many shapes and colors. Honor is given to technical studies and respect to economic complexity, yet it is demanded of both that they recognize individual value; science and philosophy are made guardians of the great ideas, subject to the influence of religion and education with respect to individual nurture; the harmony of the parts is maintained not by coercive edict but by the humane vision of history and the sensitive stimulus of art. The canvas has what Whitehead calls "scale," and it is his contribution to the present time, of which he once said: "We are at the threshold of a democratic age, and it remains to be determined whether the equality of man is to be realised on a high level or a low level." [29] The canvas illumines much that Nunn took for granted about our way of life, confronts the planner Mannheim with an effective option, and sketches in shapes above the horizon of Dewey, yet is weak in one crucial dimension—the ethical.

This lack has philosophical roots, which take us on to the second stage of our enquiry, into Whitehead's philosophical speculation. Within the limits of this study it is proper to make two criticisms. The first concerns the problem of ethics and the second the concept of evolution.

We have already observed that Whitehead tends to treat ethics as incidental to other categories of discussion, and Schilpp asks him a pertinent question: Is there such a thing as a "bad life"? [30] Also, Goheen shows that the emphasis on the bipolarity of strife and harmony may be taken to mean that, even in the moral realm, "it may be better to have conflict

---
[28] Price, *Dialogues*, p. 82.
[29] *Aims of Education*, p. 107.
[30] Schilpp, "Whitehead's Moral Philosophy," p. 607.

than to resolve it."[31] Discussing immortality, Whitehead identifies it with the world of value, which "contains within itself Evil as well as Good."[32] The term "evil" appears from this and other contexts to be generalized in typical fashion to mean "destruction as a dominant fact in the experience," and one therefore feels that as a concept it goes beyond the special case of moral discourse. Hence Urban contends that Whitehead "dissolves value" and that one is left with a highly esoteric hedonism or aestheticism as the ground of moral obligation. "God," says Whitehead, "is the measure of the aesthetic consistency of the world."[33] Understanding this, we can see that Whitehead has in fact consulted purely personal preference in selecting those great ideas which he actually treats in *Adventures of Ideas,* rather than building on some systematic framework. One case in point is the contrast between his sweeping remark that "the life of Christ . . . has the decisiveness of a supreme ideal, and that is why the history of the world divides at this point of time," and his repudiation of those elements in Christ's life which do not suit his purpose, especially moral and religious absolutism. For goodness he tends to substitute a quality called "peace," whereby the pursuit of truth, beauty, adventure, and art is rescued from being "ruthless, hard, cruel"; but the concept is a shadowy one and, along with goodness, finds no place in the admittedly scrappy index of *Process and Reality.*

The second criticism concerns the function of "evolution" in his thought. Whitehead has a Jamesian view of a "universe with the lid off," which is preserved from anarchy by the eternal objects or permanences which structure experience. By locating value in the emergence of novelty, he is then able to equate evolution with progress and to identify human life as the noblest form yet to emerge. The base line for evolution is the growing complexity of organisms, or "societies," and these have proceeded from societies enduring in both time

[31] John Goheen, "Whitehead's Theory of Value," in Schilpp, *Whitehead,* p. 456.
[32] Whitehead, "Immortality," in Schilpp, *Whitehead,* p. 692.
[33] *Religion in the Making,* p. 86.

and space to those "personal" societies enduring only in time, and from "democracies" of co-ordinated organisms to "hierarchies" where a subordinate society co-ordinates the larger congeries. If this is the direction of evolution and evolution is progress, then what is to stop us from arguing that collectivized human society is the next level of complexity to emerge,[34] and that we are moving towards co-ordination of a kind that will produce great progress, as witness the integration of effort that has made space travel a fact? Why stop at "qualified individualism"?

For Whitehead, then, progress depends on the freedom of the individual to create, but his power to contribute to the slow rise of humanity comes from his participation in and through social institutions. A healthy society possesses institutions sufficiently independent of the state to criticize in a constructive manner, effects change by persuasion rather than force, and fosters the whole spectrum of human interests. With such views Whitehead has contributed considerably to democratic ideology. However, the coherence of his viewpoint with respect to the sanctity of the individual is affected by his neglect of ethics as such, and by his use of the evolutionary analogy for social theory. Philosophically we are forced to take somewhat on trust the qualitative difference between the human and other kinds of individual organism.

[34] Cf. Mannheim's "man in super-individual group solidarity."

COUNTERPOINT

DEWEY : WHITEHEAD

SCIENTIFIC COSMOLOGIES AND SOCIAL THEORY

The status of the individual in the eyes of both Dewey and Whitehead is ultimately established by their scientific cosmologies, just as their general ideologies are. Whitehead of course unashamedly extends his scientific cosmology into metaphysical speculation, whereas Dewey claims not to be speculating at all but generalizing from the clear facts of the immediate situation. However, Dewey has decided that the rise of science is the central fact of our time, and he has a definitive view of what science is. These two things color all his thought and produce, whether he would or no, a distinctive ideology. If for no other reason, our contention is substantiated by the difference between the two thinkers' views concerning what science is and how it affects social life.

For Dewey, science is problem-solving, and its method is generalizable to social life. For Whitehead, science is theory-building, and its method constitutes but one of several ways of apprehending human existence. Also, scientific theory abstracts from the total manifold of experience and is therefore a mental construct, which has value not only because it is useful but because it gives aesthetic fulfillment. Both Dewey and Whitehead have things to say about art, but Whitehead grants to the artist a degree of autonomy in the pursuit of knowledge that Dewey fails to do. Indeed, one senses that Whitehead sees human culture as a many-layered thing; he accords to art, religion, history, science, technology, and politics their several legitimate spheres of discourse and canons of truth. The binding cement is value, the intrinsic worth that some entities in each sphere possess, recognized in the human mind by a sense of fitness. Dewey's binding cement is method, a pragmatic criterion which brings value in after the fact and focuses attention not on that which abides but on that which succeeds.

Far-reaching in effect though these divergences are, it would be unwise to overlook views that Dewey and Whitehead hold in common. Both lay stress on the organic nature of life and, derivatively, the biosocial nature of man. Both proclaim the theoretical power of the notion of evolution, and even Whitehead ultimately opts like Dewey for a relativistic view of value, notwithstanding those eternally debated "eternal objects."

Both see man as a creature in whom consciousness is a late arrival and reason a puling infant; both affirm that our hope lies in the enhancement of rationality. Despite the purported practicality of the one as compared with the other's penchant for abstract thought, Dewey and Whitehead are fundamentally at one in their conviction that modern man's authority resides in reason. Again, both see society as a changing structure in which rational argument is slowly gaining the upper hand and overleaping national barriers, through the employment of such universal languages as science and mathematics. Politically they lean to a qualified individualism which is more carefully spelled out in Dewey's case than in Whitehead's. The final evidence of their humanistic kinship is the parallelism between *A Common Faith* and *Religion in the Making*, in particular the reverent relegation of God to such a high level of abstraction that the focus of attention settles on man and his efforts.

It is no surprise, then, to find that both would provoke the philosopher to become a man of social purpose, involved directly in the refinement of understandings basic to human behavior. Dewey asserts that philosophy is the general theory of education, and Whitehead that speculative reasoning is the necessary follow-on from analytic. Both begin with theories of knowing rooted in scientific discovery, and move on to value theory and cosmology. Comparisons in these three areas need teasing out, because of the light they throw on the views taken of the individual.

With regard to theories of knowing, Dewey and Whitehead clashed explicitly on one occasion, Dewey insisting that Whitehead was vacillating between two kinds of explanation. As we might have expected, Dewey was asking for a decision as to which should be regarded as all-embracing, opting himself for the instrumental or functional kind. Whitehead replied:

> John Dewey asks me to decide between the "genetic-functional" interpretation of first principles and the "mathematical-formal" interpretation. . . . But I must decline to make this decision. . . . The historic process of the world, which requires the genetic-functional interpretation, also requires for its understanding some insight into those ultimate principles of existence which express the necessary connections within the flux.[1]

The result is that the dualism we have previously noted in Whitehead[2] hints at a differentness in man which he fails to explore and Dewey denies. This element is man's capacity to transcend the time-flow and to have experiences qualitatively different from those of animals. It is our view that this unexploited dualism opens the door to that kind of discussion, undertaken by neither of these thinkers, which occupies all of Kierkegaard's writings and those of many of his modern disciples.

[1] Whitehead, *Essays*, p. 94. See also Dewey's comment in "The Philosophy of Whitehead," in Schilpp, *Whitehead*, p. 653.
[2] This is also commented on in F. S. C. Northrop, "Whitehead's Philosophy of Science," in Schilpp, *Whitehead*, p. 186, and Harry S. Broudy, "Actual Entities and the Learning Process," *Educational Theory*, vol. 11, Oct. 1961, p. 223.

Value theory has different origins in the writings of the two thinkers. Dewey's criterion is extrinsic or functional; it depends on the working out of the situation. Whitehead's criterion is intrinsic, in that the creative power of an actual occasion determines its worth. Yet in the balance Dewey provides a more effective criterion for practical action than Whitehead, because the creativity criterion is much harder to apply and has been pilloried as an aestheticism. The two thinkers are ultimately agreed, however, that moral categories of explanation are derivative from other categories—for Dewey social, for Whitehead perhaps aesthetic—and Dewey would concur with Whitehead's relativism when he says: "There is *no one* behaviour-system belonging to the essential character of the universe, as the universal moral ideal."[3]

That Whitehead's philosophy moves on into speculative metaphysics he himself makes explicit; and that Dewey's does too, despite his disclaimers, we have sought to demonstrate. Relative to our topic the metaphysical notions they hold in common are more impressive than those at variance. Both stress change, especially on the social level; both embrace an evolutionary view of human affairs and equate this kind of change with actualization or progress; both applaud individuality in human behavior but stress social influences. Dewey defines the individual within the social matrix, while Whitehead in *Process and Reality* defines him within the natural matrix. On both counts individual man is a transient phenomenon, whose glory and immortality consist in the lively ideas he bequeathes to those who follow after. This makes both thinkers doughty champions of democracy, but at the same time quietly bestows the accolade on those individuals who are most intelligent and well endowed. This is a contradiction inherent in naturalism. The premium placed on education in the United States is of a piece with the tributes paid by Whitehead to the results of English élite education. One may talk about the worth of the ordinary man, but the "meritocracy" are in no doubt as to who are the men

[3] Whitehead, *Modes of Thought*, Cambridge: Cambridge University Press, p. 20. Cf. Dewey, *Human Nature and Conduct,* pp. 77–81.

of the future. The classless society is as utopian on this view as it has proved to be for Marxism.

It is contended then that, while Whitehead sees more clearly the relevance to human existence of fields other than science, both he and Dewey hold a naturalistic view of man which lays stress on his rational potentiality. Whitehead is more attracted to the operation of "pure" reason, though he does not follow this through into a consistent dualism. Both acclaim the worth of the individual as a practical notion but exhibit shortcomings in defining human individuality. Whitehead reminds us of the complementarity of several realms of discourse; and perhaps we may at this point suggest that our studies from Marx to Whitehead have demonstrated that the kind of talk which has its roots in scientific explanation fails to grapple with man as man. Other realms of discourse are needed to fill out the picture.

EDUCATIONAL THEORY

Dewey and Whitehead both put into print their views on education, though Dewey spoke as a professional educator and published far more. Whitehead's views are generally regarded as the perceptive comments of a layman, though it is our view that they cohere generally with his ideology and are based on a considerable acquaintance with diverse educational practices. It remains therefore for us to look at the educational theory developed by the two thinkers, especially in Dewey's *Democracy and Education* and Whitehead's *Aims of Education*.

For Dewey, the importance of education resides in the fact that it is the means whereby social life is transmitted. As civilization advances, education is of course all the more necessary, to "transmit all the resources and achievements of a complex society." This might seem to imply a major role for the school as social conditioner. However, education is more than the school; it is the whole of experience, apart from routine and capricious activities. Therefore the school is the special agency in which experience is enhanced by the simplification, purification, and extension of the environment with which the school is continuous. Furthermore, it is inappropriate to speak of the school as a conditioner, if one means to imply that some external objective governs the curriculum, for the fact of change rules this out, and the only durable aim for education is to facilitate growth. "The educational process has no end beyond itself; it is its own end."

We note two consequences that flow from this. The first is that the school policy cannot be entirely pragmatic, since it is necessary for the school to select experiences from the wider manifold, and selection involves value judgments. It is clear that for Dewey the criteria of selection are the promotion of democracy as he understands it by the cultivation of intelligence as he defines it. Therefore, as we have already noted, the neutrality of the school with respect to ideological issues is a myth and should be so recognized by pragmatists. Secondly, the growth emphasized as the aim of education can only be interpreted as individual growth (for it is biological things that literally grow), and therefore education is to be seen as the enhancement of the powers of every single child for its own sake. No larger objective squeezes the child into its own mold; aims are intrinsic and personal. But at the same time the individual grows within a social matrix, and it often seems in Dewey's writing that socialization of the child is held to be an end in itself, especially since in his social theory the concept of growth is extended analogically to account for the reconstruction of society.

The consequences for educational method are far-reaching. Learning is not instruction in past knowledge by the schoolmaster, but reconstruction in one's own experience by the pupil, assisted by the resources of past knowledge that are relevant at that moment. The teacher becomes a guide, the most mature member of the learning group, making information available from more distant environments when the learner is at the point where it will have relevance to the problem he is solving. Classroom discipline is not something externally applied but derives from the interest the child has in his own problem-solving. Having reacted from the Herbartian "schoolmaster," Dewey found himself having to oppose Progressivist stress on child activity to the neglect of purpose, and in *Experience and Education* he chides Progressivist teachers whose laissez-faire attitudes lead them even to the point of fearing to make suggestions to children.

The curriculum of a school is considerably modified by such an approach. Subject matter does not disappear but is brought in as required—a much more demanding standard than that set down for the traditional subject teacher or the teacher in a school based on "child activity." An understanding of science as "the sole instrumentality of conscious, as distinct from accidental, progress," a reinterpretation of "liberal education" to emphasize functional, practical, and industrial studies, and the humanizing of factual studies like traditional history and geography are all requirements of a modern curriculum. When one unites the psychology of method with the theory of curriculum, one is prompted to work for integration of educational experiences as in Kilpatrick's "project method."

It will be clear from this survey of some of Dewey's educational doctrines that they are intimately bound up with his total ideology. Equally clearly, an evaluation of the degree to which they shelter the sanctity of the individual is a reiteration of the evaluation we have already made. We have an education for individuality, whereby in theory no child may be subordinated to the social system. In practice, because ethical criteria are regarded as instrumental and socially derivative, the social pressures of the school environment take on peculiar significance, and social adjustment looms large to the individual pupil as nearly the main problem he has to solve. There will also be a stress on doing, and a premium placed on visible success as opposed, say, to inner contemplation. Hullfish and Smith have popularized a Deweyan derivative called "reflective thinking,"[4] and Brian Holmes analyzes Dewey's educational theory under the rubric of "the reflective man";[5] but the fact remains that Dewey intends

---

[4] Gordon H. Hullfish and Philip G. Smith, *Reflective Thinking: The Method of Education*, New York: Dodd Mead and Co., 1961.
[5] Brian Holmes, "The Reflective Man," pp. 305-338.

reflection that leads back to action, not reflection leading to experienced harmony in abstraction, as valued by Whitehead.

Much of what Whitehead says is reminiscent of Dewey. In *Aims of Education* he insists that education should be useful and studies integrated: beware, he says, of "inert ideas . . . merely received into the mind without being utilised." On the subject of aims, he observes that "we should banish the idea of a mythical, far-off end of education. The pupils must be continually enjoying some fruition and starting afresh." On liberal education: "The antithesis between a technical and a liberal education is fallacious," for a liberal education is dependent not on the subjects taught but the attitude taken towards knowledge. Whitehead's intriguing concept of rhythm in education reminds us that there is an oscillation in learning between romance and precision, freedom and discipline, intake and output; and he says in one place: "Get your knowledge quickly, and then use it." All this suggests Dewey's problem-solving cycle, except that Whitehead seems to probe deeper and stress the adventures of ideas even more than the performance of deeds.

It is indeed at this point that the differences begin to emerge. There is nothing in Dewey's writings to parallel Whitehead's comments on the place of the classics in education, or his appreciation of the autonomy of the pursuit of historical understanding for its own sake, or his conviction concerning the liberalizing value of mathematical ideas. Not only in style of writing but in catholicity of thought Dewey is pedestrian compared with Whitehead. Henry Holmes suggests that Whitehead's theory "saves *largeness* in the character of education, as Dewey's often fails to do."[6] In Whitehead's advocacy of art education, what he says is sufficient to identify aesthetics as the core of the process. What is wanted from education, he insists, is "an appreciation of the infinite variety of vivid values achieved by an organism in its proper environment." Education of the aesthetic sense is the groundwork even of morals, for humane conduct arises from "receptive-

[6] Henry W. Holmes, "Whitehead's Views on Education," in Schilpp, *Whitehead*, p. 636.

ness to beauty and humane feeling." Broudy has summed up the matter thus: "Despite *Art as Experience* the learning paradigm for Dewey is problem-solving whereas for Whitehead it is more akin to artistic production of selfhood." [7]

In the balance one may believe that moral education is more effectively catered for in Whitehead's educational theory because, though his metaphysics skimps this dimension of experience, his cultural analysis exemplifies it constantly, so that Whitehead's personal magnanimity and Christian-classical training accomplish that for which his philosophy of organism does not explicitly provide. But is this approach more substantial than Dewey's? Neither man grants to morality its own sphere of discourse; instead they both derive moral education from the side effects of other elements in the educational process, especially the rational. Whitehead speaks for both in saying:

> The moral of the tale is the power of reason, its decisive influence on the life of humanity. . . . the entire transformation of human habits and human mentality produced by the long line of men of thought from Thales to the present day, men individually powerless, but ultimately the rulers of the world.[8]

We may be permitted to suggest in conclusion that Dewey recognizes Truth in use and Whitehead Truth in beauty; but the creature that is man persists in setting store as well by Truth in goodness, and the language he uses to talk about it is not reducible to other terms without the evaporation of important elements. In Part Five we revert to modes of modern thought which, like Kierkegaard, lay stress on ethical and religious experience, to see if they afford any better protection of the sanctity of the individual in the present-day world.

[7] Harry S. Broudy, "Actual Entities and the Learning Process," *Educational Theory*, vol. 11, Oct. 1961, pp. 217–227.
[8] *Science and the Modern World*, p. 208.

part five:

modern

religious

thinkers

At the beginning of the present century, secular liberalism and scientific humanism were gaining in ideological influence, while traditional religious views were being undermined by their own "higher critics" and obscured by acrimonious debates about church-state relations. However, in the somber stock-taking that has followed two world wars, ideologies derived from religious premises have commanded increasing respect even from many outside the respective traditions. The views of Martin Buber, Jacques Maritain, and Reinhold Niebuhr are here contrasted with scientific and rationalistic world-views, such as those we have considered from Marx to Whitehead, which build on man's continuity with his biological environment. These three thinkers search in their own ways for a vocabulary that will, without doing violence to sophisticated understanding of the physical and social milieu, explain the behavior of man as a creature radically discontinuous from its predecessors in certain respects.

Each of these men owes a debt to the Judaeo-Christian heritage as mediated through a particular tradition: Buber to Judaism and a pietistic movement within it called Hasidism; Maritain to Christianity via Aquinas and Catholicism; and Niebuhr to Christianity via Augustine and the Reformation. Each is contemporary in his appreciation of the effects of science, technology, and world politics. Finally, each is indebted to existentialism, that multifarious wave of protest wherein Kierkegaard and Nietzsche speak to the age whose emergence they foresaw.

MARTIN BUBER

1878-1965

Martin Buber,[1] born in Vienna, spent fourteen years of his youth in the home of his scholarly grandfather Solomon Buber, a Polish Jew. Later, studying philosophy and art history at the universities of Vienna and Berlin, he became estranged from his Jewish heritage and responded with interest to Nietzsche's challenge to the superficiality and complacency of his age. The same influence encouraged in him a mystical tendency that endured for some years. Meanwhile his search for roots led him into the new Zionist movement, where he supported the concept of a new Jewish state, not so much for political as for cultural reasons, becoming editor at twenty-three of the Zionist periodical *Die Welt*. However, he was still seeking a principle of life, and was later to say of this period: "I professed Judaism before I really knew it." Through his disposition toward mysticism, he also became interested in Hasidism, an eighteenth-century movement among village Jews in Poland, and he withdrew from active involvements for five years to study it. The result was a personal transformation, as

[1] Biographical details were culled from introductions in volumes of his writings, to which reference will be made below, and from the most comprehensive source available at the time of writing: the first chapter of Malcolm L. Diamond's *Martin Buber: Jewish Existentialist* (New York: Oxford University Press, 1960). A more recent volume, in the Library of Living Philosophy, offers still more comprehensive biographical information: *The Philosophy of Martin Buber*, ed. Paul Arthur Schilpp and Maurice S. Friedman (La Salle, Ill.: Open Court, 1967).

he responded to the emphasis on community life and the "hallowing of the everyday" which characterized the *hasidim* ("pious ones"). Through the books he was later to write, Buber won for Hasidism public recognition as one of the great pietistic movements of history. His return to public life coincided with the European rediscovery of Kierkegaard's writings, and his reaction was both warm and critical. He was very receptive to Kierkegaard's existential mode of address, which led him further toward repudiating his own mysticism in preference for a holiness wrought out in the setting of daily life; but he rejected the solitariness of the "Single One." The main lines of Buber's thought were now established.

From 1916 to 1924 he edited *Der Jude,* which became the leading organ of German Jewry. In 1923 he produced the famous *I and Thou,* epitome of all he was ever to write. In that same year he accepted the newly created chair of Jewish philosophy at Frankfurt and occupied it till the Nazis ousted him in 1933. During this time he collaborated with Jewish theologian Franz Rosenzweig in an experiment in adult Jewish education, to which end they began a German translation of the original Hebrew Old Testament. He also co-edited, together with a Catholic and a Protestant, a journal devoted to social and educational problems related to religion. After losing his position in Frankfurt, he proceeded with rare courage to travel around Germany, strengthening the Jewish community, until 1938, when he was persuaded by anxious friends to leave Germany and take up a chair of social philosophy at the Hebrew University in Jerusalem. Here his advocacy of Jewish–Arab coexistence and the "liberal" attitudes he held in contrast to orthodox Judaism lessened somewhat the impact he might have had on his own people. Meanwhile the communal settlements of Israel and the specifications of his post prompted him to develop the social philosophy expressed in *Paths in Utopia;* and from 1949 to 1953 he directed the university's Institute of Adult Studies, founded to train teachers of immigrants. On retirement he traveled extensively in Europe and on a few occasions in the United States, lecturing by invitation. One of his last public gestures was to beg Israel not to execute the war criminal Adolf Eichmann.

His writings may be seen as comprising three groups. First there are his studies of Hasidism, written with feeling and style that survive translation. Then there are his Biblical studies, whose insights have powerfully influenced many Christian interpreters. Finally there are what may be called his philosophical writings, beginning with *I and Thou;* and these are most germane to our study. *Between Man and Man* (1947) contains essays brought together for English readers by Buber, to serve as commentary on *I and Thou*.[2] *Paths in Utopia* (1949) deals with social theories, *Eclipse of God* (1952) with the relation between religion and philosophy, and *Pointing the Way* (1956) with various themes of the same kind. In 1965 a very rich addition to the wisdom of Buber was *The Knowledge of Man*, which provides in a more systematic way than any previous work an exposition of his "philosophical anthropology," breaking new ground with an ontological explanation of the twofold character of human awareness first described in *I and Thou*. It includes lectures on psychiatry delivered in the United States in 1957.

Buber's influence continues to grow. His impact on Christian theologians in Europe has been profound, perhaps most notably through Karl Barth and Emil Brunner; and Paul Tillich, Reinhold Niebuhr, and Jacques Maritain, long resident in the United States, also acknowledge profit from him. Indeed Diamond observes that "although his outlook is profoundly Jewish, he has, to date, exerted a greater influence on Christian than on Jewish thought."[3] Outside the religious fold he has contributed to the "existential psychology" born in Europe between the world wars, recruited disciples for his philosophical anthropology,[4] greatly influenced art critic Herbert Read, and commanded the respectful attention of educational theorists in Britain and America. It would seem that he offers the twentieth century a way of looking at man alternative to those of the analysts in philosophy and science,

[2] See his foreword to *Between Man and Man* (trans. Ronald Gregor Smith, London: Fontana, 1961), p. 15.
[3] Diamond, *Martin Buber*, p. 168.
[4] See Friedman's acknowledgment in Martin Buber, *The Knowledge of Man* (ed. Maurice Friedman, trans. Maurice Friedman and Ronald Gregor Smith, London: George Allen and Unwin, 1965), p. 7.

yet avoiding the rather narrow intensity of Kierkegaard's utterance and the nihilism of Nietzsche's.

DEFINING "INDIVIDUAL"

Buber's life-long concern has been to define human personhood. His inaugural lectures in Jerusalem were entitled "What is man?" He described them as studies in "philosophical anthropology." It was only in the last of his writing published to date that he went any distance beyond phenomenological description into ontological speculation. Always the concrete, self-conscious individual is his starting point.

This individual, says Buber in *I and Thou*, finds that he is capable of experiencing the world in two ways. In each of these primary types of awareness, we are "saying," as it were, one of the "primary words." One of these, the primary word *I–It*, refers to our capacity to objectify our experience by describing and cataloguing the world and thereby gaining material control over it. To do this we must always suspend some of our own involvement in it, like the scientist who tries to minimize the effect of the observer in his experiments, and therefore we cannot say *I–It* with our whole being. Necessarily, by detaching ourselves from things and even persons in this way, we make them objects for our use and manipulation. This is normal and natural; however, if we are content to live on this plane of awareness all the time, we are not fully human but only spectators on the sidelines of real living.

The other way of experiencing the world is when we say *I–Thou*. When we do this, we make a response with our whole being. But it is not something we switch on and off at will; we cannot just say *I–Thou* whenever we wish. We can, however, prepare the way for this kind of awareness, in which human existence attains maximum expression, by nurturing a higher regard for the "world of relation." That is, we can be seekers after "dialogue" with other beings ("All real living is meeting") as contrasted with merely observing or manipulating them. On occasion, as we seek to be involved in living relationships (at the risk of being hurt and disturbed), we momentarily glimpse the *Thou* — the autonomous being — in someone or something else, and reality is shared *between* us; we live wholly and deeply in the present. It is inevitable that we will afterwards want to reflect on that moment of meeting, and in doing so we will convert it to a thing, for every *Thou* has to become an *It*. Indeed, without the benefit of *It*-knowledge man would not survive; but "He who lives with *It* alone is not a man."

Thus does Buber create a new vocabulary with which to talk about man. He does not deny the usefulness of historical, psychological, and sociological data concerning man, but he does insist that such data belong to the world of *I–It* and therefore miss the essential thing about man. Even when all the scientific data are in, one is not in a position to reassemble the abstractions into a living man.

> ... in every one of those disciplines the possibility of its achieving anything in thought rests precisely on its objectification, on what may be termed its "dehumanisation."[5]

He seeks therefore to develop a philosophical anthropology, which will counter the philosophical tendency to universalize by referring back constantly to the existing individual in his wholeness as a choosing, self-reflecting being. The only individual to whom one has such access is oneself, and the philosophical anthropologist must therefore involve himself in his findings, filtering his observations of other data about man through his own subjectivity. It will not be enough to *think* about his own being in relation to such data, for this will still be a reflex in the world of *It;* he must so confront the something other than himself that he *lives* in shared reality, allowing his whole being to be affected. The oft-quoted illustration for this kind of existential knowledge is Kierkegaard's commentary on the fact of human death, which, when encountered as the truth-for-me, molds much of my future response to life.

This is the first part of the philosophical anthropologist's

[5] *Between Man and Man*, p. 153.

task. The second is harder. For if he is to communicate his knowledge in order to increase the insight of his fellow men, he must do so in such a way as to provoke them into an existential meeting with this knowledge, and therefore his writing, though disciplined, must challenge and charm.[6] It is no accident that the electrifying effect of *I and Thou* is in part due to the semi-poetic form in which it is cast; in subsequent writings Buber contrives in various ways—by a frequent though humble use of the first person, by anecdotes and maxims drawn from everyday encounter, and by occasional jewels of epigram embedded in his argument—to get past his reader's guard and make him "feel" the significance of what is being said.

For the most part, Buber's method is that of phenomenological description,[7] and he evades the attempts of questioners to pigeonhole him in systematic philosophical categories.[8] He is not concerned, for example, to prove objectively that human personality lives in the two realms of *It* and *Thou;* he wants to evoke a confession that the individual reader finds it to be so for him. He does essay some anthropological speculation in *I and Thou,* based partly on the structure of primitive languages in which he sees personal being embedded as a *Thou,* rather than differentiated grammatically as a He or a She, and from this deduces that *Thou* precedes *It* in the emergence of human consciousness. He does not rest his case on this speculation, and asserts in *Knowledge of Man* that it is not useful to theorize about the dawn of the human species, since what matters is what man experiences now. He is more willing, however, to proceed to metaphysical speculations from his existential data.

Taking man as his starting point, Buber suggests that "the world" is established by man's awareness of and relation to it.

[6] Again note the comparison with Kierkegaard.
[7] Buber credits Husserl, who popularized what he called the "phenomenological method," with the discovery of an important tool, though he criticizes the way in which he wielded it. (See *Between Man and Man,* pp. 195–6.)
[8] See Diamond's testimony to his manner of coping with questions of this sort in public discussion (Diamond, *Martin Buber,* p. 4).

When a world exists, and to the extent to which it exists, there exists the man who conditions it, and he is there not in the sense of a species of living creatures, but of a category which has moved into reality.[9]

That is, existentially the world order exists in the consciousness of the individual human, as far as he can tell. One is reminded of Berkeley's Idealism, and such an association would seem to be confirmed by the discovery that for Buber the world "out there" is guaranteed by the existence of God. But the difference is fundamental. For in Buber's terms the God of Berkeleian metaphysics is a philosopher's concept belonging in the category of *I–It,* whereas Buber's God is the "eternal Thou" who confronts us in all being. This becomes clearer if we ask our two questions: "What distinguishes the individual from nonhuman entities?" and "What distinguishes him from other individuals?"

It implies differentiation whereas *Thou* implies relation; therefore an animal may be regarded as being completely and dumbly incorporated in its environment; all is *Thou,* though the creature does not "know" this or utter the *I* of *I–Thou.* Its environment is not a "world" but the "dynamic of presences bound up with one another by bodily memory to the extent required by the functions of life." With the emergence of man, however, the world order is discovered by virtue of the twofold principle of human life, man's capacity to say *I–It* and *I–Thou.*

> The principle of human life is not simple but twofold, being built up in a twofold movement which is of such a kind that the one movement is the presupposition of the other. I propose to call the first movement "the primal setting at a distance" and the second "entering into relation." [10]

This may be interpreted as suggesting three stages. The first is the unconscious immersion of the animal in relation. The second is the first human movement of abstraction or "dis-

[9] *Knowledge of Man,* p. 62.
[10] *Ibid.,* p. 60.

tance" whereby the structure of being is held independently over against the personal being. The third follows immediately from this, that the individual may seek to re-enter into relation, not now as an undifferentiated animal, but as one who says *I–Thou*.

Thus the complete human being is not established only by the capacity to say *I–It*, for this is the vestibule of human existence; in Buber's imagery: "The *It* is the eternal chrysalis, the *Thou* the eternal butterfly." [11] Man is "sent forth from the natural domain of species into the hazard of the solitary category," [12] and the element of hazard is precisely the temptation to remain in the world of *It* and not to complete the movement whereby one enters again into relation. Reality is found not in the eye of the observer, or in the thing-in-itself, but in the relation established between two "beings" (Ger. *Seiende*): most especially—because of the possibility of fully mutual response—between two human beings.

In *I and Thou* Buber describes three kinds of relation into which man can enter—with natural things such as trees and animals, with spiritual beings (a little like Aristotelian Forms or Ideas), and with man—insisting that in each case relation is mutual. This introduces an unfortunate difficulty into his exposition, despite his attempt in the postscript to the second edition to have his cake and eat it too. For what he most wants to say, and does say in other writings, is that the relation between man and man is unique and fundamental.[13] As such, it is, as we have seen, the primary location of reality.

> "Between" is not an auxiliary construction, but the real place and bearer of what happens between men; it has received no specific attention because in distinction from the individual soul and its context, it does not exhibit a smooth continuity, but is ever and again re-constituted in accordance with men's meetings

---

[11] *I and Thou*, p. 17.
[12] *Knowledge of Man*, p. 71.
[13] Friedman reports him as saying that, if he had written *I and Thou* again, he would have sought different categories to make clearer the distinction between the dialogue between man and man and other *I–Thou* relationships. (*Ibid.*, p. 27.)

with one another; hence what is experienced has been annexed naturally to the continuous elements, the soul and its world.[14]

The world order is neither the rational construct of men's minds nor the isolated substances or beings we suppose to surround us. It is a deeper stratum of interrelation which we glimpse and are assured of by *Thou* experiences, meetings between beings.

> These meetings are not organised to make the world, but each is a sign of the world-order. They are not linked up with one another, but each assures you of your solidarity with the world.[15]

Moreover, the sphere of "between" (again, especially that of man and man) is the location of personality development. Human beings may react to things and each other at the level of either *I-It* or *I-Thou*. We spend most of our time in *I-It*, but the *I* of this primary word is individuality, the distancing of the *I* from the beings it experiences and uses. At the extreme, an "individual" is so concerned with manipulating his environment that he even treats himself as a tool. Buber's example of this is Napoleon. To the degree that we enter into *Thou* moments, we become "persons." Koo provides a helpful comparison between G. H. Mead's *I-Me* and Buber's *I-Thou*, two models for the explanation of personality development; she says that while the two thinkers are at one in believing that the self emerges from environmental process in which language plays a big part, Mead's concept of the internal dialogue between *I* and *Me* falls into Buber's *I-It* category.[16] In contrast, Buber places the onus for personality development on dialogue with another *I*, another "person," on mutual meetings in which the *It* factors of objectivity are momentarily suspended. "Where there is no sharing there is no reality." There are, of course, not two kinds of human

[14] *Between Man and Man*, p. 245.
[15] *I and Thou*, p. 32.
[16] Gladys Y. Koo, "The Structure and Process of Self," *Educational Theory*, vol. 14, April 1964, 117. See also Herberg's introduction to *The Writings of Martin Buber*, New York: Meridian Books Inc., 1956, p. 15, where the same comparison is discussed.

being, individuals and persons, but two poles of humanity between which we find human beings ranged. Among "persons" cited by Buber, together with the vector of mutuality they best represent, are Socrates, who sought dialogue with men; Goethe, with nature; Jesus, with God.

At all times, then, Buber philosophizes outward from the focal human individual. Beginning with man's twofold awareness of the world, he lays stress on the need to seek *Thou* encounters, despite their unpredictability and discontinuity, in order to become truly human. The technical and manipulative control made possible by man's augmented capacity to say *I–It* is to be regarded not as his highest achievement but as the threshold to the highest, which is the capacity to say *I–Thou*, that is, to enter into full relation with other beings. The most important form of dialogue for the development of self or personality is that which can occur between man and man.

SANCTITY OF THE INDIVIDUAL

Clearly, in view of the existential line he takes, Buber is persuaded on all counts of the sanctity of the individual, and equally desirous of so persuading his readers. His method of doing so is also existential, in that he does not strive to deduce and justify his norms, but describes human relationships in such a way as to provoke his readers into desiring certain kinds of fulfillment. At the same time he adds to persuasion warning, suggesting that human affairs are in a state of crisis through failure to honor the *Thou* in experience.

Part Two of *I and Thou* describes the modern overstress on *It* which Buber believes to be the cause of the present questionableness of man. Historically, he says, the story of man has been a gradual accumulation of scientific and aesthetic understanding, that is, of increasing ability to say the primary word *I–It*. This is not bad in itself, but if a man lets it have mastery, then he, that is the *I* in this primary word, is impoverished. It is possible for a man to be so fully equipped with information that he becomes disinclined for living dealings with men. One imagines that nuclear scientists declining to be involved as persons in the moral issues arising out of their findings are examples. Our present age is sick because *It*-knowledge has reached the point where the human person is in danger of being emptied of reality. The popularity of explanations of human behavior based on evolutionary theory, or on laws of history and economics, has produced a fatalistic conviction that man is imprisoned in the cage of unlimited causality, and that his consciousness of freedom is merely an illusion produced by his feelings.

The sanctity of the individual is impugned not only by certain claims and emphases of scientific knowledge, but by the demolition of ideological canopies. In his 1938 lectures Buber explored human history in terms of alternating epochs of habitation and homelessness. The former, illustrated by the cosmologies of Plato, Aquinas, Newton, and others, are interspersed with periods of religious and social upheaval, as in the times of Augustine, Pascal, and (though he was one of the few to see the upheaval) Kierkegaard. In the present age the anthropological problem has been brought to maturity by two factors. "The first is predominantly sociological in nature. It is the increasing decay of the old, organic forms of the direct life of man with man." [17] The first consequence of this was political individualism, but this is now giving way to modern collectivism.[18]

> The second factor can be described as one of the history of the spirit, or better, of the soul.... This concerns man's relation to the new things and connexions which have arisen by his action or with his co-operation. I should like to call this peculiarity of the modern crisis man's lagging behind his works.[19]

Thus machines are controlling men, the economy is ruling the politicians, and politics itself is trammeled by the demon of war. Underneath all these things the solitary individual experiences rootlessness and despair and runs for safety into

---

[17] *Between Man and Man*, p. 192.
[18] *Ibid.*, p. 241; also *Paths in Utopia*, trans. R. F. C. Hull, London: Routledge and Kegan Paul, 1949, p. 132.
[19] *Between Man and Man*, p. 193.

collectivism. The Great Society which Mannheim assures us is inevitable is feared by Buber as the graveyard of humanity as we know it.

Buber has one remedy for this state of affairs, though it is applied at several levels. His basic remedy is to redress the present imbalance between the two attitudes man is able to adopt toward the world. His first application may be said to be the promotion of the discipline of philosophical anthropology. We have seen how he seeks to do this, and examined both the terminology and the method that he employs. The second application is to recapture for religion the integrating office that personality requires, and we shall look at his view of religion in a moment. The third is to reconsider the healing of individuals in the light of his philosophy of dialogue,[20] upon which we shall comment in discussing his view of morality. The fourth is to advocate a form of socialism for which he finds his model in Israel; and the fifth is to develop and experiment with views on education, which we shall take up in our chapter comparing Buber with Maritain and Niebuhr.

With respect to religion, Buber analyzes Heidegger, pointing out how, by repudiating the theological ground on which Kierkegaard builds, he traps the self in a closed system and exemplifies exactly the inability of modern man to communicate. Buber goes on to assert that the universe is a "stream of mutuality" and that authentic living is living that seeks to enter into relation, to glimpse the *Thou* in the entities about us which are for the most part *It* to us. The guarantee of such a search is the eternal *Thou*, God, in whom all things hold together and who is to be encountered through every particular *Thou*. This God is not an abstraction or universal principle (for then he would be an *It*), but one whom to experience is to experience relation to a person. At least three things follow for human worship.

The first is that mysticism is ruled out of court by the fact that God is in his world, and it is in the hallowing of the everyday that he meets us. Therefore Kierkegaard comes under

[20] See his lectures to the Washington School of Psychiatry, published in *Knowledge of Man*, pp. 59–87 and 120–147.

censure for identifying the "crowd" with the dialogue between man and man. The second is that all attempts to define God are at best allegorical aids to worship and at worst bulwarks of institutionalized religion which has failed to rise out of the *It* dimension. "God is the Being that is directly, most nearly, and lastingly, over against us, that may properly only be addressed, not expressed."[21] The third is that the apparently clear dichotomy between the religious man and the atheistic man may in fact bear no relation to their respective postures before God, in that the professed atheist may, by the desire he has to encounter the particular *Thou* in others, grow "into an existential state to which the name of rebirth is due"; that is, God may choose to encounter him. "God" is not merely another name for the *Thou* experiences we may have, nor is it synonymous with the world-order, for

> the concept of personal being is indeed completely incapable of declaring what God's essential being is, but it is both permitted and necessary to say that God is *also* a Person.[22]

Consistent with the above position, Buber brings religion and morality together, not as associated systems but as associated aspects of the *I–Thou* attitude. He chides Kierkegaard[23] for regarding the religious stage as something beyond, and detached from, the ethical, saying that such a view hinges on the identification of morality with the world of *It* — with moral codes and statutory obligations. Instead Buber relates morality to the *Thou,* and insists that it is basically a sense of responsibility towards the *Thou* in another person, the advantage of this being that it ministers not only to the personal development of the other but to one's own. Hence "'truth' in this realm means 'that men communicate themselves to one another as what they are,'" and "Love is responsibility

[21] *I and Thou,* p. 80.
[22] Postscript to *I and Thou,* p. 135.
[23] Not, I submit, with justice. What Kierkegaard is saying is that the ethical stage is barren until the individual has entered the religious stage and returns a transformed man to the ethical task. This is in accord with Buber's view though not perhaps as clearly and specifically stated, nor on the other hand as prone to amalgamate the religious and moral categories.

of an *I* for a *Thou*."[24] Good is to be understood as direction and evil as aimlessness, so that one may say:

> As a condition of the individual soul evil is the conclusive shirking of direction, of the total orientation of the soul by which it stands up to personal responsibility before God.[25]

Actually, however, Buber exhibits an ambivalent attitude towards evil, in that his existential interpretation of evil as a condition of drift or lostness is assailed by the evidence, especially of two world wars, that men may deliberately and purposefully choose to do evil. On the one hand he refuses to admit the term "radical evil" as referable to man's relation to man, since so unconditional a concept can only be ascribed to the relation of man to God. On the other hand he refers to certain Germans in the Second World War as having by their intentional wickedness "radically removed themselves from the human sphere, . . . transposed themselves into a sphere of monstrous inhumanity inaccessible to [his] conception."[26] One might be disposed to treat this as a shift of position, were it not that still later he insists that "one cannot do evil with his whole soul, one can do good only with the whole soul"[27] and says that he has "never known a young person who seemed to [him] irretrievably bad."[28] Diamond suggests that Buber came to terms only belatedly with "the way of the wicked."[29] A. V. Judges identifies the problem as the difference between Christian and Jewish views of sin;[30] but we

---

[24] *I and Thou*, p. 15. In this sense of "love," the objection of Kneller that he cannot be expected to love everyone is shown to be rather superficial. (See George F. Kneller, "Education, Knowledge and the Problem of Existence," *Harvard Educational Review*, vol. 31, Fall 1961, pp. 427-436.)

[25] *Between Man and Man*, p. 104.

[26] *Pointing the Way: Collected Essays*, trans. Maurice Friedman, London: Routledge and Kegan Paul, 1957, p. 232.

[27] *Knowledge of Man*, p. 136. This is not fully reconcilable either with the description of "radical evil" in *Good and Evil: Two Interpretations*, New York: Charles Scribner's Sons, 1952, p. 140.

[28] *Ibid.*, p. 78. We can ascribe slightly greater consistency to his views by stressing the qualifier "young."

[29] Diamond, *Martin Buber*, p. 144.

[30] A. V. Judges, "Martin Buber," in *The Function of Teaching*, ed. by Judges, pp. 90-92. Friedman's analysis also suggests an ultimate conviction

would suggest that both views have been modified in Buber's thinking by his existentialist leanings. At the least there is confusion that calls for closer analytic study.

Buber's views on morality have special application in the field of psychotherapy, in that he believes that the refusal to live authentically toward oneself and others can give rise to a genuine guilt which is quite distinct from the guilt "feelings" by which some Freudians are prone to explain indiscriminately all guilt phenomena. Therefore psychotherapy should include the illumination of genuine guilt, so that the patient may come to terms with it and make the reparation that will lead to reconciliation within himself. The therapist is not judge or pastor in this situation but heals by extending love for the "isolated psyche," respect for the patient as a person, since this gives him the confidence to view his guilt in its correct dimension. Buber goes on to express a Judaistic conviction that the man can then accomplish his own reconciliation or salvation. Some Christians part company with Buber at this point, and Diamond in particular is prompted to express the fear that he is overoptimistic about the results of dialogue.[31]

In *Knowledge of Man* Buber devotes considerable space to discussing social interaction, having not gladly suffered critics seeking to equate his philosophy of dialogue with fashionable social-science concepts of socialization. He distinguishes between group membership and personal encounter, that is, between the "social" and the "interhuman." The social level involves psychological interaction, mainly partaking of the world of *It*. It may vary from the mutual problem-solving in which Dewey anchored his social theory to the subrational corporateness of the muttering crowd which Kierkegaard anathematized. However, the interhuman realm is dialogical, noncontinuous, and the source of personal development. It is the way whereby men mutually confirm each other's being.

that even radical evil is ultimately redeemable by human effort (See Maurice S. Friedman, *Martin Buber: The Life of Dialogue*, New York: Harper and Bros., 1955, pp. 111–112.)
[31] Diamond, *Martin Buber*, p. 201.

In dialogue "I affirm the person I struggle with." The sickness of our age is that

> the perception of one's fellow man as a whole, as a unity and as unique . . . is opposed in our time by almost everything that is commonly understood as specifically modern. In our time there predominates an analytical, reductive and deriving look between man and man.[32]

Just as Buber distinguishes between "social" and "interhuman," so he attempts a distinction on the same lines between "political" and "social," as we shall see in the next section; and the outcome there as here is some perplexity as to how to reintegrate the data from such closely associated realms of discourse. While believing that Buber has done us a service by making such distinctions apparent, we consider that he overstates the case to the exclusion, ironically, of dialogue between the existentialist and the scientist.

SOCIETY AND THE INDIVIDUAL

Buber's stress on dialogue and community preserves him from both extreme individualism and oppressive collectivism. However, so disparate a thinker as Dewey also avoids these pitfalls while promoting a radically different view. This suggests that we must test Buber's thought against some of the modern realities that bulk large in Dewey's thought: science and politics. We must beware in doing so of talking loosely about Buber's "ideology," as though he purports to supply us with a finely articulated system enveloping all the major concerns of life. He insists that his thought is geared to "philosophical anthropology" and declares unequivocally: "I, myself, have no 'doctrine.' My function is to point out realities of this order."[33] Nevertheless one may take leave to doubt

---

[32] *Knowledge of Man*, p. 80. He specifically adds at this point that he is not attacking scientific analysis as such; but Judges considers that he refuses to "come to terms with any empirical and scientific formulation of reality." (See Judges, "Martin Buber," p. 96.)

[33] *For the Sake of Heaven*, trans. Ludwig Lewisohn, New York: Meridian Books, 1959, p. xiii.

whether he is quite free of the systematizing instinct or of bias against certain realities in the human order which do not fit readily into his system: science and politics.

In theory, Buber allots a distinguished place in his view of man to science and analytic procedures, for he acknowledges that the primary word *I-It* is indispensable, that "the world of *It* is set in the context of space and time," that we spend most of our lives in this world, and that it is part of man's glory to have greatly increased his abstractive and manipulative powers. Furthermore he describes human history as a spiral movement, oscillating between *It* and *Thou* experiences, with each new advance of *It* making the corresponding *Thou* harder to attain but richer when attained. However, Diamond points out that Buber "fails to elaborate the sense in which detached knowledge, gained in the *I-It* attitude, may enrich the meaning conveyed within the *I-Thou* relation." [34] We would suggest that this is due partly to a laudable desire to correct an imbalance, but also to a certain rigidity in the categories he set up. We have already noted the lack of an integrating office between psychological interaction and *Thou* dialogue, and Simon considers that, while he has acknowledged that "without *It* man cannot live," Buber has not paid sufficient attention to the ramifications of this insight.[35] While he has done us a service by enlarging the vocabulary we must use to describe human behavior, he has tended to present an either-or instead of indicating an effective relation between both. One cannot turn back the clock of a technological age.

We must now probe further into Buber's thought to see whether his concept of society offers sanctuary to the individual. The textbook for this is his *Paths in Utopia*. In this book he defends those to whom Marx applied the smear-word "utopian socialists" from the imputation that they were unrealistic in their views while he was himself correct. Buber shows that Marx's own vision is utopian, in his own sense of the word, and that there is in his writings an ambivalent attitude to the question of the internal transformation of society —

[34] Diamond, *Martin Buber*, p. 75.
[35] Quoted in Diamond, p. 166.

an ambivalence his disciples resolved in favor of centralized political control, so that those socialists who favor smaller social units under a federal form of control are thereafter automatically "utopian."

Buber then reasserts the feasibility of a federalized socialism, in which communities small enough to be social organisms conduct consumer-producer co-operatives. He claims that the paradigm, in a provisional sense, is "an experiment that did not fail," referring to the Jewish village commune, or *kvuza*, as found in Palestine. Some commentators refer loosely to the kibbutz as Buber's model, but as Crane reminds us, his heart is in the smaller community of the kvuza.[36] However, both give rise to the federal network that is dear to his heart. The last pages prophesy that the capitalistic societies of the West will disintegrate economically and be forced to choose between two forms of socialism, sloganized by Buber as "Moscow" and "Jerusalem"—collectivism and communalism.[37] It is clear that his heart and mind are in that unique and peculiar modern phenomenon, the nation-state of Israel.

This is indeed the ground of our criticisms, in that Buber's understanding of world affairs is rather restricted. His own compatriots still in other lands, the Dispersed Jews, complain that he has neglected them,[38] advanced technological societies may well claim that he has not comprehended them, and the specialized character of Israeli politics produces in his writings a suspect dichotomy between "society" and "politics." Buber accuses Bertrand Russell of confusing the social and political principles, nevertheless insisting himself that society is a flexible and organic thing whereas the state should be a nontechnical and constitutionally limited agency. The implication is that societies are established by *Thou* relation-

---

[36] A. R. Crane, "The Educational Thought of Martin Buber," *Australian Journal of Education,* vol. 5, July 1961, pp. 91–99.

[37] Niebuhr's strongest objection to Buber's social philosophy applies at this point, when he insists that Buber has become utopian in the Marxist sense. (See correspondence cited by Friedman in *Martin Buber,* p. 222.)

[38] Thus *Writings of Martin Buber,* ed. Herberg, p. 36.

ships and may therefore refer to themselves as *We*,[39] whereas political entities are of the world of *It* and encourage collectivism. Here again Buber's basic terminology has led him to paint the issue in an either–or way, and to that extent his social theory reverts to earlier social patterns which are too simple for the present age. It is left to the American thinker Niebuhr to relate Biblical-existentialist insights to the Great Society in a way for which Buber is not equipped.

We have endeavored to suggest that the sureness of Buber's touch when describing the human individual, or enriching our modes of discourse on personal life, is less apparent when he attempts to extend his categories to the wider spheres of science, technological society, and national politics. He is for all that well beyond Kierkegaard on such matters, and provides substantial incentive for religious thinkers and others to apply themselves to social problems and the enhancement of community life.

[39] See *Knowledge of Man*, pp. 105–109, and *Between Man and Man*, p. 213.

JACQUES MARITAIN

1882-1973

Jacques Maritain [1] is a philosopher initially trained in positivism who has become the most widely acknowledged prophet of a renascent Thomism. Though some of his writings, especially those written in France before the Second World War, sometimes present Catholic ideas in a way that repels non-Catholic readers, in the main he speaks with force and clarity to major problems of our time.

Born in Paris to a lawyer father and a mother with political connections, he was raised a nominal Protestant and went on to university in Paris, to study philosophy and natural science, without any particular commitments or beliefs. Positivism in philosophy and bold empiricism in science left him dissatisfied, and he testifies that his teachers made him "despair of reason." Despair was staved off while, together with his future wife Raissa, he attended lectures by Bergson; and in 1905 he met the Catholic thinker Leon Bloy and both he and Raissa were prompted to study Catholicism, joining the church within a year. Supposing that this shut the door on philosophy,

---

[1] Biographical information was obtained from Will Herberg, ed., *Four Existentialist Theologians* (New York: Doubleday, 1958), pp. 27f., and A. C. F. Beales, "Jacques Maritain," in *The Function of Teaching*, ed. A. V. Judges, pp. 67–88. A useful up-date is the just published volume 46 (Winter 1972) of *The New Scholasticism*, dedicated to Maritain on his ninetieth birthday. Appraisals of Maritain by other than partisan commentators are as yet few; therefore this critique must plough a lone furrow to an extent not necessary in other cases.

Maritain turned to the study of biology at Heidelberg and Rome; but he returned in 1908 to Paris, where for a time he did hack work for publishers. On advice he began to study Aquinas, found that he was "already a Thomist without knowing it," and recognized that his mission was to be a philosopher after all. First as a college instructor and then as professor of philosophy from 1914 in the Institut Catholique in Paris, he blazed a trail as a Thomist. Initially concerned more with metaphysical, aesthetic, and logical aspects, he found the social and political ferment of Europe in the 1920s provoking him to move over into political philosophy, enlarging the scope of his writings. Lecturing abroad in such places as England and the Americas, he extended the influence of renascent Thomism and prepared the soil for his self-exile from Vichy France in 1940. He served as visiting professor at Columbia and Princeton Universities and the Catholic Institute of Medieval Studies in Toronto, and added educational writings to his output. After the war he returned to France, was appointed ambassador to the Vatican by General De Gaulle, and took part in the early formative sessions of UNESCO,[2] managing all the while to keep up the production of scholarly works. In 1948 he returned to Princeton as professor of philosophy and retired from that institution as professor emeritus. In 1965 he was made a lay cardinal of the Catholic church.

The range of his publications has already been suggested. Among the early moderately technical works, we consult *Degrees of Knowledge* (1937), which deals with epistemology, and *True Humanism* (1938), which lays out the foundations for all subsequent analyses of the person and society, such as *Scholasticism and Politics* (1940), *The Person and the Common Good* (1947), and *Man and the State* (1951). Educational speculations are launched in the now famous *Education at the Crossroads* (1943); they are developed further in a chapter of the 54th yearbook of the N.S.S.E.,[3] in a contribution to a

[2] See for example his inaugural address to the second international conference of UNESCO in Jacques Maritain, *The Range of Reason*, London: Geoffrey Bles, 1953, pp. 172–184.
[3] "Thomistic Views on Education," in N.S.S.E. 54th Yearbook, 1955, pp. 57–90.

symposium on Christian education in 1957,[4] and in the collection of essays brought together by the Gallaghers in 1962.[5] Of special interest in view of our concern here with several existentialist writers is Maritain's study of *Existence and the Existent* (1948), in which he presents Thomism as the only authentic existentialism.

It is to be stressed that Maritain does not remove himself from the open forum by his prior commitment to and aggressive accrediting of Thomism. He is well aware of the disparaging view generally taken of the medieval scholastics, having added to his early grounding in European positivism a discerning encounter with American Pragmatism. Far from ignoring these schools of thought, he meets them head-on and seeks to show that what is valuable in them is compatible with, and anticipated by, Thomism. Nor will he concede that his own stance is *neo*-Thomist, for he declares that in Aristotle and Aquinas human reason acquired permanently valid structures for making reality intelligible.

> If Aristotle could be baptized by St. Thomas, it is because his metaphysical principles were founded in objective reality. . . . what a relief to play truant and to dispense with the disciplines of the *philosophia perennis!* But culture cannot dispense with these disciplines, it will never be able to dispense with the Greek Aristotle transfigured by the Angelic Doctor.[6]

> Intelligence demands that we hold one philosophic system out of all others — if it is true — as alone valid.[7]

---

[4] "On Some Typical Aspects of Christian Education," in *The Christian Idea of Education*, ed. Edmund Fuller, New Haven: Yale University Press, 1957, pp. 173–212.

[5] Jacques Maritain, *The Education of Man*, ed. Donald and Idella Gallagher, New York: Doubleday, 1962.

[6] Jacques Maritain, *St. Thomas Aquinas*, trans. Joseph W. Evans and Peter O'Reilly, New York: Meridian Books Inc., 1960, pp. 75–76. First published in 1930, this book was described by Maritain in his 1958 Foreword as "a kind of Thomist manifesto, especially directed to the French Catholic public" (p. 11). It is distasteful reading for a non-Catholic; Maritain apologized for his "youthful emphasis and rhetoric" (p. 12) but without repudiating the lavish adulation and crude miracle stories he associated with Aquinas.

[7] *Ibid.*, p. 20. I would dissent, remarking on the necessity to hold simultaneously in the mind disparate rational constructs, between and even within

Consequently we are placed in the by now familiar position of showing careful respect to an intelligent man's diagnosis of modern views and trends while recognizing the ideological character of his recommendations.

DEFINING "INDIVIDUAL"

Whereas the Thomism of Aquinas has as its starting point God and his attributes, the Thomism of Maritain sets out from the human person, inviting Lawson's comment that "what is new with [neo-Thomism] . . . is the re-assertion of personal values and the primacy of man in the visible creation." [8] It is therefore reasonable to discern in Maritain's reaction to the contemporary crisis an existential element. It is not that he is subjectivist like Kierkegaard or Buber, for indeed his analytic objectivity is as formidable as that of the philosophers Kierkegaard criticizes.[9] But he is consistently at pains to prove the

---

the same realms of discourse, which modern research imposes. If Maritain really means "valid," then he is referring to an empiricological criterion, but what he seems to mean is "true" in a metaphysical and normative sense. If so, then the Thomist criterion he promotes is not such as to command common consent, but competes with other ways of looking at the structures of knowledge. For Thomist reasons Maritain cannot allow this, since the theology of Aquinas teaches that God may be discovered ("proved") by rational means, even without the enlightenment of revelation. Therefore this and other authoritative first principles are available and infallible, and it is not the weakness of reason but the disobedience of will that causes so many scholars to deny the *philosophia perennis*. This is a dogmatic and drastic way to deflect sincere dissent. My point of view is that at this second level of validation Maritain passes over from philosopher to ideologist, thereby taking his place appropriately alongside the other thinkers we are studying. He is not like Whitehead, who acknowledges that he is engaging in metaphysical speculation, but rather like Dewey, who claims to be redefining philosophy so as to bring it into line with the real world as he sees it. It is no accident that Maritain's tilts at Pragmatism are sharp and frequent. The clash is not merely philosophical but ideological.

[8] W. Lawson, "Neo-Thomism," in *Education and the Philosophic Mind*, ed. A. V. Judges, London: Harrap and Co., 1957, p. 46.

[9] Maritain claims that existentialism is essentially a religious posture, tricked into becoming a pseudophilosophy by the strength of Hegel's philosophicoreligious synthesis, which it opposed. It therefore asserts subjectivity at the expense of intelligibility. Thomism is the only authentic existentialism, for it asserts that "truth follows upon the existence of things" (*Existence and*

uniqueness, worth, and particularity of the human person, and to define all other phenomena in relation to this "end in itself."

Maritain believes that the essentialistic question "What is man?" can and must be put, and that the answer in our civilization derives from the integration of Greek, Jewish, and Christian answers, which he summarizes respectively as follows:

> man as an animal endowed with reason, whose supreme dignity is in the intellect; and man as a free individual in personal relation with God, whose supreme righteousness consists in voluntarily obeying the law of God; and man as a sinful and wounded creature called to divine life and to the freedom of grace, whose supreme perfection consists in love.[10]

This is, as Maritain himself points out, a definition in philosophicoreligious terms, but inasmuch as he claims that Thomism is derivable from experience and reason alone, though analogous in its conclusions to the data of faith, our analysis may proceed for the most part at the philosophical level.

Man, says Maritain, is an animal endowed with reason. With respect to his animality he is a biological organism which acquires its data via the senses. But by virtue of his intellect he is also a soul and inhabits another plane of existence — has "spiritual superexistence through knowledge and love." This unites him with the community of spiritual beings, although (quoting Aquinas) "the human mind belongs to the lowest stage of minds."[11] It is important, however, to stress that, as against the dualism of ancient Greek and modern Cartesian

---

the Existent, trans. Lewis Galantiere and Gerald B. Phelan, New York: Doubleday Image Books, 1961, p. 21) and that "the concept of existence cannot be detached from the concept of essence" (p. 34). Rationality is therefore the premier existential attribute, and requires Thomistic analysis.

[10] Jacques Maritain, *Education at the Crossroads*, New Haven: Yale University Press, 1960, p. 7. It is reiterated in "'Thomist Views on Education," p. 63.

[11] Jacques Maritain, *The Degrees of Knowledge*, trans Bernard Wall London: Geoffrey Bles, 1937, p. 102.

thinkers, the resultant creature is a unity. While the soul, separated from the body, is no doubt an entity, it is not one in which human nature is complete; that is, it does not constitute a "person."[12] Man is "a spirit united substantially with matter and implacably subject to a bodily condition," yet "an individual who holds himself in hand by his intelligence and his will." The degree to which he realizes the aspirations of spirit is the measure of his conquest of freedom.

Like Buber, Maritain distinguishes between "individuality" and "personality," and the two writers have by some been bracketed together on this basis. But whereas Buber uses both terms for specifically human attributes, Maritain regards individuality as the material pole, linking us with our organic inheritance, and personality as the spiritual pole, linking us with our fellow persons and God.[13] The second category for Maritain therefore incorporates both the *I–It* and *I–Thou* notions of Buber, or, in Maritain's terms, man's capacity for both knowledge and love.[14] There is here reflected, via Aristotle, the Greek subordination of the flesh, which in Aquinas and Maritain provides the ground for admiration of the celibate and the mystic, sometimes at the expense of the dignity of sex and family and even of the bodily functions generally. Maritain tends to associate evil with materiality; he declares that

> personality, which it is metaphysically impossible to lose, suffers many a defeat in the psychological and moral spheres. It risks

---

[12] "On Some Typical Aspects of Christian Education," in *The Christian Idea of Education*, ed. Edmund Fuller, New Haven: Yale University Press, 1957, pp. 173–212.

[13] Jacques Maritain, *The Person and the Common Good*, trans. John J. Fitzgerald, New York: Charles Scribner's Sons, 1947, p. 23. I take it that he is not using the word "individuality" in the same sense in *Degrees of Knowledge*, p. 287, when he names it as an attribute of personality and distinguishes it from "individuation."

[14] *Person and the Common Good*, p. 31. That "knowledge" and "love" do denote much the same as Buber's categories is further illustrated by Maritain's distinction between the "two fundamentally different postures of the mind," i.e., "cause-seeking" (in philosophy), which is theoretical and detached, and "saving my all" (in religion), which is the struggle for salvation of the self. *Existence and the Existent*, p. 130.

contamination from the miseries of material individuality. ... For the same being who is a person, and subsists through the subsistence of his soul, is also an individual in a species, and dust in the wind.[15]

The human person is at the lowest degree of personality.[16] Maritain also identifies the "world" as a sphere of "things existing in themselves ... a *symposium* of individuals and personalities in interaction," [17] thereby relating his doctrine of personality to Thomist Realism. It is because man exists on two planes that we must employ two levels of discourse in order to comprehend him: one is ontological or essentialistic, related to "being"; the other is empiricological or phenomenal, related to "becoming." Insofar as science is making great strides on the latter level, this is good; but insofar as scientism belittles the former, this is to be resisted as a betrayal of human reason. Maritain unashamedly pursues the "science of being" in his quest for an understanding of man.

He contends that only thus can the freedom of the person be established. In words that echo both Buber and Niebuhr, though he arrives at his thought by different routes, Maritain says that

> only the person is free; only the person possesses, in the full sense of these words, inwardness and subjectivity—because it contains itself and moves about within itself. ... The paradox of consciousness and personality is that each of us is situated precisely *at the centre* of this work. Each is at the centre of infinity.[18]

However, again like the existentialists, he qualifies this statement, tilting at Rousseau, in the remark: "Man is not born free save in the basic potencies of his being." There is no disregard of conditioning factors, but an assertion of freedom achieved only as man by knowledge comes to understand the

---

[15] Jacques Maritain, *Scholasticism and Politics*, ed. Mortimer J. Adler, London: Geoffrey Bles, 1940, p. 135.
[16] *Person and the Common Good*, p. 50.
[17] *Degrees of Knowledge*, p. 100.
[18] *Existence and the Existent*, p. 75.

power of these factors and by will comes to know his self through its decisions. As always, Maritain is eminently quotable:

> Man must gain his personality like his liberty, and it is dearly bought. He is not a person in the order of action; he is only *causa sui* if his rational energies and virtues and his love—and the Spirit of God—gather his soul into their hands . . . and into the hands of God. They give a face to the torrent of multiplicity of which he is the streambed, freely seal him with the ontological seal of his radical unity.[19]

What has thus far been said about human freedom is derived from philosophical enquiry into being, but one moves over into Christian theology to obtain the additional datum of original sin. Maritain follows Catholic dogma in assuming that original sin is a state of privation into which the newborn child enters, that is, deprivation of such infused virtues as grace, faith, hope, and love. Thus the soul breathed by God at birth into the body inherits from Adam a wound which can only be healed by the grace of God, pre-eminently available through baptism into the visible Catholic church which is the body of Christ. Even that prime faculty the intellect is wounded— not incapable of right reason but unwilling to follow it through to first principles. Terms like "faith" and "love" are expressive not of intellect but of will, and it is the restoration of these virtues that causes intellect to turn toward the light of "being" and discover the eternal validity of the *philosophia perennis*. Hence it emerges that it is a pointer to one's redemption that one becomes a Thomist![20]

It is therefore understandable that Maritain does not say very much about human evil except insofar as it is a political fact or a fault in our neighbor's philosophy. It may be coun-

---

[19] *Degrees of Knowledge*, p. 286.

[20] At this point the value judgments implied in Maritain's castigation of atheists, existentialists, pragmatists, etc. (see, e.g., *Range of Reason*, pp. 84–98) merit O'Connor's derisive comment that this is a shrewd way to dispose of one's critics (D. J. O'Connor, *An Introduction to Philosophy of Education*, London: Routledge and Kegan Paul, 1958, p. 113, n. 2).

teracted by identification with the life and thought of the Catholic church. A subtle argument showing how God can know of but not be the author of moral evil relies on a definition of evil as negation, privation, or non-being into which man may retreat instead of taking up the tasks of personal freedom and religious faith.[21] As with Buber, radical evil is admitted by the back door of a deliberate willing of the negation, the act of an "absolute atheist."[22]

Again, in a passage in the *Range of Reason,* where he describes how a child enters upon his life as a person in the first moment that he deliberates about himself as a self, Maritain says, quite obscurely, "If the child decides upon the good in his first act of freedom, he is set free from original sin and receives sanctifying grace"; and he goes on to suggest that a religious background will predispose the child to make this right choice "by virtue of divine charity received in baptism together with grace." One is driven to observe that if from common observation one concludes that radical human sin is a datum to be accounted for in one's definition of man, then Maritain's way of doing so is of little help to any but those already persuaded to his view by their allegiance to his church. On this point the apologist has failed his audience.

SANCTITY OF THE INDIVIDUAL

As an unabashed metaphysician, Maritain has no hesitation in grounding the sanctity of the individual in the very constitution of reality, and therefore we must examine his attitude to "natural law," leading on to the moral law and the rights of man. With this yardstick we then follow his criticisms of the humanisms that have brought us to this hour of distress, as contrasted with what he views as the true humanism, from which he derives a vision of "Christian democracy."

It is a continuing theme in the writings of Realist philosophers that because the stuff of reality is material objects, as

[21] *Existence and the Existent,* p. 116.
[22] *Range of Reason,* p. 97.

opposed to ideas or mere flux, there inhere in these objects essential natures which determine the way in which they will behave; that is, there is a natural law. Thomism carries this principle through into human nature.

> Since man is endowed with intelligence and determines his own ends, it is up to him to put himself in tune with the ends necessarily demanded by his nature. This means that there is, by virtue of human nature, *an order or a disposition which human reason can discover and according to which the human will must act in order to attune itself to the necessary ends of the human being. The unwritten law, or natural law, is nothing more than that.*[23]

Maritain takes care to stress that the law and knowledge of the law are two different things, and that the actual discovery of the natural law is progressive and difficult. Scientific investigation (which for Maritain ranges from sense experience to metaphysics) is discovering the inner constitution of matter, but when one crosses the threshold of human nature, there comes into play "knowledge through connaturality." This has to do with knowledge through the intellect modified and informed by "affective inclinations and the dispositions of the will," such as mystical and poetic insight and supremely moral experience.

Knowledge through connaturality thus goes beyond mere intellectual understanding, for it reveals the "ought" not only as an article of moral philosophy but as an imperative of moral conduct. In this sense Thomistic ethics are existential, and Maritain commends the emphasis of modern existentialism on the "creative importance of the moral act" because it is in the act that the person defines and comes to know himself. But for man, in his fallen state, to make the *right* moral choices, it is necessary that religion come to his aid. "No effort of reason to establish among men a firm system of morality based only on natural law has ever been able to suc-

[23] Jacques Maritain, *The Rights of Man and Natural Law*, London: Geoffrey Bles, 1958, p. 35. This work was first published in 1942, prophetic of the debate soon to come, in the newly created United Nations, on an international charter.

ceed."²⁴ The ministry of religion is to facilitate the infusion of divine graces so that the hand of reason will be strengthened, for human conduct at its best *is* rational and, as such, disposes the worshipper to the beatific vision.

As to what is known intellectually about the moral law at this present time, the enlightenment of the conscience has proceeded under the guidance of Aristotle, the Church Fathers, and Aquinas. It is apparent that other influences have also played a part; Maritain speaks approvingly of the American Constitution, an eighteenth-century achievement, mainly Protestant, as "an outstanding lay Christian document." We have now progressed, he believes, to the point where we have become aware not only

> of the rights of man as a human and a civic person, but also of his rights as a social person engaged in the process of production and consumption, especially of his rights as a working person.²⁵

It is appropriate to test this last insight against the false humanisms that in Maritain's estimation have successively weakened the life of Western society since the decay of the Middle Ages.

> In broad outline, the image of man which reigned over medieval Christendom depended upon St. Paul and St. Augustine. This image was to disintegrate from the time of the Renaissance and the Reformation—torn between an utter Christian pessimism which despaired of human nature and an utter Christian optimism which counted on human endeavour more than on divine grace. The image of man which reigned over modern times depended upon Descartes, John Locke, the Enlightenment, and Jean-Jacques Rousseau.²⁶

The Protestant image, based on grace without freedom, was rejected in the bright morning of scientific achievement in favor of the humanist image, based on freedom without grace,

---

²⁴ *Education of Man*, p. 116.
²⁵ Jacques Maritain, *Man and the State*, Chicago. University of Chicago Press, 1951, p. 104.
²⁶ *Range of Reason*, p. 185.

which launched the bourgeoisie on its confident climb to affluence. A new humanism has latterly emerged, born of resentment against the Christian world and the bourgeoisie: the atheistic humanism of Marxism. Marxism remains rationalistic in order to decapitate reason and therefore misjudges and maltreats human nature. The cumulative effect of these humanisms has been the evaporation of human integrity and dignity, and the latest upsurge of error has been a reaction into racism, wherein "man is unmasked, the countenance of the beast appears." Nazism and Fascism only brought to fruition the secularizing tendency operative in Western culture for the last three centuries. We cannot stand still; a new age must emerge from the world conflagrations that have sealed the tomb of the "modern era," and Maritain believes that it will be a new Christendom, inaugurated perhaps not without generations of suffering by Christians.

The humanism Christianity has to offer is one that honors the historic ideal of the democracy of the person, as opposed to the myth of the democracy of the individual.

> Such a humanism, which considers man in the wholeness of his natural and supernatural being, and which sets no *a priori* limit to the descent of the divine into man, we may call the *humanism of the Incarnation*.[27]

This humanism, then, is a personalism dependent upon an acknowledging of God and the Christian gospel. "The world has done with neutrality. Willingly or unwillingly, States will be obliged to make a choice for or against the Gospel."[28] This is not to imply a reversion to the political ascendancy of the church as in the Middle Ages; Maritain observes often that this idea would be utterly anachronistic.[29] Nor does it mean the coerced allegiance of all citizens to the church, but a happy co-operation between church and state, wherein is recognized the institutional church's place as religious leader, exercising its leadership through influence alone, within the

[27] *Scholasticism and Politics*, p. 9.
[28] *Man and the State*, p. 159.
[29] E.g.: *Man and the State*, p. 108; *Range of Reason*, pp. 165, 193; *True Humanism*, trans. M. R. Adamson, London: Geoffrey Bles, 1939, p. 127.

context of a pluralistic society such as we shall discuss in the next section. It will be "the age of a 'secular' Christian civilization," in which the basis of co-operation between believer and nonbeliever will be a democratic charter which lists the practical objectives they have in common. This charter will be built on the rights and liberties of the "person," in the sense which this term has here acquired.

SOCIETY AND THE INDIVIDUAL

Maritain's new-found interest in Thomism began to veer towards social and political philosophy in the troubled 1920s, and he has thought further into the problem of the individual's relation to modern society than any of our ideologists save Niebuhr, so that, as we shall see, his social theory does in fact mesh clearly with his personalist theory and offers practical safeguards. The question that will remain, however, is whether his allegiance to Thomism is likely to unfit his proposals for general acceptance.

In *True Humanism* Maritain names six characteristics of the Christian order he looks for. The first is "pluralism" and the third "personalism," the rest being changes rung on these two.

Frequent references to pluralism throughout his writings demonstrate its centrality in his social theory and help to account both for the hostility he arouses in some Catholic circles [30] and for the respect shown him by many non-Catholic thinkers. Maritain seeks to show that an organic democracy must resist collectivization and the over-exercise of political functions, by constant self-examination and the preservation of the autonomous functions of many spheres of social living. He claims that there is

an element of pluralism inherent in every truly political society. Family, economic, cultural, educational, religious life matter as much as does political life to the very existence and prosperity of the body politic.[31]

[30] Reported by Herberg, *Four Existentialist Theologians*, p. 11.
[31] *Man and the State*, p. 11.

Society at large may be regarded as a series of concentric circles spreading outwards from the family, but it is also a collection of overlapping circles with different centers, all within the largest entity, the body politic.

This pluralistic concept may be tested against two of the entities which have tended historically to gather unto themselves imperial powers over the body politic: church and state. With the details of Maritain's discussion of the role of the state we need not concern ourselves, except to observe that the general purpose of the state is the enforcement of social justice, and the relation in which it stands to the whole political society is that of "a part—the topmost part—of this whole." Below it operate many co-operating subgroups possessing genuine powers consistent with the preservation of good order, and in one place Maritain suggests that universal suffrage would be better exercised through such groups than on the direct, collective level now in use.[32]

The church, he says (thinking of institutional Catholicism), is one of the societies within the body politic, maintaining diplomatic relations with the state, exercising leadership through moral influence alone, and recognizing that Christian citizens are no more legally privileged than any other citizens. Maritain scoffs at the charge that the Catholic church would be oppressive or intolerant if in power by a majority, and he lays down principles concerning the exercise by the church of social and political influence. He expresses distrust of so-called Christian political parties such as are common in Europe, and defines three planes of action for Christians. The spiritual and temporal planes are clearly distinct in his view, but the third is where the Christian acts as such in the community and to this extent commits the church. Maritain favors his acting as an individual rather than as a spokesman for the Catholic church.

A test case for these criteria of state and church relations is the heretic, either political or religious. Maritain not only acknowledges his presence but almost commends his function of shocking the populace into self-defense. He doubts the

[32] *Scholasticism and Politics*, p. 113.

long-term efficacy of censorship or suppression, saying that the main weapon is education. One must not in any event be too hasty because it may be a prophet one is dealing with, and democracy cannot do without prophets and "prophetic shock-minorities." So here again the principle of pluralism is supported, as also the second note of Christian democracy: personalism.

Maritain's definitions are not arbitrary but go right back to his personalist metaphysics. The ultimate social unit is the person. "Society cannot live without the perpetual gifts which come from persons." Of course the person is intended to live in society, and indeed it is in the society of other persons and of God that a personality is established; the person is to submit himself to the common good. But it *is* a "common good" he submits to, not a "public good" as in a beehive. The common good is "a good received and communicated."

> It includes within itself as principal value, the highest access, compatible with the good of the whole, of the persons to their life of person and liberty of expansion.[33]

The common good has two poles. The good of the society as a whole is a good in itself, and the good of each person within it is a good in itself. Therefore the common good is an ethical good, and cannot be achieved by immoral procedures perpetrated in the name of political necessity. Maritain lays great stress on the bankruptcy of Machiavellianism for this reason, insisting that its result is destruction of the common good. He does not, however, promote an immaculate and other-worldly view of politics but says rather that it must be

> situated in the order of nature and must put into practice natural virtues; . . . must be armed with real and concrete justice, with force, with perspicacity and prudence; a politics which would hold the sword that is the attribute of the state, but which would also realize that peace is the work not only of justice but of love. . . .[34]

[33] *Person and the Common Good*, p. 41.
[34] *Range of Reason*, p. 153.

In order to obtain that cohesion between persons and groups which the common good calls for, Maritain has an increasing amount to say about education in his later years, especially in connection with the democratic charter.

It is essential, he claims, that a pluralistic society bring to explicit formulation the practical tenets on which it is agreed. While conceding that "No common assent can be required by society regarding the *theoretical justifications*," Maritain provides an impressive catalogue of matters of common concern on which, in the present state of development of Western societies, practical consensus might be expected.[35] He does not, however, suggest that the theoretical justifications do not matter; indeed, since the democratic charter is the basis of moral education in schools, and moral education depends particularly on the teacher's personal commitment, he sees special problems for education, which we shall take up later when discussing his educational theory. Suffice it here to say that the formula Maritain proposes is by no means locked up within Thomist assumptions, but is accessible to all social theorists.

It is also evident from the foregoing that though Maritain's political philosophy is consistent with his general Thomist position, it is so serviced by what the Thomist would call the "natural virtues" that it offers strong competition at a pragmatic level to other "democratic" theories. Nevertheless, practical consensus may not be easy to achieve, for the human values on which, say, John Dewey would lay stress are not of the same order as those which Maritain commends, as witnessed by the latter's stringent criticisms of Pragmatism. This is immediately apparent in his succinct statement on the hierarchy of values:

> Now in the true hierarchy of values . . . knowledge and love of what is above time are superior to, and embrace and quicken, knowledge and love of what is within time. Charity, which loves God and embraces all men in this very love, is the supreme virtue. In the intellectual realm, wisdom, which knows things

[35] See *Man and the State*, pp. 112–113, and *Rights of Man*, pp. 41–62.

eternal and creates order and unity in the mind, is superior to science or to knowledge through particular causes; and the speculative intellect, which knows for the sake of knowing, comes before the practical intellect, which knows for the sake of action.[36]

Such a statement is nearly tantamount to a declaration of war on Pragmatism; it would trouble a joint curriculum-planning committee as seriously as the probable disagreement on the nature of democracy would affect statements of aims and policies.

In summary, Maritain has articulated a comprehensive theory of the state in which clear directives are provided that help to preserve the sanctity of the individual — or, as he would prefer us to say, the person. He also shows that he is not unmindful of the complexities of modern great society. It may be concluded that in defining the individual and the ground of his sanctity, Maritain is not likely to win general support, but in placing the individual in his social context he makes available a solution that deserves study because of its blend of realism and personalism, conviction and tolerance.

[36] "Thomistic Views on Education," p. 65.

REINHOLD NIEBUHR

1892-1971

Historic Protestantism wears coats of many colors, but always there is a cut of the cloth that distinguishes it from other ideologies and religions. Reinhold Niebuhr has evolved a system of thought that grew out of involvement in the social history of his time and place and is distinctively his own; yet it is quite clearly continuous with the Protestant heritage. Though he has offered few comments on education as such, he is relevant to our purpose on three counts. First, he has made trenchant criticisms of the other ideologies that are influencing educational theory. Second, Protestantism is a major, though often not clearly articulate, contributor to education. Third, Niebuhr's insights are rich in implication for educational theorizing, as writers like M. V. C. Jeffreys have begun to discover.

Niebuhr [1] was born in Missouri into the family of a clergyman of a small Lutheran denomination, and received his undergraduate education in a college and theological seminary of that denomination. He went on to the Divinity School of Yale University and acquired his M.A., but then discontinued formal study, because of family needs and "boredom

[1] Biographical detail comes mainly from Nathan A. Scott, *Reinhold Niebuhr* (Minneapolis: University of Minnesota Press, 1963) and Charles W. Kegley and Robert W. Bretall, eds., *Reinhold Niebuhr: His Religious, Social and Political Thought* (Library of Living Theology, vol. 2, New York: The Macmillan Co., 1961). The latter volume includes an autobiographical note.

with epistemology," to enter a parish in the industrial world of Detroit. This ministry, among Ford employees sweated by efficiency experts in appalling work conditions, intensified his already lively social concern and challenged the liberal optimism of his theological training. His first book, *Does Civilization Need Religion?* (1927), showed his emerging dissatisfaction with theological liberalism. Opportunity for more profound appraisal came with his appointment in 1928 to the renowned Union Theological Seminary, in New York City, as assistant professor in the philosophy of religion. His social involvement was not curtailed by the move; he continued active in pacifist and socialist groups during the thirties, sitting at one time with John Dewey on the executive committee of the League for Independent Political Action. Two things now combined to turn him completely from moral optimism: the depression of the 1930s and his study of Saint Augustine. He was won over to a statement of the human predicament in terms of sin and its cure, and to the task of composing a social theory adequate to cope with the implications of pervasive egocentricity. His theology revived the insights of the Protestant Reformers of the sixteenth century; his social theory progressed in subsequent years from a Marxist view of history through "Christian Socialism" to a pragmatic power theory accepting the shortcomings of a mixed economy.[2]

He became professor of Applied Christianity at Union in 1930, and was married in 1931. The following year saw publication of his first major work, *Moral Man and Immoral Society*, which, in Herberg's words, combined

> a sombre Augustinian emphasis on the involutions of sinful self love in the individual and corporate structures of life with a social radicalism bordering on Marxism.[3]

The tension sensed in this work between the individual and society was sharpened in *Reflections on the End of an Era* (1934), expressing his conviction that the sorry period of

---

[2] John C. Bennett traces the mutations from the twenties to the fifties in his "Reinhold Niebuhr's Social Ethics," in Kegley, *Niebuhr*, pp. 45–78.

[3] Will Herberg, "Reinhold Niebuhr," *Encyclopaedia Britannica*, 1963.

bourgeois individualism was inexorably closing and that new structures needed to be thought out for social life. From the flood of articles and books that followed, we single out three more titles bearing directly on our theme.

An Interpretation of Christian Ethics (1935) was an attempt to relate behavior to the Christian norm of "sacrificial love," a transcendent criterion by which the temporal must be governed. Niebuhr has since repudiated this work, but insofar as it is consistent with his later thought, we have made use of it. The invitation to deliver the Gifford Lectures in Edinburgh in 1939 gave him the opportunity to draw together his views on man and history in his acknowledged masterpiece, *The Nature and Destiny of Man* (1941, 1943). That this two-volume work survives comparison with the greatest works of human thought is due in part to "the author's seeming to carry in his head the whole of Western intellectual tradition and to have a constantly simultaneous vision of all its myriad strands."[4] A succession of slighter works took up themes relevant to the changing times; the approach of age (he would retire in 1960) found Niebuhr's mind still alert and contemporary. In 1955, despite having suffered severe illness, he penned another substantial work, *The Self and the Dramas of History*, which he prefaced with a warm tribute to Martin Buber. In it he accepts the dialogic view of interhuman relations but requires that it be modified by the social deposit of history.

It is illuminating to note the springs from which Niebuhr has drawn in developing his thought. Scott observes that he broke with liberal theology because

> the secular tradition of Locke and Jefferson and Stuart Mill and John Dewey appeared to him to be very largely the ideological expression of bourgeois mentality.... Nor could he find Protestant liberalism to be any less brankrupt; in fact ... he had come to regard it as involving little more than a reinterpretation of the Christian faith in accordance with the system of secular values descending from the Enlightenment.[5]

[4] Scott, *Niebuhr*, p. 81.
[5] *Ibid.*, p. 14.

In search of new resources, Niebuhr discovered in his Lutheran heritage an uncompromising and astringent answer: the Pauline view, amplified by Augustine and the Protestant Reformers, of man as a fallen creature.[6] His liberal training prevents him from accepting the literal-historical view of the Bible with which the Reformers developed their thesis, but he is receptive to the "dialectical theology" of Karl Barth — itself a reaction to liberalism — in which Reformation concepts are defended with existentialist weapons. Emil Brunner, disciple of Barth, declares that Niebuhr has profited most from dialectical theology,[7] and his opinion carries weight; Niebuhr admits to learning most about theology from Brunner. Also, since dialectical theology is heavily indebted to Kierkegaard, Kroner is entitled to claim that Niebuhr was primarily informed by Kierkegaard about "the mystery of human selfhood." It is not only in this respect, but in respect of method, that Niebuhr owes much to Kierkegaard, for he replaces the propositional logic of systematic theology with the dialectic of existential psychology. To this extent he is not at one with the Reformers, and his theology is not Reformation theology.[8] Rather is he to be compared with Buber, whose final court of appeal is the responding reader who says: "For myself, this analysis rings true." Niebuhr advances beyond his mentors in his brilliant utilization of the dialectical approach for purposes of social and political analysis, and it is this especially that accounts for the wide public interest in his views, warranting Brunner's tribute that "with him theology broke into the world."[9]

DEFINING "INDIVIDUAL"

Convinced that Western civilization is at a low ebb, and that radically fresh insights are the only alternatives to collapse,

[6] The extent of his debt is brought out by Richard Kroner in "The Historical Roots of Niebuhr's Thought," in Kegley, *Niebuhr*, pp. 177–192.
[7] Emil Brunner, "Some Remarks on Reinhold Niebuhr's Work as a Christian Thinker," in Kegley, *Niebuhr*, p. 29.
[8] Edward John Carnell makes this point convincingly in *The Theology of Reinhold Niebuhr*, Grand Rapids, Mich.: Wm. B. Eerdmans, 1960.
[9] Brunner, "Niebuhr's Work as a Christian Thinker," p. 29.

Niebuhr locates the weakness in defective views of human nature—views leading to emphasis on the wrong aspects of technological development and to either optimistic or inhuman political solutions. His strategy is to point up the errors in classical and modern anthropologies, countering them with a reassertion of the Christian view of man in Protestant and contemporary language.

At the outset of *The Nature and Destiny of Man,* he asserts the primary dialectical fact that man is both a child of nature and a spirit who stands outside nature. This is not only his starting point but his destination, in that he does not adopt a take-it-or-leave-it attitude but seeks to demonstrate what superior explanatory power his dialectical analysis possesses. The axiom governs his three main observations about man: that he is a unity, that he is made in the image of God, that he is a sinner. We shall investigate each of these points, concluding with a note on the "new man" who might be expected, in Niebuhr's view, to result from the reorientation which the Christian religion claims to be able to give to human personality.

It is essential, says Niebuhr, to recognize that human individuality is derived from the bonding of body and soul, not from the one or the other. "There is no place for individuality in either pure mind or pure nature." Idealism, especially as inherited from the Greeks, places all the emphasis on "mind," but then relates this to the universal and the divine, causing individuality to be eclipsed.[10] Naturalism seeks to reduce

---

[10] Reinhold Niebuhr, *The Nature and Destiny of Man: A Christian Interpretation,* vol. 1: *Human Nature,* London: Nisbet and Co., 1941, p. 3. (The two volumes of *The Nature and Destiny of Man* will be referred to hereafter as *Human Nature* and *Human Destiny.*)

Niebuhr's terminology is difficult, in that shades of meaning represented by "soul," "mind," "self," and "spirit"—as he uses them to express concepts he finds variously expressed in the Scriptures—are subtle and in some cases deliberately overlapping. I explore the main point, the individual's powers of transcendence, in the first chapter of Part Six; but I will venture here to attempt some clarification of Niebuhr's usage. He seems to mean by "soul" that degree of conscious co-ordination of bodily activities which is apparent in the higher animals, and by "spirit" the transtemporal sharing of human individuals in the personal existence of God. When these are brought together in the one entity, the result is a "self." "The self is 'soul' in so far as it has an experience of the bodily organic unity" (*The Self and the Dramas of*

spiritual phenomena to streams of consciousness or behavioral outcomes of the organism, thereby also absorbing the individual "self." For example, in the biological analogies with which Freud builds his psychological theory, the "id" which plays so vital a role turns out to be "armed with the guile of spirit." Unlike animals, man has not only a central nervous system but a spiritual organizing center which enables him to see himself as an object. Therefore "genuine individuality, embodying both discreteness and uniqueness, is a characteristic of human life." Whereas discreteness is established by the mere fact of being born, the uniqueness of the human individual is a datum to be nourished by the growth of body and spirit together. This is evident in the development of a child, who is initially "held within the 'primeval we' consciousness of the family," and also in the development of the race:

> Primitive man is inserted with comparative frictionless harmony into the "primeval we" of group life. He emerges from this group consciousness only gradually as an individual. But what emerges is an original endowment, present from the beginning.[11]

The individual therefore comes to know that he is an individual by virtue of the invasion of his body-soul by spirit. He can think of his body as an object even while being himself "an inner experience of the bodily organic unity." How can such things be? The answer lies with Niebuhr's second observation about man: his creation in the image of God.

As against the Hellenistic tendency to regard this as a pleasing metaphor for the fact that man is a rational animal, Niebuhr sets the Christian view that "God as will and personality" creates finite creatures with these marks of the infinite upon them, enabling them to transcend their space-time location.

History, London: Faber and Faber, 1956, p. 38). Hence the Greek doctrine of immortality, based on a view of "mind" (*nous*) as immaterial universal reason, is no part of Hebrew or Christian thought (*Human Nature,* p. 13). "Mind" is one, and only one, of the attributes of the unified self, and is not the ground of that self's immortality.

[11] *Self and the Dramas of History*, p. 38.

The self knows the world, insofar as it knows the world, because it stands outside both itself and the world, which means that it cannot understand itself except as it is understood from beyond itself and the world. This essential homelessness of the human spirit is the ground of all religion.[12]

Godlike attributes of this self include reason, not in the merely abstract Greek sense, but as a vital power, including the force of memory whereby the self lifts itself above the time-flow and maintains its identity amidst the flux. The self also conducts dialogues with itself, not always or only at the rational level,[13] and is capable of a dialogue with others that goes beyond the "category of social life as usually defined." [14] Actually, it is not so much in conscious self-realization as in being drawn out of itself into the life of others that the self finds fulfillment.[15]

Will and conscience are also elements in the transcendence of the self over itself, involving not only reason but "intuitions of the self about the essential nature of its selfhood." However, here again the dialectic applies. Conscience is not purely individual, for it is strongly influenced by socializing factors; yet it is not purely social either, as shown by the frequency with which conscience defies the community. This defiance is usually related to some higher loyalty or community of purpose, occasionally known only to the dissenter himself.

Such observations draw us into the vexed debate on free will, and Niebuhr discusses this in an existentialist frame. Characteristically, he criticizes the frame of reference which has become accepted in our "empirical culture," leading to the restriction of the term "fact" to the sense data examined by "traditional scientific empiricism." He objects that the self's freedom is a reality recognized by common-sense jurisprudence and the arts, and criticizes much psychology for prejudging the issue by accepting only data of a behavioral type.

[12] *Human Nature*, p. 14. The debt to Kierkegaard is unmistakable.
[13] Hence both Aristotle and Freud are partly right and partly wrong.
[14] *Human Nature*, p. 42.
[15] *Ibid.*, p. 44. This time the palm goes to Buber.

Our responsible freedom can be established introspectively because we know that, though there are always previous causes which can explain our actions, we ourselves stand above the flow of causes and are ourselves the causes of our actions.[16]

Unlike Buber and Maritain, Niebuhr does not stress the need to expand this freedom by growth and exercise because he wants to say that this happens anyway, whether for good or evil ends, and that it is in the misuse of this freedom, to rebel against our creaturely dependence on God, that we become sinners. That is, his concern is less with the listless and vegetative mass man of our time than with the egoistic abusers of freedom who, at all social levels, are stifling the liberty of their fellows. It is ironic that when scientists and philosophers play down human freedom they not only contribute to the dehumanization of the masses but also spur the demonization of the power élites; they are, paradoxically, tools of bourgeois individualism.

This is because (to return to the axiom) man is a sinner. This is not a palatable doctrine to modern man, who since the Renaissance has been busy justifying in every possible way a conception of man as "fundamentally good, as sufficient, as the measure of things." Evil is therefore located in factors external to man: in the eighteenth century it is traced to religion and political tyranny; in the nineteenth Marx blames class organization; in the twentieth Dewey and Whitehead, despite their variant definitions of reason, ultimately agree that the villain is cultural lag. All such explanations founder on the fact that sin is ultimately not in the situation but in the human actor and his will-to-power.

Alternatively, some have sought to locate evil in one part of the human personality, so that the solution is to build up the remaining parts and starve the one. Nietzsche isolates the will-to-power, justifying it when he should be in some circumstances reproving it, but erring further in that he treats it as purely biological, whereas in fact it partakes of both body

---

[16] *The Godly and the Ungodly: Essays on the Religious and Secular Dimensions of Modern Life*, London: Faber and Faber, 1958, p. 127.

and spirit because man is a unity. "The beast of prey ceases from its conquests when its maw is crammed; but man's lusts are fed by his imagination." Or again, the Greeks and some modern rationalists despise the body and commend the mind, an attitude not entirely absent from Catholic thought. What confounds all such diagnoses is the unity of the self, which in Reformation terms is totally implicated in its sin.[17]

In essence, what is sin? Niebuhr's answer depends greatly on Kierkegaard, inviting Carnell's warning that he is allowing the psychological to outweigh the theological elements in explanation of its origin and nature.[18] This results in old terms being used in a new way, including to some extent the word "sin" itself. We learn that the experience of man reveals a tension or anxiety, he is a creature bounded by natural and historical limits, yet with the spiritual attribute of transcendence which enables him to see himself as finite. His proper reaction should then be trusting submission to his creator, but invariably he lets anxiety lead him into efforts at securing and magnifying his status, and egoistic pride ensues. Thus "the Christian estimate of human evil is so serious precisely because it places evil at the very center of human personality — in the will." [19] And, *contra* Dewey and modern liberalisms, "the root of temptation is not ignorance but anxiety."

Dialectically, Niebuhr suggests that man invariably falls into sin, but not as a necessary consequence of finiteness, and that he is therefore rightly held responsible by God and rightly experiences guilt. This is a hard saying, and Niebuhr has been taken to task for it by logicians, a fate he anticipated. But he continues to insist that, paradox or no, he is reasserting the ancient Christian insight of "original sin" because it has proved "its ability to throw light upon complex factors in

---

[17] Calvin's technical term is "total depravity." Sometimes Niebuhr seems to interpret this as psychological description as well, causing Calvin to be tarred with the same brush as Karl Barth. But Calvin is not using it existentially; his concern is with theological precision.

[18] Carnell, *Theology of Niebuhr*, p. 69: "Orthodoxy determines its view of the nature of man from propositional revelation; Niebuhr determines his from the existential witness of the heart."

[19] *Human Nature*, p. 17.

human behaviour." He also criticizes the Catholic version of this insight, which, as we have been reminded by Maritain, suggests that by sinning Adam was deprived of supernatural graces and reverted to a natural man with intact natural faculties. Niebuhr insists that we may not assume that any part of human personality has escaped the biasing effect of sin, or that human reason in particular is immune from its corrupting influence. For just as spirit pervades all parts of the body-soul, giving rise to a unified self, so it is the whole self that is affected by sin. For this reason also, the ethical Thomist categories of "natural law" and *justitia originalis* (the original state of virtue, fragments of which still linger in man) set up an untenable dualism in evaluations of human conduct.[20]

What then of the Christian view that man may be transformed by a right relationship with God? As a debtor to the Reformation, Niebuhr might be expected to acknowledge a reversal of the sinful tendencies in man by the restoration of communion with God—that is, by conversion. Certainly he does speak of the need for the self to be shattered by confrontation with a holy God, emerging from this experience with a new humility and trust. He says that "the Christian experience of the new life is an experience of a new selfhood" and that in this state one is conscious of being personally empowered by the Christ of prophetic religion, not in such a way as to lose one's selfhood, but rather to enlarge it. To illustrate this he quotes the Apostle Paul's dialectical remark: "I live, yet not I, but Christ liveth in me."[21] It is not altogether clear, however, by what means an individual man is to enter this state, though it cannot be doubted that Niebuhr is true to the Reformers in believing that the transaction is between a man and his God, without other human or institutional mediation.

[20] He illustrates this point by referring to the Catholic handling of the issue of birth control, where the sexual function in human life is treated as purely biological, i.e., for procreation, and as arbitrated by natural law, thereby denying that the unity of self alters the nature of the act (*Human Nature*, p. 298). Nor is the supernatural virtue of "love" extinguished in the natural man, as the Catholic claims, but lingers "as a vision of health which even a sick man may envisage" (p. 304).
[21] Galatians 2:20, quoted in *Human Destiny*, p. 111.

Reinhold Niebuhr

Let us grant that when a man becomes a Christian he begins to lay hold of spiritual dynamic beyond his original self. The question must then be asked: to what extent does this enable him to overcome the bias of sin? Niebuhr's answer is categorical, and it incorporates rebukes to Catholic pretensions, Renaissance optimism, and liberal utopians. We live in a compromised world; perfection is not achievable in this life.

> The Reformation took the fact of sin as a perennial category of historical existence more seriously, and maintained that there is no point in history where history is fulfilled and where man's self-contradiction is ended.[22]

One may perhaps represent Niebuhr's view of what happens at conversion as a reversal of the plane of an individual's life-direction. Previously on a downgrade into greater compromise and sin-domination, he now finds himself on the upgrade by the help of the God to whom he has committed himself. But there is much lost ground to be retrieved in his personal life, and it has to be lived out in a sinful community and world. This verdict of Niebuhr's has far-reaching implications for his social and political theory, as we shall see.

In sum, man is an organic body-soul unity invaded by spirit, which gives rise to a self-consciousness capable of transcending its own finite bounds. It partakes of eternity to the extent of knowing it is finite, and this knowledge creates an existential anxiety from which it seeks to escape by efforts to secure the self's independence.[23] Man is thus led into sinning against God, a posture which involves his whole being. In Niebuhr's words:

> The Christian view of human nature is involved in the paradox of claiming a higher stature for man and of taking a more serious view of his evil than other anthropology.[24]

[22] *Human Nature*, p. 317.
[23] I suggest that incipient in this existentialist explanation is the suggestion that scientific and technical advances are somewhat presumptuous, being products of self-assertion and the search for substitute kinds of security. Is it an accident that Buber's dialectic also tends to deprecate the attainments of the *I–It* posture?
[24] *Human Nature*, p. 18.

Man recognizes responsibility for his sin and experiences guilt, which it is the ministry of religion to transmute into forgiven-ness and trust. However, to become a Christian is not to overcome the inroads of sin forthwith, though reformative energies are now at work.

SANCTITY OF THE INDIVIDUAL

Niebuhr's concern for the sanctity of the individual is paramount, and his strategy is symbolized by the title of the chair he held from 1930 to 1960: Applied Christianity. He works in two ways: by a pulling down of inadequate social concepts, and by a building up of new ones based on the "prophetic religion" of Christianity. We shall consider first his criticisms of modern technology and social theory, then his reconstruction of moral and social theory in the light of prophetic religion.

Niebuhr suggests that if we take equality of justice as the touchstone of minimal respect for the sanctity of the individual, then the coming of technological society has not eased but accentuated the problem. Scientists and industrialists are replacing the soldiers and the priests as controllers of social life, and (echoing Marx) their sense of responsibility to that life is far less while their power has multiplied.[25] Fortunately, socialist and religious agitation has forced some scruples upon them, but the effectiveness of such agitation will not fully appear until it is buttressed by more realistic assumptions about the nature of man and society. Technology is with us to stay, and it has conferred many material boons; but it has also magnified the perennial problems of human relations, in which sin is an ever-present reality.

That social theories and sciences have not met the need of the hour is due to errant and optimistic views of man. Niebuhr persistently criticizes John Dewey as a representative of secular liberalism and the trust it reposes in the social

[25] *Moral Man and Immoral Society*, p. 7. See also Reinhold Niebuhr, *Reflections on the End of an Era*, New York: Scribner's, 1934, pp. 101f. and chap. 9.

sciences. Dewey, he says, has underestimated the powers operative in political life, believing that education can answer the need by helping students to achieve "a significant critical detachment from a contemporary culture and its official propagation in the public schools." Such a view is "incredibly naive" and could "only have arisen in a period of comparative social stability and security." What Dewey does not take into account is the disobedient will in man and the social checks that this necessitates.

> In his thought the hope of achieving a vantage point which transcends the corruptions of self-interest takes the form of trusting the "scientific method" and attributing anti-social conduct to the "cultural lag," that is, to the failure of social science to keep abreast with technology.[26]

Dewey's hopes for social science are shared by many thinkers. Under the heading of "scientism" Harland discusses the nature of Niebuhr's polemic against them, pointing out that it is not the method or achievements of science that he deplores but the "assumption that the methods of the natural sciences are the avenue to the understanding of all human problems."[27] This usually results in an untenable determinism, a neglect of the historical character of man, and a naive dream that "sociocracy" will supersede all other forms of government. It is needful for social scientists to realize both that complete rational objectivity in a social situation is impossible and that the cause of conflict is basically not ignorance but self-interest. If they do not, then they will be the unwitting militia of the power élites. Had Reformation theology gained the victory over Renaissance humanism, the social sciences might well have been more insightful about man and society in the present day.

There is another element in modern social theory which

[26] *Human Nature*, p. 117. See also M. L. Story, "Dewey and Niebuhr: A Brief Juxtaposition," *Educational Theory*, vol. 3, Apr. 1953, pp. 182–184. The article is short and simplistic, but seminal.

[27] Gordon Harland, *The Thought of Reinhold Niebuhr*, New York: Oxford University Press, 1960, p. 70.

Niebuhr finds pernicious, and this is the tendency to think in terms of realizable utopias. Perhaps some of his ire is due to the lingering utopianism of his own social thought. Schlesinger detects a commitment to doctrinaire socialism which prevented him, even late in the thirties, from recognizing how a political policy of realistic check and experiment was in fact adjusting the American economy in a manner consistent with his scruples.[28] His resignation from the Socialist party in 1940 was an action belatedly in accord with the objections he had lodged against all doctrinaire political solutions, which look forward to utopias or perfected societies in this world order. Such are Marxism, secular liberalism, and liberal Christianity. As usual, their error is said to be that they overlook the historical inevitability of human sin, especially when magnified by collective association.

Reconstruction of moral theory, says Niebuhr, must begin with the revision of current concepts of man, along the lines of the paradoxes of prophetic religion. It must proceed at two levels, individual and social. At the individual level, the point must be made that

> the individual never comes to full self-consciousness, and therefore to a consciousness of what is nature and what is spirit in him, until he strains after the absolute and the unconditioned.[29]

This fulfillment comes about from religious experience. At the social level, there must be constructive thought about politics, economics, and the social sciences, in the light of our knowledge of man as a unified creature, made in the image of God, but prone to sin. The attempts of twentieth-century liberal Christianity to develop a social gospel have been made in quite other, and inadequate, light. Niebuhr's own social thought will be further traced in the pages following under the heading "Society and the Individual."

Moral theory must also be reshaped along more realistic lines. We must debit to the accounts of the Renaissance and

[28] Arthur Schlesinger, "Reinhold Niebuhr's Role in American Political Thought and Life," in Kegley, *Niebuhr*, pp. 125–150.
[29] *Reflections on the End of an Era*, p. 114.

the Enlightenment that "easy conscience of modern man" which has blinded him to the injustices in modern societies and prompted him to expound optimistic and perfectionist ethics. Niebuhr insists that morality must take equal account of inclination and obligation, that it must have set before it the "impossible possibility" of the love commandment of Jesus, recognizing that it necessarily prohibits anyone from claiming full truth and authority. He also refutes the extension of the love principle to all areas of life, since love,

> whether it expresses itself in transient sentiment or constant goodwill, is baffled by the more intricate social relations in which the highest ethical attitudes are achieved only by careful calculation.[30]

That is, the bigger the collectivity, the weaker becomes love as a binding principle, and the more power relationships come into play which must be so balanced against each other as to produce approximate justice for all. This is the main thesis of *Moral Man and Immoral Society*, which takes the view that, while individual men are not morally perfect, they are "moral" relative to the behavior of collectivities, where the restraints on egoism are lowered by the impersonal nature of the interaction within them, proportionate to their size. It is a delusion to attempt to amalgamate the moral and political realms. As Niebuhr replied to a pacifist, it is an error to suppose that one can live in history without sinning, that is, without being forced into compromise.

SOCIETY AND THE INDIVIDUAL

Niebuhr is determined to describe society in such a way as to keep the door open for continuous adjustments of the status quo in favor of greater individual liberty. No rosy vision of millennium achieved in this historical order guides him, but rather the dialectical tension between what he understands by the transcendental Biblical symbol of the "judgment" at

[30] *Moral Man and Immoral Society*, p. 74.

the "end of the world" and the ever-present reality of an imperfect and changing society. This becomes clearer from his analysis of Western capitalism and Marxism, and the terms in which he refers to democracy.

In the industrial hell of Detroit in the twenties, Niebuhr was drawn to the Marxist analysis of society, which in 1932 he said was

> a true enough interpretation of what the industrial worker feels about society and history, to have become the accepted social and political philosophy of all self-conscious and politically intelligent industrial workers.[31]

He went on to say that the greatest ethical contribution of Marxism is its demonstration that inevitably special privilege and opportunity are associated with power, and that the ownership of the means of production is the significant power in modern society. He accepted the view that the commercial classes, or bourgeoisie, have carried us into a mechanical civilization lacking any concern for the individual. Paradoxically, this was because the creed of individualism articulated in the Renaissance both liberated the commercial classes and led to the suppression of the remainder in the name of liberalism. In 1934 he was convinced that civilization had come to the end of this road, and that society must either capitulate to Marxism or develop a democratic socialism.

However, as Schlesinger demonstrates, Niebuhr was not then altogether free of the doctrinaire and utopian elements in Marxism, and his "commitment to socialization was both the price of indifference to the achievements of piecemeal reform and a symptom of despair."[32] Subsequently he relinquished his membership in the Socialist party and in 1947 became a leading figure in the ADA (Americans for Democratic Action), described by Schlesinger as a group of "pragmatic liberals opposed to all dogmatisms, conservative, socialist, or communist, and dedicated to piecemeal and gradual reform."

[31] *Ibid.*, p. 144.
[32] Schlesinger, "Niebuhr's Role in American Thought and Life," p. 141.

Never content with the anthropology of Marxism, Niebuhr became progressively more critical of other elements in it. Its historicism is overplayed; it errs in identifying personal power purely with property ownership and therefore cannot see the beam in its own eye, which is the power possessed by those who control the processes of production in and for the Marxist State; and it seeks "consciously to reduce the family unit to even less significance than bourgeois culture has unconsciously done." The utopian element in Marxism is productive of great evil because it uses a spurious historical possibility—the classless society—to justify crimes against humanity in the present. Considering his early recognition of the power of the Communist bureaucrats, spoken of by Djilas as the "new class," his own journey to pragmatic liberalism was perhaps rather protracted.

Regarding his view of democracy, we are now in a position to appreciate how profoundly apt as a summary of Niebuhr's thought is his famous aphorism: "Man's capacity for justice makes democracy possible; but his inclination to injustice makes democracy necessary." As Bennett rightly observes, this "reveals the essential balance of his thought, which is as far from cynicism as it is from utopianism." [33] Insofar as democracy has been in some measure realized, it has its roots in Calvin and the "Christian radicals on the left wing of Cromwell's army"; it was secularized (i.e., shorn of its transcendental reference) by the French Enlightenment, and it has been implemented by the commercial classes because it is an ideology suited to their purposes. After an all too brief and sickly life, it is about to be overwhelmed by technological collectivity, unless the transcendental reference is restored as keystone. Of this latter we have already spoken, but some implications follow: the need to preserve ways of expressing resistance to the government; the need constantly to scrutinize shifts in power relations in order to readjust the checks and balances that constitute justice, recognizing that there will never be an end to such negotiations because "the dream of

---

[33] Bennett, "Reinhold Niebuhr's Social Ethics," in Kegley, *Niebuhr*, p. 50.

perpetual peace and brotherhood for human society is one which will never be fully realised"; and the need to affirm the fallibility of all human institutions, including the church, and to subject them continually to constructive criticism. As against all humanist confidence in the advance of the human race, Niebuhr holds this somber thought (now deemed more valid than in earlier decades of this century):

> Human history is indeed filled with *endless possibilities;* and the Renaissance saw this more clearly than either classicism, Catholicism or the Reformation. But it did not recognize that history is filled with endless possibilities of *good and evil.*[34]

Niebuhr's conception of democracy is mostly free of doctrinaire elements, making him in some ways more pragmatic even than Dewey and considerably less rationalistic. This is both the strength and the weakness of his view, in that while proposing a more realistic approach to the sanctity of the individual than most of our thinkers, it provokes the critics to ask for more guidance on the "middle principles" that bond the transcendental and permanently valid religious symbols upheld by Niebuhr to the practical expediencies of personal and social living.[35] A related difficulty is that the way Niebuhr addresses himself to Biblical data and speaks of the church's errors, coupled with the pragmatic criteria he commends in community life, suggests a relativism — indeed, a skepticism — that he is far from wishing to espouse. The problem is only accentuated by his observations on Mannheim's *Ideology and Utopia.* He commends Mannheim for his recognition of the "all-pervasive character of ideology," but rebukes him for supposing it possible

> to eliminate ideology by developing a high degree of consciousness of the conditioned character of human knowledge. Such a consciousness may indeed purge knowledge of many overt idealogies [*sic*], but it cannot produce an unconditioned mind.[36]

[34] *Human Destiny*, p. 160.
[35] E.g.: Scott, *Niebuhr*, p. 24; and Paul Ramsey, "Love and Law," in Kegley, *Niebuhr*, p. 109.
[36] *Human Destiny*, p. 246n.

Yet the religious symbols and "myths" he invokes to provide a transcendental stratum of absolutes are basically his own selection of those elements in the Bible that buttress his own ideology.[37] He therefore deprives himself of the ground of certainty which the Reformers, whose doctrines govern his thought, upheld. As other theologians are finding, existentialist dialectic is a two-edged sword.

If, for these reasons, disciples of Niebuhr's political "realism" sit loose to the personalist ethic he calls upon to supply a light for navigating in the cross winds of politics, it may not always happen that their actions are free of the taint of Machiavellianism. Living in a country where not even a moderate socialism has had genuine opportunity to try its wings, Niebuhr may be swinging unnecessarily far in his horror of utopianism. But this is a debate that moves outside our scope, and is mentioned only in order to suggest that Niebuhr's own practice must be looked at closely in order to see whether it fulfills the promise of his major axioms in safeguarding the individual as far as can be.

In conclusion, the society of which Niebuhr speaks is not the scientific brotherhood of Dewey, or the cultural organism of Whitehead, or the planned collective of Mannheim, but the practical situation of human beings in the present mechanized society. No structures are recommended as final, but the principle whereby existing structures are to be judged and modified is justice for the individual, having regard to the need for political realism in balancing collective demands and power groups against one another, and keeping open the avenues of resistance and criticism. However pleasing to the rational intellect a theory which resolved the tension between the individual and society would be, it would falsify the actual human situation; for the theorist, however saintly, would be a sin-affected man conditioned by the peculiarities of his own situation. For these reasons the democratic ideal is the most

---

[37] Ironically, my view is supported by a self-declared religious naturalist, who recognizes the procedure because he himself frankly follows it, regarding the Biblical revelation as subordinate to reason. See Henry Nelson Wieman, "A Religious Naturalist Looks at Reinhold Niebuhr," in Kegley, *Niebuhr*, p. 339.

expedient to work for, not because one is likely to attain final equilibrium but because it derives ultimately from the transcendental criterion of love or dialogue and provides a norm for the dynamic adjustments that need constantly to be made. Ultimately, therefore, Niebuhr arrives at a position very close to Dewey's in relation to political commitment, but it is informed by a very different view of the individual it is meant to serve.

COUNTERPOINT
BUBER : MARITAIN : NIEBUHR

THE STUDY OF MAN

The prestige of science has fostered a contemporary view that human understanding progresses most surely when harnessed to the scientific method, and this view has been applied, particularly since Comte and Freud, to the study of man. Though acknowledging the practical benefits that this realm of discourse has bestowed upon us, Buber, Maritain, and Niebuhr all hold out strongly for the need to employ other vocabularies as well, and each proposes and employs terms which are intended to prove their value by the explanatory power they exhibit.

Buber adopts a language he claims is appropriate to "philosophical anthropology"; Maritain works from the speculative philosophy of Thomism; and Niebuhr employs existential-theological explanation. All three men invoke personal and purposive categories, which partly shift the onus of proof from the objective to the subjective sphere; that is, agreement comes through personal assent rather than published results, and is inevitably less than total. Yet if, as these writers insist, man is a personal being with a private plane of existence, a plane on which decisions can be reached that initiate action rather than being (*vide* Marx) always and only rationalizations accessory after the fact, then clearly one will need disciplines that grapple with the nature of man at this level, however exasperating it may be that the final test of adequacy is personal appropriation.

Nor are they saying that introspective, historical, and ontological descriptions are simply to be added to the functional and experimental as equals, for in the study of man they are ultimately superior. The life of man has not been fulfilled when he attains adjustment to or equilibrium within his environment, for only then in fact does his life properly begin, when he starts to act in that climate of choosing freedom to which he is native. His conduct now becomes ethical and his objectives religious (whether for good or demonic ends). Thus Buber places *I–Thou* above *I–It*, Maritain calls for reconsideration of the importance of aims in human behavior, and Niebuhr insists that evil flows not from ignorance or maladjustment but from "self"-assertion beyond the bounds of biological need.

It must be noted that the three thinkers are not unanimous as to what is the precise field in which they are working. They move freely between philosophy and religion, but philosophy is for Buber existential, for Maritain essentialistic, and for Niebuhr mainly political, and as regards religion Buber weights the intuitive while the other two put greater stress on revealed knowledge. But they all concur in the conviction that the concept of a personal, creative God is the key to understanding human personality. All maintain that the spiritual plane is not merely an adjunct of some human lives but the environment in which all human beings have their definitive experiences. As such, it has to be talked about and tested by personal involvement, and this is a finding that affects life and education. It appears therefore that Whitehead was counseling what other ideologies fulfill better than his own when he said: "The essence of education is that it be religious. . . . A religious education is an education which inculcates duty and reverence."[1] This is language of the spirit; "duty" and "reverence" are begotten of ethics and religion, which are categories not to be subsumed under aesthetics or science.

[1] Whitehead, *Aims of Education*, p. 23.

The definition of "individual" to which these three men come, then, is more than biosocial, and it lays stress on the significance of human consciousness. Buber notes man's twofold awareness of the world in distancing and dialogue, and Maritain also posits such awareness, referring to it as "superexistence in knowledge and love." Niebuhr analyzes the powers of the consciousness under the category *imago Dei*, and in his discussion of sin he makes it clear that this somber datum is peculiar to man because it is an experience within the self-conscious being. Far from seeking to reduce the conscious life of man to biosocial categories, as Freud and Marx do, these three writers bring the study of the consciously existing self to the fore and locate in it man's uniqueness. They speak, that is, of a kind of existing which operates above the biosocial but descends upon it so that no biosocial function remains unaffected.

The previous sentence points up an important difference between these views and others current today. Not only are they implacably opposed to naturalistic explanations that reduce everything to the biosocial; they are also equally opposed to dualistic explanations which distinguish the body from the soul. Man is a unity, bringing body, mind, soul, and spirit together in what Buber and Maritain usually refer to as a "person" and Niebuhr a "self." Buber stresses that this unified being is more capable than any other of entering into relation with other beings. Maritain alone of the three exhibits traces of the classical embarrassment about the body, but he too emphasizes its essential involvement in the "person." Investigators are not talking about different entities when they refer separately to "body" as over against "mind" or "soul" but to different and complementary aspects of the same total functioning phenomenon, for one kind of technical discourse will not cope adequately with all the data it generates. Niebuhr's analysis is perhaps most effective, treading with great skill the knife edge between dualism and monism (whether idealistic or naturalistic) and achieving the most effective association of transcendental categories to biosocial phenomena.

It is these men also who have grasped, with varying degrees of firmness, the nettle of human sinfulness. They all agree that it is a datum which cannot be dissolved into genetic or functional disorders. It is related to the life of "persons." Niebuhr again provides the most hard-headed rationale. Buber is somewhat hindered by the existentialist emphasis on failing-to-choose, which is hard put to accommodate positive evil; and Maritain does not free himself entirely from the Greek stigmatizing of materiality. A strength of Niebuhr is his warning against utopianism, which invariably places the individual in jeopardy. All three insist that scientific "progress" does not remove the root of evil but increases the possibilities of both good and evil.

Such considerations produce estimates of social life which resist the functional and statistical tendencies in much current thinking. Buber's distinction between collectivity and community is echoed by the others, and Maritain builds a political theory around the concept of the "common good" which is the most positive of the three and safeguards personal relationships. Niebuhr adds to these a sense of history akin to Whitehead's, but coming to grips more adequately with the cumulative and personal evil running through the story. On all counts we are offered a theory of democracy richer than Dewey's, with a greater awareness of its moral perils. In reaction to overstatements about the achievements of science and technology, the religious thinkers give the impression at times of undervaluing these, but they do show they are aware of them, Niebuhr in particular working from the given of technological Great Society.

In the context of this study, it turns out to have been helpful to play off the scientists and the religious philosophers against each other, to get the best of both worlds (not the Here and the Hereafter but the biosocial and transcendental aspects of human life). That is, we submit that support has been obtained for the claim that we need to employ several complementary realms of discourse to discuss the nature and sanctity of the individual, and that we should strive to give due honor to the various spheres of life, knowledge, and education that correspond to them. Such an outcome has substantial repercussions on educational theory, as we shall now see.

EDUCATIONAL THEORY

Buber and Maritain have both spoken explicitly and at some length about education. Niebuhr has said little directly bearing on it, but we shall offer here observations on what might be inferred from his general attitude, assisted by the one educator who to the author's knowledge has drawn substantially from the same springs and from Niebuhr himself — M. V. C. Jeffreys, recently retired from the chair of education at Birmingham.[2]

There is infused through Buber's remarks on education a warm, wholehearted awareness of the child as a person, as a *Thou* for whom too much cannot be done to ensure that he develops as an autonomous self. With exquisite sensitivity he detects behind the often deceptive outward appearance a divine spark awaiting release. Therefore the educator

> does not merely consider individual functions of his pupil, as one intending to teach him only to know or to be capable of certain definite things; but his concern is always with the person as a whole, both in the actuality in which he lives before you now and in his possibilities, what he can become.[3]

Education then is directed toward the formation of character, that sequence of consistent and ethical actions which gives evidence of the unified and responsible personality within. Such an education is neither individualist nor collectivist, for "Genuine education of character is genuine education for community."

---

[2] In *Mystery of Man* (London: Pitman, 1957) Jeffreys draws constantly on Kierkegaard and Niebuhr and shows appreciation of Buber. In *Glaucon: An Enquiry into the Aims of Education* (London: Pitman, 1955), he confronts the datum of sin in chap. 7; and in the rather more popularly written *Personal Values in the Modern World* (Penguin Books, 1962) he speaks at length on the education of the "person."

[3] Buber, *Between Man and Man*, p. 132.

Clearly Buber is mainly concerned with moral education; and he offers us, as Judges points out, insights rather than a pedagogy: "Only the broadest suggestions about the content of teaching are left in our way."[4] The emphasis is on the teacher-pupil relationship rather than the pupil-pupil or group relationship, and what he says about it is subjective rather than methodological. He explicitly criticizes Dewey's *Human Nature and Conduct* for stressing the subrational elements of habituation and "the accumulation of maxims." The moral imperative is not an *It* but comes out of relation.

> The command addresses us really in the second person, and the Thou in it is no one else but one's own self. Maxims command only the third person, the each and the none.[5]

Therefore moral education depends on the promotion of freedom and dialogue, and the teacher becomes more than an instructor; he must achieve a meeting with the child. If he tries to give instruction in ethics he will produce the opposite result. What he says will be "accepted as current coin of knowledge; nothing of it is transformed into character-building substance." He must submit to the more exacting labor of winning the confidence of the child so that he accepts the educator as a person, as someone who is in turn "accepting him before desiring to influence him." Buber does not deny the external reality of norms, though in our view he says too little about social codes of behavior; but he insists that responsibility means responding and is not merely a matter of concurring,[6] and this implies a higher objective for social education than mere "adjustment."

The nature of the child is regarded as going beyond what behaviorist psychologists have so far described. In particular, the child possesses an "originator instinct" which is the chief factor in the emergence of the *I* that confronts the world in a

[4] Judges, "Martin Buber," p. 106.
[5] Buber, *Between Man and Man*, p. 144.
[6] Maurice Friedman clarifies this point further in "The Existential Man: Buber," in Nash, *The Educated Man*, p. 365.

twofold way. It is most closely identified with the *I* of the *I–It*, for it does not lead to relations with others. That comes through the "instinct for communion . . . the longing for the world to become present to us as a person." The educator is he who prepares conditions whereby these instincts may be expressed. He is not the unobtrusive scene-shifter of progressive education any more than he is the authoritarian bearer of assured values of traditional education. He is a person seeking a meeting with a person-in-the-making. The relationship he is seeking is not one of full mutuality, for the teacher-pupil axis is lopsided, and the teacher must exercise restraint in order not to violate the autonomy of the child. He must be a man "who is wholly alive and able to communicate himself directly to his fellow beings" yet able to accept sincere dissent from his views on the part of the child while continuing in love for that child. Here is a criterion fulfilled by few teachers, but one calculated to prevent complacency or preoccupation with techniques to the exclusion of personal factors.

In *Pointing the Way* Buber speaks about ideological education. Confronting the propaganda drive of the Nazis in the thirties, he had opposed the *Weltanschauung* which declares that the group defines the educational objectives, insisting that the "person" one proceeds from is the primary reality, not the goal one goes toward. In 1951 he goes further, in line with his later thinking on the social principle versus the political principle, and defines social education:

> Education is the great implement which is more or less under the control of Society; Society does not, however, know how to utilize it. Social education is the exact reverse of political propaganda. Such propaganda, whether spread by a government or by a party, seeks to "suggest" a ready-made will to the members of the society, i.e., to implant in their minds the notion that such a will derives from their own, their innermost being. Social education, on the other hand, seeks to arouse and to develop in the minds of its pupils the spontaneity of fellowship which is

innate in all unravaged human souls and which harmonizes very well with the development of personal existence and personal thought.[7]

His final word on the issue distinguishes between propaganda and education as between "imposition" and "unfolding." The propagandist, he says, "concerned simply with *more* — more members . . . ," looks upon individual qualities as a burden, whereas the educator lives gladly in a world of individuals who are coming into being.

Buber does not offer the modern educationist an articulated educational theory. He has nothing to say about curriculum, teaching aids, special methods, measurement and evaluation, or administration. But his insights do provide invaluable pointers in the confused areas of educational aims and values, moral education, and teacher-pupil relationships.

Some of Maritain's views on education relate specifically to denominational education, but for the most part he speaks more broadly, exhibiting a more liberal recognition of the achievements and objectives of the public school than we have come to expect from Catholic theorists. His comments have therefore deservedly found a wide audience. He begins by acknowledging the great advances made in educational method and learning theory, especially through the application of scientific findings. However, he believes that education is in sore straits because of the very success of these advances, in that it has lost sight of its objectives. The "scientific idea" has exalted means into ends, Pragmatism has aided and abetted that tendency by refusing to contemplate ends outside the process, and "sociologism" has made social conditioning primary at the expense of the person.

Maritain's own views on educational aims are, characteristically, clearly stated. We are primarily concerned with "*making a man,* and by this very fact in preparing a citizen." "The prime goal of education is the conquest of internal and spiritual freedom to be achieved in the individual person."

[7] Buber, *Pointing the Way*, p. 176.

This means that social adjustment and group problem-solving come in as subsidiary aims, measured by their effectiveness in promoting the primary goal. There is in fact another subsidiary aim which Maritain rescues from the Pragmatist assault, affirming that "knowledge is a value in itself and an end in itself."

This leads on into recommendations for liberal education that reassert the place of philosophy and the humanities, for it shifts the focus of syllabus integration from *use* to *truth*. Maritain also places bounds on the function of the school as a specialized agency, suggesting that it is "not primarily to shape the will and directly to develop moral virtues in the youth, but to enlighten and strengthen reason."[8] At this level the public school is capable of going a good part of the way from a secular rationale, and Maritain does not deny the secular school its place in the educational program of a community, but proposes a theory of curriculum which may be applied in any school, secular or church, leaving it to the community to judge where it is being best implemented.

His theory of curriculum is geared mainly to upper secondary and junior college years in the American system. Maritain proposes a "liberal education," available to all students, geared to universal knowledge (i.e., of first principles) rather than vocational or academic expertise, catering for the development of the soul (*vide* Aristotle) through the imaginative to the reasoning stage, and based on the humanities. An intriguing reconstruction of the liberal arts follows, designed for the age of democracy and technology, deranking but retaining the classics and humanizing the study of science. The new *trivium* consists of the creative activities of eloquence, literature, and fine arts (including the technological arts), and the new *quadrivium* comprises the rational activities of mathematics and physics (with their histories), human sciences, and philosophy in all its branches (including psychology and sociology). The categories are rather arbitrary, the attempt to contain them in the medieval schema of *trivium* and *quadri-*

[8] Quoted and discussed by Beales, in "Jacques Maritain," p. 80; see also Maritain, *Education of Man,* pp. 103–106.

vium precious, and the omission of languages surprising; but as an organizing framework the proposal has promise. At one point Maritain makes the provocative suggestion that college education in the humanities would be built around two different kinds of institution:

> a centre of manual-service training, and a centre of intellectual-service training, each one with its own various institutes or schools of oriented humanities. And though intellectual service is in itself or in its nature more spiritual and therefore of greater worth than manual service . . . they would be on a completely equal footing in the educational system.[9]

Such an Aristotelian bifurcation of the human race is surely not to be countenanced in the light of modern knowledge about man.

As to the moral attitudes which it is proper for all schools to promote, Maritain considers that the practical tenets of the democratic charter would be our guide. However, if a teacher is to inculcate them effectively he must believe in them firmly from a standpoint which for him supplies their justification, though in a pluralistic society many such standpoints will exist. Neutrality cannot be an option, says Maritain (in criticism of many Pragmatists), not only because no human being can help infecting a pupil with his attitudes but because there must be moral education if children are to grow up as persons. Hence we must accept the problem as given and look for effective administrative alternatives, such as geographically homogeneous schools, or schools with a purposely heterogeneous staff, or the creation of a special subject called "the democratic charter" which would be basically a history of ideas. Whatever solution was adopted, teachers would be allowed and indeed encouraged to teach with strong and open conviction.

Ultimately the role of the school in moral education is not the direct formation of the will, which is a job for the family and the church, but the indirect formation of the will through

[9] Maritain, "Typical Aspects of Christian Education," p. 195.

intellectual enlightenment. Maritain is sympathetic to the program of his friend Mortimer Adler to enrich tertiary students' awareness of great formative human ideas through a course in the "great books," in particular because it acquaints them with developed ethical notions and prepares the soil for right volition. Of religious instruction he says that, despite the scoffing of logicians, it is apparent that morality is linked with religion; "What I maintain is that with regard to the average behavior of mankind, morality without religion undermines morality, and is able to sustain human life for but a few generations."[10] Therefore the school that can promote religious knowledge unashamedly is in the best position to make gains in moral education. Even the public school, however, if true to its mandate, should be representing the cultural component of religious knowledge in its curriculum, and Maritain deplores the fact that the American concept of the "secular school" has prevented it from doing so. As we have already seen, a pluralistic solution is offered in preference to so-called neutralism. In the space available we have only hinted at the rich mine of insight into moral education which is there for the digging in Maritain's writings, but a last quotation fixes its priority in educational theory:

> This moral task of education is growing today, it seems to me, more and more important, as mankind is confronted with materialist or positivist philosophies which make moral standards completely relativized, and with the "other-directed" or sheeplike cast of mind which our industrial or technological civilization tends to develop.[11]

It is appropriate finally to remind ourselves of Maritain's stress on the integrity and autonomy of the child, as a counterweight to the advice he gives about promoting ideology in the school. We are seeking, he says, to make "persons," and this ties in with the view of Aquinas that the principal agent in education is the child himself, responding out of his own inner

[10] Maritain, *Education of Man*, p. 117.
[11] *Ibid.*, p. 106.

freedom and in his own way. While the teacher is "a real giver whose own dynamism, moral authority, and positive guidance are indispensable," we are working towards the freeing of personality, that is, "the mastery and independence of my spiritual self." One may infer that education is viewed as a course steered between authoritarian indoctrination and progressive neutralism, or between imposition and free expression, with one's respect for the sanctity of the person plotting the path. This is, like Maritain's recommendations generally, a more balanced and realistic educational theory than Buber's. Yet we must draw from both, allowing the cumulative logic of Maritain to be tempered by Buber's undisguised partiality for the particular person.

What direct comments Niebuhr has to make on education are mostly negative, in that he speaks of it as an instrument by which inadequate ideologies are being passed on. This in itself is a point that has to be made, denying yet again the neutralist stance. All education contains coercive and propaganda elements, says Niebuhr. "Even the most honest educator tries consciously or unconsciously to impress a particular viewpoint upon his disciples." [12] Hence education is at one and the same time "a tool of controversy as well as a method of transcending it." The fundamental ideological springs of Western education are the Hellenic and the Hebraic. Because the Hellenic has attained dominance, we are in the situation of needing to apply a corrective.[13] One result of the bias has been a naive faith in reason.

> This faith of the Enlightenment is still the creed of the educators of our day and is shared more or less by philosophers, psychologists and social scientists.[14]

In a popular essay on "Higher Education in America"[15] Niebuhr deplores the deficiency of language study and the

[12] Niebuhr, *Moral Man and Immoral Society*, p. 245.
[13] Reinhold Niebuhr, "The Two Sources of Western Culture," in Fuller, *Christian Idea of Education*, pp. 237–254.
[14] Niebuhr, *Moral Man and Immoral Society*, p. 24.
[15] Niebuhr, *The Godly and the Ungodly*, pp. 24–38.

separation of the sciences from the perspective of the humanities, and notes a "general mood of soft conformism." He also contrasts the secularism of daily American life with its strong allegiance to religious institutions, and suggests that what knits the American community together is a strong sense of the dignity of man. He urges, however, that the Christian faith speak in a balanced way of both the dignity and the misery of man.

Taking these warnings to heart, what may we then say constructively about educational theory? M. V. C. Jeffreys leads off from Niebuhr's baseline by highlighting the evasiveness in the Harvard Report [16] regarding the relation between the ideals of free enquiry and firm personal convictions. "The weakness of the Report is the lack of clear and firm belief about the nature and destiny of man," he says, going on to develop Niebuhr's criticisms of Dewey. He proceeds to stress that man is to be spoken of as a rational and moral being. One is thereby warned against too great preoccupation with disciplines that emphasize the subrational aspects of human behavior and its deterministic character. It is helpful to distinguish the education of thinking from the education of feeling. The education of thinking includes not only freedom from the thought of others but freedom to think. The education of feeling involves helping people "to achieve depth and sincerity of feeling" and building a community of love in the school wherein moral education may take place. Neutrality is not an option; the teacher "can (and indeed must) reveal his opinions on matters of moment, but also can and should cherish the pupil's freedom to do his own thinking about what is offered to him." [17]

The obstacle to the working out of these proposals is the fact of human sinfulness. Following Niebuhr's analysis, Jeffreys says that sin is "not merely the display of an inferior side of man's nature; it is the corruption of the best in man." Therefore not just education but redemption is needed, and the reconciliation is achieved by love, supremely, in relationship

---

[16] Committee on the Objectives of a General Education, *General Education in a Free Society*, Cambridge, Mass.: Harvard University Press, 1945.

[17] Jeffreys, *Personal Values in the Modern World*, p. 136.

with Christ. For moral education, therefore, the development of personal relationships of warmth and love in community are the best foundation for that turning of the soul to God which will reverse the processes of evil. We do not find Jeffreys, for all his recognition of sin in human life, providing us with clear guidelines for the integration of this fact into educational theory. He seems not to follow Niebuhr far enough into his social analysis of the effects of sin, nor to come down clearly enough on the necessity for facilities beyond those which education can provide for the conversion of persons to God, such as Niebuhr's profounder appreciation would seem to require.

Along with Nunn, Dewey, and Whitehead, our three religious thinkers focus education on the development of the individual. However, they enrich the connotation of "individual" in such a way as to strengthen the case for a wide curricular offering, of Whiteheadian magnitude but with emphasis on moral rather than aesthetic or pragmatic principles of organization. Truth in goodness, for which we earlier sought in vain, becomes the touchstone of personal development. But the full import of the datum of human evil as expounded by Niebuhr has not been adequately accounted for in any educational theory here cited. And it is needed to inform our understanding of learning processes, of administrative problems, and of all human studies (including moral education) in the school curriculum.

The individualism of Kierkegaard and Nunn is moderated by the visions of community upheld by these three thinkers, without swinging to the opposite pole of collectivity as with Marx and even Mannheim. This "community" does not debase reason as Marx and Nietzsche do; rather, it provides a major point of contact with Dewey and Whitehead, but sets a higher value on "love," "meeting," "dialogue," and "responsibility." Aims of learning are thereby considerably modified.

With the illumination of ten acute minds on the problems surrounding the individual and education, we should now be in a position to bring together some implications for sound educational theory.

PART SIX:

toward adequate educational theory

THE SANCTITY OF THE INDIVIDUAL

BASIC ASSUMPTIONS

Can it be said, in light of the ideologies we have investigated, that the problem of the sanctity of the individual is of sufficient moment in the modern world to have warranted our study? I submit an affirmative answer, for three main reasons. First, with a single exception the ideologists sampled cast a solid vote in favor of viewing the individual as an end in himself. The exception is Nietzsche, who is to be taken as a warning rather than an example. Even Marx claims to be working towards a society of truly free individuals. Second, the individual in question is Everyman, identified not by birth, not by intelligence or personality quotient, but by the fact of being human. Third, it is not human individuality in general but the particular and unique individual who is defended so spiritedly and whose sanctity is felt to be in special jeopardy in the modern day. It will be taken as given, therefore, that there is in Western culture today a strong, articulate belief that each individual matters for what he is intrinsically, prior to any accounting of what he has achieved or received.

The problem is not to gain assent to such a proposition but so to define it that we are provided with a guide to practical action.

Preserving the sanctity of the individual requires action on two planes. The first is protection: shielding the individual from forces that would reduce him to a means in the accomplishment of impersonal ends. The problems this poses are largely political and lie beyond the scope of this study apart from the comments made in each case on the social safeguards proposed by each thinker. It is recognized that at times people must be treated as means in the accomplishment of certain ends of social organization or scientific investigation, but the way people are thus used must be consistent with agreed-upon rights of man, remembering that it is a delusion to think that the rights of the man of the future may be ensured by depriving some men in the present of their rights without their consent. Avoiding protracted political theorizing, I would simply express a belief that the most advisable political structure is some form of dynamic democracy.

The second plane of action involves promotion: providing opportunities for the self-enlargement to which human individuality lends itself, a task that is initially educational. It may be said that all the notion of individual sanctity directly implies is the first plane of action, the removal of hindrances to individual liberty; but I would argue that a satisfactory understanding of what an individual is, and how he becomes fully developed as an individual, points to the need to take positive steps to promote that development. The dangers to individual liberty created by such intrusive agencies as education (dangers seen by J. S. Mill and others) are to be avoided not by minimizing the influence of the agencies but by placing their goals and procedures under the judgment of the concept, as I shall attempt to do in the last chapter.

One looks of course for the rise of a culture which has realized the democratic pattern on a wide and generous scale; and this can only be built upon an adequately designed education of the young, for the evidence is strong that the die of adult personality is cast in the formative years of childhood and youth. It must be added that without a positive program of individual enrichment, any political scaffolding of democratic freedoms is mere bones without flesh.

If it is accepted that, as will be argued in the next chapter, education aims to develop persons, then a basic task of clarification must be attempted concerning the view of human nature which governs our theorizing. I have maintained that the shortcomings of ideologies as regards the sanctity of the individual usually stem from a defective view of man and from the resulting neglect of certain realms of discourse. One might further claim that the same defects give rise to errant political and social science; and one may hope that the correction of educational theory will ultimately influence these fields of enquiry also, provided that it has not itself fallen victim meantime to the exigencies of a particular political or social science theory with normative pretensions. In matters of the kind we are dealing with, it must fall to the philosopher of education to adjudicate. The next and major section of this chapter is therefore the crux of this study, for it sets out what I deem to be essential elements in a balanced view of human nature.

DEFINING "INDIVIDUAL"

Most descriptions of man are preoccupied with one large aspect of this complex entity and tend to demand that all other aspects shall be expressed ultimately in the same language. Educational theorists often do the same, building on narrowed sets of basic assumptions. Religious, philosophical, aesthetic, scientific, and utilitarian writers have all been prone to this error, and we stand in need of more generous syntheses. This is not to imply that we should fall into the opposite error, illustrated by many school syllabuses, of a vague and diplomatic eclecticism. There must be a ranking of the several kinds of knowledge, and the principle I propose here is that of determining the priorities given to various learning activities by the degree to which they reflect what is distinctively human in the individual. That is, all knowledge is our province and none should be neglected, but the knowledge that is of most worth is that which bears on those attributes of the individual which account for his uniqueness.

I am now fairly entered upon speculation with a view to recommendation, in token of which I have adopted first-person address. My excuse for doing so can only be a claim that no theorist, whatever his procedure, can avoid being committed to a speculative conviction regarding human nature, and it were well that more theorists were explicit about their beliefs in this matter, instead of sheltering behind ostensibly neutral scientific description or an inadmissible agnosticism. Furthermore, my account purports to have profited from the analyses of other views in the previous chapters of this book. The reader must be the judge of the extent to which this is so.

What then is man?

Man has a body, and is continuous by this fact with the dust of the ground. As Whitehead has reminded us, physicochemical components are basically not stable lumps of solid, inert matter but "life"-histories of units of energy. The development of theories to account for the behavior of the energy in matter has contributed remarkably to the growing dominion of man over such entities, and therefore to his own material condition. But this same dominion and manipulation remind us: man is more than body.

Man is an animal; that is, he exhibits a complex range of physiological processes which are co-ordinated within the total organism. This enables the organism to achieve a high degree of individuation, sharing with other higher animals various co-ordinated responses of considerable complexity, such as emotions and a certain power of practical reason. However, the human animal has so largely suppressed instinct, advanced in reasoning, and refined emotional responses that there is a limit to the usefulness of equating animal and human behavior. Undoubtedly much remains to be discovered by the employment of this equation, and improved knowledge of organic and functional processes has greatly aided man's constant effort to maintain a healthy adjustment to his environment; but man is more than animal.

From a behavioral point of view man is a social animal. As with any large societies of entities, one is able to arrive at very useful probabilities of large group behavior, given adequately sophisticated instruments. However, just as McDougall's "gregarious instinct" has failed to cope with the weight of social theory it was once made to bear, so have biological and statistical vocabularies proved liable to distortion unless supplemented by more distinctively human realms of discourse. The extension of behavioral social theories is imperative if man is to cope with the highly sophisticated environment he himself has developed; but man is more than social animal.

It is my contention that the physical, biological, and social levels of being with which I have so far dealt, far from accounting for the phenomenon of man with little or no "remainder," do but deal with the preliminaries. Man exhibits capacities to manipulate these realms, to conserve past experience not only as discrete memories but as integrated interpretations and rules, to initiate new experiences, and to know himself as the possessor of experiences. That is, he functions on a higher level of being. I shall say he exists as a "self," and in order to identify those aspects of his behavior which are distinctively human, I shall employ the adjective "spiritual," and shall mean the same sort of thing when I speak of the "marks of spirit" generally or of various attributes or expressions "of spirit." [1]

Some attempt must now be made to catalogue the marks of spirit, and two preliminary comments are needed. The first is that "spirit" is to be understood as infusing all human func-

---

[1] I have avoided using "mind" or "soul" because of their varied usage and consequent ambiguities in both ordinary and technical language. "Mind" in particular suffers from the limitations of the Greek overstress on objective rationality. It can be argued that "spirit" is in the same situation, but I believe that the meaning I stipulate above shares many features with common usage. Also, it is a word less likely than the others to be reified through the use of the definite article. I shall not in any case refer to "the spirit," and when I speak of "the spiritual realm" I shall be indicating that environment or level of functioning which is unknown to animals because it is a distinctively human experience, to which the best clue is the testimony of language. While it is possible to extend the argument to make God accountable for spiritual life, I do not so argue here, nor is this essential to the case being argued here.

tions, and therefore no rigid boundary may be drawn between, say, "natural" and "spiritual" or "social" and "spiritual." I am in entire sympathy with those who for various reasons have deplored the Hellenistic dualism reflected in Descartes' description of what Ryle derided as the "ghost in the machine," whilst being equally antipathetic to those who have simply deleted what truth there was in the ghost and spoken only in machine terms. The marks of spirit in human behavior require enriched discourse, to be sure, but the self is a unified entity, and it is safest to speak adjectivally about the various facets of its behavior rather than employ nouns with the definite article ("the body," "the spirit," "the mind"); one must avoid being tricked by grammatical structures into creating substances instead of expounding qualities.

The second preliminary comment is that in singling out marks of spirit, I do not mean to imply a faculty psychology based on the supposition of certain "powers" separate from each other in essence. The marks of spirit are aspects or facets of the self's total response and interdependent upon each other, like the several planes of a cut diamond which may be looked at individually but derive their brilliance from the relations they bear to one another and to the heart of the stone.

The first mark is endurance. Chemically the bodily constituents replace themselves entirely over a period of time, and functionally there is growth and new experience, yet existentially the self endures at least until bodily dissolution or radical psychic disruption. When Hume objected that apart from successive perceptions he could discern nothing by introspection, and when James surrendered the existing subject as such because, he said, "my thinking is first and last and always for the sake of doing, and I can only do one thing at a time,"[2] both men underestimated the enduring "I" that owns the experiences and knows them subjectively. One need not enter into debate as to whether animals experience enduring identity at the conscious level, for the endurance of a human self is much the richer by virtue of its capacity for

---

[2] Quoted approvingly by Dewey in *Problems of Men*, p. 401.

language, which develops symbolic meanings that increase and refine feelings, actions, and the storage capacity of memory. Our memories go beyond the immediate and concrete into recollected growth and interpretations of experiences. Nor is human endurance confined to present and past, for the self has power to anticipate future outcomes and to subsist by long-term goals.

We are thus brought to the second mark: transcendence. An animal is able to react as a total organism to alterations in its environment, but a human self possesses in addition the power to stand off from its external environment and its own body with its memories. It moves therefore in a private environment with its own space and time, from which it is able to endow the "world" with purposes and to influence the course of events. The impressive achievements of this objectifying power have often been hailed as proofs of rational mind underlying the universe, but since this is usually understood in the Greek sense, it does not do justice to the creative energy of the self. Reason is not the hallmark but the tool of spirit, and is used to bridge the gap between the meanings the self imparts to life and the functions of empirical living. It would be more appropriate to speculate that the "world" is sustained and infused by transcendent, creative spirit which, mute in lower forms of life, produces in man a creature capable of initiation.

The third mark of spirit is therefore creativity. The Greek rationalist fled from the flux of life into contemplation of the bloodless abstract. The modern empiricist spurns metaphysics for practical explanation. Both expect too much of reason, for creativity springs from deeper wells. The self is urged beyond the requirements of survival and adjustment by the creative thrust of spirit. It must reveal itself, become explicit, build upon its former manifestations. The result is human culture, a testimony to man's incapacity to be at rest. No sooner does a human being pause to regain stability of personality than he finds he has once more discovered something to say and do. Art, philosophy, and science are not calm achievements but continuous adventures beyond the call of duty (i.e., beyond survival requirements), and reason pants doggedly after, indispensable to their advance but subsequent to their inspiration. Because all men are spiritual, so it must be said that every individual is creative, even when he happens to be intellectually below average. To focus education on academic achievement is to produce a few scholastics and many spiritually maimed drop-outs, to the neglect of resources more fundamental, which then overflow into unintended channels, not all beneficial.

The fourth mark of spirit is dialogue. The enduring, transcendent self is conscious that it is neither supreme nor alone. The world which is over against it both indulges and limits its creative urge. The limitations are not only physical and biofunctional but spiritual, in that there are other selves to be reckoned with. Being also uniquely enduring and transcendent, they constitute not only a limitation but an opportunity for the expansion of oneself. It is well-nigh impossible to conceive of a human self in isolation from dialogue with other selves, whereas the common ground of spiritual being makes possible discoveries through the group that would be beyond the isolated individual, on condition that the individuals in the group are each free to contribute creatively. Dialogue in this sense will occur whenever two or more individuals are able to communicate by word or gesture.[3] That is, whatever the biofunctional character of their encounter, there will be spiritual intercourse of some kind, whether recognized as such or not. For educational theory this fact is pivotal.

Each of the marks of spirit gathers up the others into itself, but this is specially true of dialogue. Buber depicts dialogue as *I–Thou* and tends to commend it without reserve, suggesting that when individuals abuse each other all the fault lies on the *I–It* plane. But it would seem to be more helpful to allow that on both planes individuals may encounter each

[3] It is tempting to suggest that even these signs may not be essential, since the private time-space of the transcendent self may interlock with another's regardless of "objective" time-space, as in Buber's wordless communion, or in prayer, and even perhaps in phenomena of the kind J. B. Rhine and others call extrasensory perception.

other with intent to do good or ill. The spiritual impact of one self upon another may produce either communion or corrosion. Such is the freedom available to a transcendent self that it may, even knowing the destructive effects of self-assertion and isolation, choose that dialogue shall go this way. That men do so choose, and often, suggests that the fact of sin must be accounted for in my analysis.

The ends which determine man's life are spiritual. Ends relating to the physical and biofunctional areas of human life are immediate, as Dewey suggested, and turn out to be means toward more inclusive goals whose profundity he missed. Spiritual ends include long-term and even eternal objectives ("ideals"). For example, endurance and transcendence allow the self to view its distant past and plan for its distant future. Unlimited at this level of existence, the self experiences frustration and anxiety because of its biofunctional limitations and eventual death, giving rise to that search for meaning and purpose which I shall define as the province of religion, a province formerly thought to be contiguous with philosophy because of the overly exalted status accorded to universal reason.[4] Likewise creativity and dialogue, which both conflict and co-operate with each other, give rise to aesthetics, science, and society. These with the help of reason become enduring and transcendent as historical culture. The self that engages in all these transactions is a choosing being, and its choices reflect not merely the objective evidence of reason but the subjective passion of existence.

Human choices prove, according to many observers, to be suffused with a tendency to egoism. The destiny of the physical particle is to endure; of the organism, to achieve survival adjustment. But the destiny of man is to gain self-enrichment through the effective use of his spiritual energies. So far has he transcended the finite limits of his biosocial existence that he may even run counter to its creature needs in the fulfillment of

[4] The assertion that religion is a search for meanings more profound than meanings of a rational or analytic kind is buttressed by the observed capacity of higher religions to minister to all strata of society; though not necessarily irrational, they have other weapons in their armory besides rationality.

spiritual objectives, good or evil. A weak character is one who has failed to co-ordinate the elements of self toward consistent purposes. A strong character is one who has succeeded in this, though his consistent purposes may be either good or bad. Good purposes are defined as those which promote communion between selves, fostering creativity on behalf of such communion. Bad purposes are those which destroy communion and divert the creative energy to securing the autonomy of self, reflecting indifference or unawareness that the self is thus severed from the stem of its spiritual life.

Egoism does not merely derive from a biological principle of survival of the fittest, for biology is silent on the making of value judgments of this kind; and if one insists on arguing by analogy, then certain other biological facts offer equally useful principles of co-operative living. Moreover, human egoism does not stop at the fulfillment of creature needs but craves limitless satiation. That this spiritual datum is a towering fact of human life is borne out by the persistence of social disorder even, and perhaps especially, in the most advanced societies. A more extreme example is provided by the atrocities of war. Unlike the other marks of spirit, however, egoism is not ontologically necessary; nor is it always irresistible, for its expressions result mainly from conscious choices made by the self. It may therefore be spoken of in moral terms as "sin" — the tendency of selves knowingly to make choices that destroy communion with other spiritual beings.

Into the origins of sinful tendencies we need not further enquire, but it is important to appreciate their extent. As a datum of spirit, egoism cannot be compartmentalized or related to only one plane of selfhood. It is of the self and prone to affect anything the self does. Children are less likely to "grow out of it" than they are to grow further into it; and neither habit nor reason alone will cure them of it. Only in the influence of self upon self through communion may hope be held out that a growing self will be prompted to make an existential decision to eschew as far as possible choices and actions that will destroy or inhibit communion. Even then there will be more ground to be retrieved than most naturalists and idealists bank on, and for this reason alone all visions of perfectibility in this world order are dangerous. It is as well to take a tough, albeit extreme, line, and treat the tendency to sin as though it were a fifth mark of spirit.

The problems of meaning and purpose which I assigned to the province of religion then become doubly important, for the fact of sin cuts across all easy answers and demands that the problem of redemption be grappled with. The rationalist explanation — that the characteristic concern of religions with redemption is to be traced to the fear of the unknown which led primitives to postulate angry gods — not only begs the question it purports to answer but fails to cope with the sins and anxieties of scientific civilization. Education, in intentionally guiding the development of persons, must awaken a recognition of the problem of redemption in human living, in the hope that each individual will be prompted thereby to come personally to grips with it.

What humanists have attributed to ignorance and existentialists described as despair, I have described as sin attributable to egoism. Correspondingly my remedy has been previsioned in different terms: not just enlightenment or self-affirmation but redemption. At the least it is generally agreed that we ought to educate the child not merely up to what man is, but to what it is considered he ought to be. The goal of most educationists goes beyond producing the type. In defining "individual" it may therefore be deemed appropriate to add to the description of what the individual *is* a speculation regarding what he ought to *become*.

I look to the emergence of a self which knows both its capacities and its limits. Regarding its capacities, it is aware of what is distinctively human, and it orders its behavior in such a way as to enhance this; that is, it covets opportunity to reason, to create, and to enter into dialogue. To this end it seeks to exercise more efficient control over physical and biofunctional phenomena, profiting but not profiteering from the accumulated wisdom of the community of selves. Regarding its limits, it is aware of the physical and biofunctional (i.e., hereditary and environmental) boundaries within which it moves, it recognizes its need of other selves whose integrity it must at the same time respect, and it confesses its need of redemption from destructive tendencies within itself.

Thus far a person may be expected to fulfill the moral and social requirements of human life; one will be behaving, in Jeffreys' terms, as rationally and morally as he may.[5] Many educational theories bring us to this point. My view, however, requires that for adequate self-organization one must obtain at least provisional answers to the problems of meaning, purpose, and redemption. One will therefore be a consciously religious person. Education which belittles either rational, moral, or religious concerns will not be doing justice to the distinctively human, that is, the spiritual.

To make such a claim is to point up an imbalance in present-day studies of man. It is probable that thinkers in the past tended to take physical and biofunctional development for granted and to concentrate on spiritual or, more narrowly, mental development. The pendulum swung the other way when the scientific revolution showed what enormous fields of study derived from the aspects that had been neglected, and proved that the scientific method is capable of modifying behavior considerably throughout the range of organisms. The speed and spread of scientific achievement have resulted, however, in an imbalance in the studies of modern man. While studies in areas like history, philosophy, literature, and religion, loosely identified as "the humanities," are still very much alive, the prestige and power belong to the sciences.

Many of the older disciplines are succumbing to the pressure to become more "scientific" in method and judgment, and there are many advocates for the view that the social sciences have assumed full responsibility for the advance of mankind. Yet insofar as the social sciences underrate the spiritual liberty of the self, partly because the nature of their tool requires them to assume causal determinism, thus far do they fall short of coping with the human datum. As Jeffreys points out,

[5] Jeffreys, *Mystery of Man*, p. 19.

it is all too easy to forget the role of the individual as a rational and moral person. In other words, the sociological method tends to eliminate from the picture the distinctively human quality of behaviour. The approach is one that highlights the irrational elements in behaviour; the more irrational the behaviour, the more easily can it be accounted for in terms of social pressure. Little light is shed on the problem of how man can become more rational and responsible.[6]

Similarly, Story contrasts the titles and contents of Dewey's *Human Nature and Conduct* and Niebuhr's *The Nature and Destiny of Man*.[7] Dewey's interest is in psychological habituation and the use of intelligence—that feeble emergent power—to fix more efficient habits, whereas Niebuhr's concern is with the spiritual powers of the self and the realm of ethical choice. Dewey's social psychology is arresting and insightful, but rather than a remodeling of ethics, as he is prone to claim, it is better regarded as another way of viewing ethical behavior, a way moreover which is less competent to account for what is distinctively human about that behavior.

It is also necessary to recognize the automatic element in spiritual growth. Physiology and psychology inform us of certain aspects of growth which take place automatically unless arrested by conditions of extreme deprivation or malfunction; such growth is often referred to as "maturation." It is essential to my view to regard the development of spiritual functions as in part due to maturation. The self is already present, as a potential, in the newborn infant, and forthwith the behavior of the organism begins to diversify in patterns that bear increasing evidence of the marks of spirit. Of adult behavior it is therefore essential to insist with Niebuhr that it is shot through with spirit; the most "natural" of activities are so transmuted by purposes which are ultimately spiritual that even a concept like "natural law" is perilous when utilized for, say, ethical theory.[8]

[6] Ibid.
[7] Story, "Dewey and Niebuhr: A Brief Juxtaposition," p. 182.
[8] E.g., Niebuhr, *Human Nature*, pp. 42–45, 163–165.

Maturation of spiritual powers does not result necessarily in a well-knit personality or a "good character"; it does make it inevitable that the self will exist in ethical categories. For endurance and transcendence make man a choosing being, and creativity and dialogue are the channels through which his choices are actualized. Therefore the direction of spiritual development is to a significant extent at the discretion of the self, and the possibilities are bipolar: self-extension may be promoted either at the expense of or in co-operation with other selves. Buber's *I–It* and *I–Thou* in my view do not adequately accommodate this polarity, nor Maritain's distinction between materiality and spirituality. Dewey's equation of evil with ignorance is only sometimes plausible; Whitehead's aesthetic criterion, though closer to the mark because it requires the more direct employment of spiritual powers, fails to establish that we are dealing with a distinctively human polarity. A man may fail to rise to the ethical task that Kierkegaard claims is the core of his response to life, but he cannot thereby escape its demands upon him.

From birth, then, man develops physically, biofunctionally, and spiritually. There is increasing scope for optional kinds of development as one moves across from the physical and biofunctional to the spiritual. Therefore culture and education are most concerned with the spiritual or distinctively human. The marks of spirit are endurance, transcendence, creativity, and dialogue, resulting in selves who are free to remember, reason, create, commune or corrode, and control. How they employ their freedom is substantially influenced by the universal tendency to strive for self-autonomy beyond the limits of what is rational and moral. Because both reason and conscience identify such acts as destructive, it is proper to speak of human sin and the problem of redemption. By proposing that educational theorizing should focus on the spiritual, I have implied that the desired educational outcome will be a self which is consciously concerned with the problem of making consistently good choices and is intelligently aware that its choices lie in religious as well as rational and moral categories.

EDUCATION AND THE INDIVIDUAL

AIMS AND VALUES

There are many problems associated with educational aims. Aim statements vary from Dewey's insistence that the only aim is growth to Maritain's goal of a liberally enlightened Christian, while developing countries often reflect that view of education for national superiority which characterized nineteenth-century Prussia. R. S. Peters even questions the whole point of aims statements.[1] The problem is further complicated by the gap that exists between theory and practice, a gap due not only to conservatism but to the difficulty of stating aims in an operational form that will give some guide to method and evaluation procedures. This difficulty is all the greater with formulations relating to spiritual objectives, which, because of their holistic character, introduce what are commonly called "intangibles"—that is, they do not yield their secrets to functional quantitative measurement.

[1] R. S. Peters, *Ethics and Education,* London: George Allen and Unwin, 1966, part I. Interestingly, Frankena compares Peters' attitude with Dewey's, in that both spurn long-term objectives in favor of immediate purposes. (See W. K. Frankena, *Philosophy of Education,* New York: Macmillan, 1965, p. 12.) In more recent writing, Peters has chosen to talk about "the educated man," which in my view modifies this judgment.

Peters notes that statements of general aims are so vague that educationists of quite different outlooks can appear to be in agreement, until they reveal their principles of procedure. Whereas an ultimate aim sets up some vague future goal, an ultimate value governs the procedures employed in the on-going process. Therefore, says Peters, let us settle for "principles of procedure," based on the values we hold dear, and avoid use of the term "aim" in its general sense. "In the spheres both of intellect and character it is the manner that maketh man."[2] This is in effect Dewey's "process aim," though Peters appears to be rather more hospitable to external standards of morality and says that "the crucial valuative questions, when we come down to *moral* brass tacks, are questions of principles and procedures."[3]

These distinctions are helpful. They remind us that an educational theory is normative through and through, not only in its goal statements but in the values behind them and the processes they sanction. In particular it is clear that if the sanctity of the individual is a basic ideological belief, as I have suggested, then it is a basic value by which educational practice must be judged. Teacher attitudes, methods of teaching, classroom management, school administration — all must be constantly scrutinized in the light of the conviction that the individual is an end in himself. More will be said of such matters subsequently.

However, I would also contend that we must be aware of our ideological environment and keep general goals before us. The point was made earlier that Dewey's refusal to look beyond process aims reflected his view of man as a biosocial being, which I criticized as shortsighted because it neglected spiritual elements. Similarly, Peters in his later statements about "the educated man" seems to suggest that the criteria by which one judges the appropriateness of applying this description to a person are logically implied, when in fact

[2] R. S. Peters, *Authority, Responsibility and Education*, London: George Allen and Unwin, 1959, p. 118.
[3] *Ibid.*, p. 96 (my italics).

they are indebted to an English intellectual climate which he tends to take for granted as Nunn did.

The marks of spirit in man — his temporal endurance and objective transcendence, his creativity and dialogue, even his ravening ego — suggest not only that long-term goals are important but also that there is considerable scope for variation at the spiritual level of development, especially of the moral sense. The child will not mature into the adult we hope for by himself, but needs correction and enlightenment, some of which education can give him. It is ncessary to have before us a norm for human nature. Dewey in fact is not without such a norm, and offers us a portrait of a problem-solver, in which the character traits are those he considers vital to scientific research.[4] The end product he has in view is not a "natural" consequence of growth but an ideologically influenced norm. "Natural development," first dreamed of by Rousseau, is literally out of this world. Similarly, Maritain castigates existentialists for being so concerned with existential becoming that they have decried essential being.[5] The initial self-datum has definable potential and needs most help in spiritual development.

The point I am defending is that there is value in specifying goals as well as process aims, most especially when one is thinking of some kind of staging point in the lifelong process of education, such as the attainment of adulthood in an educational sense. In doing so we must make clear what understanding of human nature governs our specification, and at this point the value with which this study is concerned is of prime importance.

Just as the sanctity of the individual requires both protection and promotion, as we saw in the previous chapter, so in education it affects the two kinds of aiming that I have been discussing. As the value by which process aims are judged, it protects the child from administrative or ideological presumption. But just as the concept needs promotion at a cultural

[4] Thus Dewey, *Democracy and Education*, p. 413.
[5] Maritain, *Existence and the Existent*, p. 10.

level, and such promotion hinges on a view of man, so in education it must act as a future objective, whereby the curricular balance of learning experiences is assessed for its effectiveness in bearing the child toward what we understand to be mature selfhood. Mature selfhood involves, as we have seen, not merely freedom from hindrances to the exercise of spiritual capacities, but adult maturity with respect to understanding and accepting responsibility for using those capacities in ways which honor rational, moral, and religious dimensions.

A rather different aims debate concerns the extent to which education, especially state education, can perform such tasks. An unequivocal declaration by a leading Australian educator brings the issues clearly into focus. He says of education that

> the essential part of that task is that of fostering the development of individual boys and girls to the full extent of their powers. I believe that, as members of the profession, we must be eternally vigilant in maintaining this point of view. For we are rarely free from pressures that would bid us yield. There are those, for example, who look to the schools primarily as the means of improving the socio-economic future of their offspring. Again, never a month passes but we encounter the view that the justification of schools is the production . . . of industrial and professional workers. Within our own ranks [we commit] the error of thinking that examination results are ends in themselves. . . . [6]

This statement reminds us of Nunn's cardinal principle, to which reference will be made again later. The main point here is that there are possible alternatives to the goal I have stated, and Wyndham hints at some of these. We have already noted how Mannheim declares that the ultimate educational unit is not the individual but the group, stressing that youth are the most malleable in the hands of those who would build the democratic personality type. At a more mundane level Wyndham hints at parental ambitions, employer demands,

[6] H. S. Wyndham, "Presidential Address," in *Each to His Full Stature*, published for the Australian College of Education, Melbourne: F. W. Cheshire, 1965, p. 4.

Education and the Individual

and even teacher designs which threaten to violate children's rights to an education for mature personality. I am therefore bound to defend the priority of this goal.

Phenix's definition of education is especially acceptable in this context (it is "the process whereby persons intentionally guide the development of persons")[7] because, as he articulates it, the emphasis is on the sanctity and creativity of the individuals we are attempting to influence. Toward what goal are we guiding them? Various answers may be summarized as: social adjustment, economic efficiency, citizenship in the state, and membership in the church. Suppose that we give priority to "social adjustment." We find that personal values begin to be depressed, methods of conditioning and pressures to conformity are encouraged, and social relations themselves decline from dialogue between selves to the establishment of a pecking order amongst diplomats. Maritain makes this point very effectively.[8] If, however, the development of mature personality is made primary, then the dialogue which is a mark of spirit requires that we foster social relations and moral responsibility, and social adjustment enters in as a by-product.

With respect to "economic efficiency," the case has become even clearer in this day of accelerating technological change than it was in Marx's day. To force an individual's education along a particular vocational track because his abilities point in that general direction and society at the moment needs that specific skill is not only to trammel the individual now but to condemn him to future loss of usefulness because of the changing requirements of industry. If on the other hand the individual is fully developed, his chances of adapting to new vocational requirements are enhanced by his greater personal flexibility. "Citizenship in the state" is an aim that must be similarly subordinated, for the goose-stepping youths of Hitler's Germany were only the final shame in a process begun after Prussia's defeat at Jena in 1806, when state education was reorganized primarily according to this criterion.

---

[7] Philip H. Phenix, *Philosophy of Education*, New York: Holt, Rinehart and Winston, 1958, p. 13.
[8] Maritain, *Education at the Crossroads*, pp. 15f.

"Membership in the church" or in any other culturally important body is now seldom championed over and above education for mature personality, especially since Maritain and others have moderated the educational theory of the most authoritarian church by appeals to the personalism of Aquinas. Nevertheless it is still necessary to emphasize the higher goal because, for whatever good motives the other is pressed, it can very easily encourage indoctrinative pressures which defeat their own ends. Of all agencies the church stands to gain the most from selves who are free to choose responsibly.

The point was made that Wyndham's statement echoes the sentiments of Nunn, especially when the latter asserts:

> We shall stand throughout on the position that nothing good enters into the human world except in and through the free activities of individual men and women, and that educational practice must be shaped to accord with that truth.[9]

It is therefore advisable that I define my goal in such a way as to show how I stand in relation to the incipient individualism of Nunn. Difference arises from our views of the nature of the individual. As has already been said, the marks of spirit, especially dialogue, suggest that one's spiritual development occurs mostly in association with other selves. Therefore education for mature personality implies that we do provide for the development of the person in a social context, but do not make a coercive doctrine of "sociality" or cast aspersions on those who seek "privacy." Our stress will be not on how much the individual fits into the group but on how much he contributes to the group from personal reserves. Moral criteria of valuation will always outweigh social.

Nunn's proposition is probably overstated for emphasis, since he seems elsewhere to commend self-formation through group processes. It is surely as likely that something fresh will enter into the human world through group interaction as through individual creativity. This is not because the group stands higher than the individual but because the group is

[9] Nunn, *Education*, p. 12.

the recipient of the favors of individuals. Even thus does a complex technological society produce artifacts too intricate to have arisen in only one man's mind, though it is important to add that such gifts can only be expected to continue as long as the individuals involved are allowed and indeed encouraged to challenge party lines in their field of endeavor and beyond.

"Education for mature personality" suggests that there is an *end* or terminus to education, taken in one sense of the word, as well as aims for the educational process. I have already implied that my interest here is chiefly in that phase of education relating to the guidance of children towards mature adult personality, and that interest includes the belief that formal learning takes on a different character when the educand assumes full responsibility as an adult for his own further training and development. I have spoken of the educated man as one who consistently applies rational, moral, and religious criteria to his experiences. There is value in suggesting some desired outcomes that stem from norms of this kind.

The problem is how to state such educational objectives. Educational theorists owe much to Bloom and his associates for their two volumes classifying educational goals;[10] but despite the wise cautionary remarks in the explanatory chapters of both books, I take issue with their approach on three counts. The first is that the authors originally resolved to formulate objectives that would be descriptive of behavioral outcomes, since these lent themselves to the evaluative procedures of a social science. While this principle has proved very useful in studying the "cognitive domain," and will presumably be readily applicable to the motor side of the "psychomotor domain" if the authors produce the projected third volume, it breaks down in the "affective domain." It is not that psychology is unable to measure attitudes and beliefs, but that the self conscious unity of the person in his behavior

---

[10] Benjamin S. Bloom, ed., *Taxonomy of Educational Objectives: The Classification of Educational Goals. Handbook I: Cognitive Domain*, New York: David McKay, 1956; *Handbook II: Affective Domain*, by David R. Krathwohl *et al.*, London: Longmans, Green and Co., Ltd., 1964.

cannot be accommodated in the categories proposed. The authors speak of the "erosion of affective objectives" and suggest that this is not due only to difficulties of evaluation but has these other causes: the "public-private status of cognitive vs. affective behavior [which] is deeply rooted in the Judaeo-Christian religion"; slow attainment of affective goals compared with cognitive; a policy of "neutralism" in schools; and a stress in American life on public achievement. I surmise that some blame also falls on the influence of the rationalistic strand in philosophy which, since the Greeks, has overplayed the hand of objective reason and observation. Also, the affective domain is made to carry too diverse a load. There the authors include "receiving," "responding," "valuing," and organizing a value system and philosophy of life; that is, they lump together feeling, believing, and willing and divorce them equally from the cognitive domain.

Secondly, the behavioral approach obscures the distinction between the inner and the outer, for it is committed by its measurement criteria to the outer. For example, knowledge is all of the outer, and no regard is paid to knowledge of other selves in the personal sense indicated by Jeffreys' distinction between objective and subjective knowledge.[11] Or again, the moral sense seems to appear purely as a feeling tone because the inner life of spirit does not fit the classificatory schema.

Thirdly, the whole realm of "willing" or volition is subsumed under other categories, because it is apparently assumed that willing is doing, doing is outer, and the outer is what we measure. Thus the cognitive domain incorporates both intake and output of knowledge, the affective both receiving and responding. But willing is becoming as well as doing; it is creating and communing as well as psychomotor performance. The statement of educational objectives must be existential as well as behavioral; the criteria of evaluation, personal as well as quantitative.

[11] Jeffreys, *Mystery of Man*, p. 27. Note that he explicitly resists the equation of his terms "thinking" and "feeling" with "cognitive" and "affective."

I shall say that our educational objectives are to be grouped around the need of the person adequately to receive, process, and respond to the human environment.

"Receiving" is dependent largely on physical and biofunctional factors. Sensations are received, coming together at the threshold of consciousness as perceptions of facts. This minimal awareness is the first operation of spirit. We aim to enhance the reception of facts, and the basic tool is language. There are facts to receive relating to things, skills, values, and persons. Valuative facts include both propositional data and personal attitudes. Personal facts include both knowledge about (objective) and knowledge of (subjective) persons.

"Processing" is the inner response to the data received, and is dependent largely on spiritual factors, though organic alterations in chemical structure are probably the carriers of the process. The first movements of spirit are cognizing and appreciating—that is, the objective and subjective reactions of the transcendent self. Cognition involves comprehension, analysis, and synthesis. Appreciation involves attending to and liking or disliking. These primary inner movements are fused in "evaluation," [12] which involves weighing of all the facts, choosing on the basis of adequacy, and lastly becoming a subtly different self by virtue of their incorporation in the spiritual manifold, which is "integration" into be-ing.

Much of our educational effort will be expended on the inner functions I have just described, but measurement must be by overt response, and this will inevitably leave the essential self un-computed. At best the educator must rely upon personal acquaintance with the student to tell him how far he is getting with the true self of the learner.

"Responding" is the outer response to received and processed data; it is an act of the whole self, in which the spiritual infuses the behavioral. All the responses that we deem most significant for education are loaded with spirit, though our

[12] It will be seen that I am insisting that evaluation is an act of the self drawing on both objective and subjective criteria, a point which Bloom's taxonomy obscures.

quantitative and attitudinal tests deal only with behavior segments. Behavioral evaluation makes the outcomes appear as separately itemized behaviors in discrete categories, thus:

intellectual
physical
socioemotional
moral
religious
(et cetera)

In fact, however, all behavior segments are intertwined in a total behavioral response in which at any one time one component is uppermost, as in these diagrammatic examples:

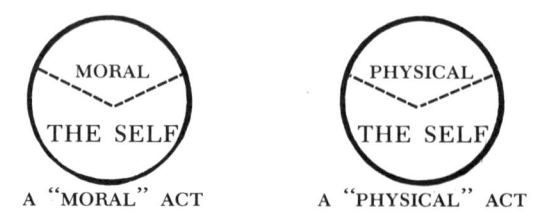

A "MORAL" ACT A "PHYSICAL" ACT

Truly human responses are more than immediate reflexes; they endow the satisfaction of immediate needs with the perspective of enduring purposes. A mature self responds not merely by putting to use but by improving use, by adding refined needs to original basic needs, and by personalizing the social situation.

Education and the Individual

Most stimulus-response models are too simple for human behavior because the intermediate stage of processing usually results in a response which transcends the stimulus and becomes an efficient cause in its own right. The spiritual marks transform what might otherwise be a biofunctionally determinate situation. Our responses tend to improve use, explore truth, create beauty, communicate love, and express faith — or to have the opposite effects. One is tempted to turn these verb phrases into imposing nouns — respectively: practice, science, art, morality, religion — except that, as so often happens, the noun forms obscure the functional nature of the phenomena.

Though indebted to Bloom and his associates, then, I have proposed a different basis for a taxonomy, on the ground that the nature of the individual is not adequately accommodated by their categories: cognitive, affective, psychomotor. I have also implied value loadings for experiences, something they were careful to avoid for good and sufficient reasons. There may, I have suggested, be value in attempting to order our educational objectives along the lines of the following schema:

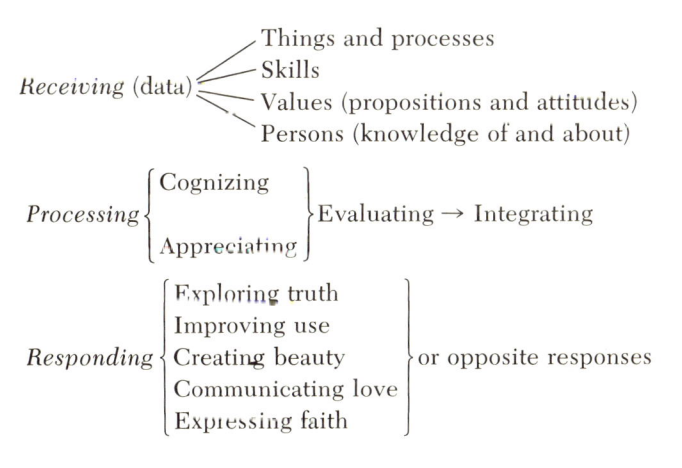

$$Receiving\ (data) \begin{cases} \text{Things and processes} \\ \text{Skills} \\ \text{Values (propositions and attitudes)} \\ \text{Persons (knowledge of and about)} \end{cases}$$

$$Processing \begin{cases} \text{Cognizing} \\ \text{Appreciating} \end{cases} \text{Evaluating} \rightarrow \text{Integrating}$$

$$Responding \begin{cases} \text{Exploring truth} \\ \text{Improving use} \\ \text{Creating beauty} \\ \text{Communicating love} \\ \text{Expressing faith} \end{cases} \text{or opposite responses}$$

CURRICULUM AND METHOD

Strictly speaking, "curriculum" encompasses all formal learning experiences, but for our present purpose it will be convenient to refer separately to the content of learning and the procedures of learning.

Any educational agency must exercise selection to determine the learning experiences in which it will seek to involve the pupils. In search for an organizing principle by which to govern this selection, I shall say that those materials which bear most directly on the distinctively human in the child's personal environment are to have priority. The meaning of this principle can be enlarged by criticism of two extreme cases.

The one is the "classical" curriculum which stresses literary knowledge from past (mainly Western) cultures, on the ground that the primary notions that govern man's spiritual life have been stated for all time. There is truth in this reasoning, but it is overshadowed by neglect of the child as a biofunctional entity and of his immediate environment. Not for nothing have Dewey and Whitehead caviled at "inert ideas."

At the opposite pole is the "scientific" curriculum, which exalts quantitative and empirical studies and in some cases introduces studies of considerable abstraction in very early years, on the ground that the explosion of scientific knowledge requires a stepping-up of the informational intake of children. The consequence is again, paradoxically, neglect of the child's immediate environment and of the existential side of his life. Scorn has been poured on the Soviet Union for its reversion ˋ a stringent academic approach in the late 1930s after a flirta- with Dewey; but post-Sputnik America tended the same ᾽loom found affective objectives ill defined and psycho- ᾽jectives virtually nonexistent—and that in the land

ɩp next the question of what are to be appropriate ᾽ans. One begins where the child is: in an ᴀre people are living together, probably nall way from technological devices but greatly concerned also with earning a living, with taking advantage of mass entertainment, and with maintaining family and wider social relationships, political allegiances, and religious affiliations. Even in a society strongly oriented to material objects, man is man and spiritual development is bound to occur, however warped it may become.

Some educational theorists suggest a criterion of "use" for the selection of human studies; but this begs the question "Useful for what?" and it also pitches education at the level of biofunctional means instead of spiritual goals. Others suggest the criterion of "truth," and Maritain leans in this direction; but in the education of children and youth this can easily lead into an intellectualist curriculum as it did for the medievals. "Socialization" has its supporters, but falls not only under the strictures of my comment in the previous section of this chapter, but also under the disability that when one focuses objectively on social relationships, those same relationships become self-consciously artificial. Group dynamics as an objective can only sustain fervor for learning when made for the most part incidental to other learnings.

Maritain's most promising suggestion is "meaning," as when he says: "We grasp the meaning of a science or an art when we understand its object, nature and scope, and the particular species of truth or beauty it discloses to us." [13] But it is Phenix who carries those notions forward into what he terms a philosophy of the curriculum for general education, based on "realms of meaning." [14] He contends that human beings "are essentially creatures who have the power to experience *meanings*. Distinctively human existence consists in a pattern of meanings." I find his view congenial because of his recognition of the many-sidedness of man, and because he anchors his description in the unifying idea of "meaning" — a spiritual criterion. In particular he criticizes the traditional idea that man is primarily a rational animal because "the life

[13] Maritain, "Thomistic Views on Education," p. 80.
[14] Phillip H. Phenix, *Realms of Meaning: A Philosophy of the Curriculum for General Education*, New York: McGraw-Hill Book Co., 1964.

of feeling, conscience, imagination, and other processes that are not rational in the strict sense are excluded by such a construction."

For Phenix, "meaning" performs the offices I have attributed to the marks of spirit, and therefore his proposals for curriculum organization are of special interest. It is not my province to attempt excursions into the specialized field of curriculum theory, but the following specification of the realms of meaning and their associated fields of study, abstracted from Phenix's book (pp. 18f.), appears promising:

Realms of Meaning	Disciplines
Symbolics	Ordinary language, mathematics, non-discursive symbolic forms
Empirics	Physical sciences, life sciences, psychology, social sciences
Esthetics	Music, visual arts, arts of movement, literature
Synnoetics (personal knowledge)	Philosophy, psychology, literature, religion, in their existential aspects
Ethics (moral knowledge)	The varied special areas of moral and ethical concern
Synoptics	History, religion, philosophy

Phenix goes on to stress the need to develop our professional expertise in synnoetics and ethics, suggesting that "academic man" has taught us to feel reasonably secure in the other areas but to neglect these.

Concerning teaching procedures, discussion ranges in the modern day from the "operant conditioning" of the pioneer of programmed instruction—B. F. Skinner [15]—to the *I–Thou* interaction theory of Buber. It is apparent that when the decision has been taken on what studies are to be pursued, it is then mainly for educational psychology and sociology to determine the methods appropriate both to the subject and the

[15] See the helpful summary of what Skinner's ideological assumptions amount to in Mary Jane Aschner, "The Planned Man: Skinner," in Nash, *The Educated Man*, pp. 389–421.

child at various stages of his development. But there is an imperative need, frequently pointed up in these pages, for the social sciences to take account of all the data, both inner and outer, and to check more carefully the philosophical presuppositions that govern their theoretical framework.[16] All teaching methods are ways of "guiding" the child, but not all possible ways will be always or equally admissible. Skinnerian conditioning will be admissible for some kinds of learning, particularly for lower orders of psychomotor functions and even for some cognitive learnings; but if made focal in the total learning situation such conditioning will violate the right of the child to develop in distinctively human ways. What is necessary here is not to try to invent new ways of teaching, but to suggest how to weight the value of those that are or will be known so that a principle is available.

Methods must be evaluated not only by their psychosocial efficiency but by the degree to which they invoke the spiritual capacities of the child. It is a question not so much of excluding certain low-level methods—rote learning, crude conditioning, physical punishment—as of giving higher priority to certain other procedures. Speaking generally, one should expect to find considerable attention being given to setting up social matrices, nurturing personal relationships, encouraging creative art and play, and challenging students to think logically and critically. Opportunities for individual excellence will vie with situations where the student is encouraged to give loyalty and service to the group, applying his learnings in responsible conduct toward others. The breadth of learning experiences here implied suggests both that the "school" as it is understood today cannot be held responsible for doing the

[16] See also G. W. Allport on psychology, referred to in the opening chapter, and his "psycholinguistic trifle" in which he shows that terms which represent man as a reactor to stimuli are five times as numerous in the technical vocabulary of psychologists as those implying that he is an initiator of action. Note Rogers' rebuttal of Skinner on this same point: "A prior subjective value choice is necessary for any scientific endeavor, or for any application of scientific knowledge." Carl B. Rogers and B. F. Skinner, "Some Issues Concerning the Control of Human Behavior," in *The Self in Growth Teaching, and Learning: Selected Readings*, ed. Don E. Hamachek, Englewood Cliffs, N.J.: Prentice-Hall, 1965, p. 107.

whole job, and that the school has perhaps become too omnipresent in educational theory.

The teacher, on any view, must be one who understands and exemplifies the values and goals of the educational process. On the one hand there have been psychologically deficient persons who entered the teaching profession unconsciously seeking compensation of their own lacks through the dominance and absorption of immature psyches, whether by winsome or violent devices. Such excess of subjectivity produces crippled persons; it has been partly eradicated by more effective selection, supervision, and school rules. On the other hand there are many teachers, themselves products of a literary-academic training, who have responded to modern pressures for a scientific-academic curriculum by setting their sights on good results in examinations and assuming neutrality toward moral and social side effects. Such excess of objectivity also produces crippled persons, not all of them low-IQ rejects of the system.

The need is for teachers who are in themselves mature personalities, capable of mingling subjectivity and objectivity in their attitude to learners and the learning experience, encouraged by administration through clearly stated objectives and appropriate procedures. Buber's portrait of the teacher who nurtures with love and pain the developing self within each child, yet keeps sufficient subjective distance so as not to overwhelm him, has yet to be bettered, though it could have been expanded to accommodate group relationships. And Maritain's point must be recalled: that if the child is to acquire convictions he must not only engage in cognitive learnings about them but see in the teacher an example of someone with convictions. The tendency in present public school systems is to concentrate on academic development, though that itself is only part of learning to live rationally, and to skirt almost entirely, due to a mistaken policy of "neutrality," guidance in moral choice and religious integration. I shall return to this point under the heading "Education and Values."

AGENCIES AND ADMINISTRATION

It is not enough to consider the education of the child only in terms of the formal school situation. Our locus of concern requires that I investigate also the responsibilities of other agencies which attempt to guide the development of children.

The danger inherent in professionalization of teaching is a tendency to arrogate to the school all the functions of education and to speak mostly in disparaging terms of other agencies, particularly the home. Yet even in impoverished home environments there is usually a recognition at some level of the worth of the individual, an acceptance of him as a person prior to any accounting of his abilities or achievements, which outstrips the attention that any other agency can offer. After a period when the school has been credited with extraordinary powers and prerogatives of child-molding, we are becoming aware, through research [17] and the very limitations of our schools in practice, that the vision was illusory. This is the rock on which totalitarianism from Plato to the Chinese communal experiment founders, and it is a problem to which educational planning must give far more attention than hitherto. The home is the place where the firmest lines are laid in the personality toward good or evil, and on a realistic view moral problems begin here.

The implication of these remarks is not, however, that increasing formalization of home educational influences is desirable; the genius of the family is precisely the casual interaction that occurs, the acceptance of the child-self not for what he achieves but for what and who he is, and the spontaneous dialogue of persons. It has already been remarked that socialization suffers from formalization and explicit structuring; nevertheless these are necessary as rationality develops, and the home and voluntary agencies in the community are essential supplements to anything the school achieves in this respect. What is being implied, therefore, is a strengthen-

---

[17] Such as, for example, Frank Musgrove's iconoclastic *The Family, Education and Society*, London: Routledge and Kegan Paul, 1966.

ing of the community image of family, together with promotion of opportunities for parents to confer with and assist people involved in the formal school situation. The school is limited by size and circumstances in the amount of remedial attention it can give to selves who have been violated spiritually in earlier years. The enthusiasm with which some publicists of the public or private school recommend the extension of their responsibilities beyond what now obtains in advanced countries is to be treated with sober caution.

For similar reasons the contribution of voluntary agencies should be investigated more systematically. Diversity of subgroups within a culture is held by most democratic theorists, especially those who take human sinfulness seriously, to be a strength of free society, particularly if there is considerable overlap of group memberships, as Maritain advises. This not only gives free play to the diverse interests of human beings and encourages constructive criticism but also shields the individual from envelopment by impersonal monoliths. Educationally, the strength of voluntary agencies is precisely that they are voluntary; the person may exercise choice in his allegiance and acceptance of responsibilities, and fulfill the promptings of spirit in his own unique way. Uncoerced, he may even be expected, I suggest, to seek out those who can help him to answer questions of meaning, purpose, and redemption; but it may well be questioned whether churches, viewed by many as custodians of religious insights, have not suffered from the identification they have often sought with governmental and formal educational agencies, where a certain benevolent coercion or compulsion is unavoidable. Supremely in religion, of all human concerns, indoctrination in a coercive and conditioning sense defeats its own ends. For the same reasons, church schools would be advised to investigate whether, having acquired control over a certain body of students, they have not lost the good will and allegiance of many through overzealous prescription and limitation of learning experiences, at the expense of opportunities for voluntary response to the attitudes they have sought to develop.

It is often forgotten what substantial educational agencies the mass entertainment media are. Proposals regarding censorship invariably meet with some kind of opposition—the ridicule of aesthetes and academics, the anxiety of assorted democrats to protect their various freedoms, the moral outrage of idealists inadequately informed about human sinfulness. The extreme situation that is tending to obtain today is one in which private entrepreneurs are given nearly free rein to exercise their own brand of conditioning purely for monetary gain. The supposedly protective diversity to which this is said to give rise is in fact a depressing uniformity, appealing to the demonic, the brutal, and the superficial. It may well be that the remedy lies not in the widening of the state's police powers (which would substitute the devil for the deep blue sea) but in the enriching of community resources for cultural life, in pressures brought to bear by lively voluntary bodies, and in the establishment of public trusts to administer such media in place of the commercial ownership whose criterion of value is ultimately the purse of the shareholder.

Returning to the school, one observes that one of its major functions is usually held to be the promotion of those learnings which contribute to a common citizenship. All schools are conducted on behalf of sponsoring bodies and are primarily answerable to their sponsors for what is done. The private school answers to the owner, who hopes that the curriculum he offers will appeal to a certain kind of cash customer. The church school is answerable to its denomination to contribute to the continuance of a consenting membership. The state or community school is answerable to its particular democratic community to produce a consenting member of a pluralistic society. The sanctity of the individual provides a principle which, translated into goals and process aims as we have done, should bring to all three types of school an impressive unity concerning objectives and procedures. Unfortunately, what unity is presently observable in many schools must be attributed to an academic curriculum buttressed by external testing services, and in human terms the wastage of spirit is tragic.

A special example of the application of our principle is in

school management. A trend towards bigness in schools has been justified as a means towards diversification of curriculum offering. Such diversification is well within our specifications; but bigness promotes depersonalization and mass handling unless great care is taken to create intimate groups within the larger school community. I would suggest that until our social theory catches up with our technological theory, most schools with more than, say, a thousand pupils are almost certainly too big for the education of persons.

Furthermore, education for mature personality implies a co-operative relation between staff and students, as well as student participation in school planning and administration. The latter is unlikely to work if there is not at a higher level staff participation in the educational policy-making of the school. The autocratic model of headmastering is especially dangerous, for not only may incapable incumbents stultify the operation of the school, but suppression of professional initiatives of the staff may dam up spiritual energies that will overflow only too readily in disruptive ways. Trends in the theory of administration away from a "scientific management" model to a "human relations" approach are to be welcomed, though they have not gone far enough if they only lead to diplomatic expediency in administrator behavior, as opposed to leadership displaying respect for persons and personal integrity.[18]

It would be attractive to digress into an examination of the effect of big school systems on the kind of education available to children in a school within such a system. Studies such as Whyte's *Organization Man* are making us aware of the degree to which bureaucratic structure can take over the executives within it and seduce them into dehumanizing responses. I must hope, however, that enough has been said here to indicate that this large field of controversy is also open to the application at various points of our principle.

In sum, education for mature personality must be conceived as a project larger than the school, to which the family and

[18] See my "Social Science and the Study of Leadership," *Australian Journal of Education*, vol. 8, June 1964, pp. 111–117.

Education and the Individual

voluntary agencies contribute — the family because it lays the foundation for existential self-acceptance or rejection, voluntary agencies because they provide opportunities for genuine choosing according to personal interest and need. By the formal learning experiences structured in the school environment the child may be helped to make intelligent commitments in the wider society. The school neither can nor should be neutral in relation to the major concerns of community life.

EDUCATION AND VALUES

Of all learnings, those which pose the greatest problems for the administrator of a state school relate to the education of values in respect of such controversial areas of life as morals, politics, and religion. The easy way out is to leave such concerns to the family and voluntary agencies, and this was the policy adopted during the nineteenth century in many countries where comprehensive state systems were first being established, church-state relations were acrimonious, and secular ideologies were at their most brash. Amidst the sober reassessments of the recent postwar period, however, the myth of neutrality has been exploded, and it has been recognized that the pervasiveness of personal and spiritual intercourse amongst humans, and especially between teacher and pupil, makes it impossible for a school to sit loose to ideological viewpoints.

On what I shall call the Secularist view, education is the business of imparting known facts and developing the skill of critical enquiry into beliefs that are built on disputed facts. Hence one seeks to inculcate not a point of view but a method of approach to all views.[19] The teacher must therefore adopt toward controversial issues (i.e., most of the distinctively human concerns) a posture of strict impartiality, or even of complete neutrality, as some advocate.

[19] Note that, since the facts least in dispute are those of the natural sciences, it is very possible that a materialistic view may in fact be inculcated by this supposedly detached approach.

Regarding neutrality indicated by the absence of any mention, it must be said that omission is itself the implicit indoctrination of a viewpoint—the view that such matters are unimportant to the real business of living. Furthermore, neutrality can itself become a philosophy of life, encouraging detachment and aloofness from personal interaction and obligation.

The less extreme Secularist posture is impartiality. On this view the teacher must strive to present both sides of the argument without weighting or even revealing his own personal position. Such counsel ignores the power of human dialogue, whereby a thousand personal cues acquaint children with teacher attitudes and convictions whether or not a word has been spoken; and it also ignores the opportunity that so false a situation gives to the evil man. One must be deeply suspicious of the man who claims he is able to be completely impartial, since in practice the most honest form of impartial teaching is likely to be the encouragement of discussion about values by a teacher who admits his partiality in the matter but is able and careful to allow the pupils to view it as one of the contributions to their discussion rather than as a covert conclusion they will be required to reach. This calls for that maturity in the teacher to which I have already referred, and requires that the teacher discipline himself to suffer dissent and deal gently with error in such a way that the child continues to be accepted by him as a person, an individual with worth.

The Secularist view itself is not impartial. Aims of critical enquiry and rational detachment are desirable ones, but to promote them above all others can lead to betrayal of the marks of spirit, especially in respect of commitment, creativity, and communion.

The term of opprobrium leveled at much moral, political, and religious instruction is "indoctrination," and its sting is the implication that the sanctity of the individual is being impugned. Observe Good's definition:

> In the broadest sense, the attempt to inculcate beliefs, a possible concomitant of any learning situation; in narrower terms, the

attempt to fix in the learning mind any doctrine, social, political, economic or religious to the exclusion of all contrary doctrines, and in a manner preventing serious comparison and evaluation.[20]

It appears that here we have a neat discrimination between two uses of the term. However, the word "inculcate" in the first definition literally means "to tread into," which is suggestively stronger than "fix in the learning mind" in the second. The pivotal word in the second definition is "exclusion," but this makes the issue too black and white, for as Andersen's study of ideological education argues,[21] this is a necessary concomitant of any learning situation, particularly in the earlier years of a child's education. Not only must we at all times exercise selection of curriculum content, making value judgments as well as empirical ones about what to include and exclude, but the young child has a primary need for personal integration in terms of an authoritative value system. Actually, then, the gap disappears. There is but one process, differing only in degree, depending firstly on the developmental stage the child has reached and secondly on the convictions the teacher holds concerning the person he is educating. All education of values is indoctrination; indoctrination may be educative or miseducative; and the only safeguards sufficient to prevent the latter are, I believe, to have as goal the education for mature personality recommended in this study, and to evaluate our teaching procedures constantly in the light of the principle of the sanctity of the individual.[22]

As Phenix has pointed out by his classification of meanings,

---

[20] Carter V. Good, ed., *Dictionary of Education*, New York: McGraw-Hill, 1959, p. 285.

[21] Andersen, *Ideological Education*, pp. 60-98.

[22] I have not attempted to trace the debate on "indoctrination" through the continually growing literature on it, since my assignment has been to show the relevance of the principle we have been examining to this debate. However, I commend in particular to the reader interested in this issue the articles on "Objectivity and Neutrality in Public Education" in *Melbourne Studies in Education, 1963*, ed. E. L. French, London: Melbourne University Press, 1964, pp. 3-82; and Brian S. Crittenden, "Teaching Educating and Indoctrinating," *Educational Theory*, vol. 18, 1968, pp. 237-252.

synnoetics, which has to do with the existential aspects of spiritual life, is to be distinguished from ethics and synoptics. The subjective and the objective are both relevant, and there is a cognitive content to the education of values, though that is not all there is to it. This is where Niebuhr improves on Buber, for Buber neglects the historical deposit by which the self's choices in the present are modified. Innate spiritual responses pass through meanings developed by civilized man, and though bodies of knowledge do not constitute the normative imperatives, they clothe them. In particular, what cognitive content should appear in the curriculum of the public school? Again, a detailed answer does not belong here, but in the light of our principle one may suggest that the administrator should obtain a mandate from his sponsors by some machinery of consensus which does not neglect his own staff, and also work towards the involvement of senior students in designing courses for the later levels of high school. Maritain has provided many useful seed thoughts for such an operation in his discussion of the "democratic charter."

It is not only inevitable but desirable that the teacher go beyond a dead-pan recital of and aloof detachment from the facts he presents. Learning involves the arousal of the emotions and the wooing of the will (the technical jargon for it is "motivation") as well as the extension of the mind. This is more and not less true of the education of ideological values. The point is not whether to utilize such powers of "guidance" or not, but how far to employ them. Personal example is the greatest power at the teacher's command, and I have spoken earlier of the dual need for a teacher who lives out his convictions and at the same time can accept and not penalize the child who rejects them, not lose respect for that child's unique worth or fairness in assessing his educational progress. Group pressures are another power he possesses, and the greater the unity within the sponsoring body the greater is the temptation to envelop the learner in an authoritarian environment, deferring for him the maturing existential moments when he consults genuine alternatives and takes his own personal stand. Hence a fine balance is to be sought between the provision of information about moral and religious ideas dominant in the child's environments (initially the local, later the wider ones) and the provision of opportunity for the student to examine critically even the views of respected elders and come to the point of choosing for himself. It is probable that the time at which such adjustments and choices become increasingly autonomous is the period including the middle and upper years of high school — the time of adolescence.

The nub of my argument is that the difficulties faced by curriculum planners and teachers in respect of the education of values in public schools cannot be skirted by a supposed neutrality or separation from experiences in other areas of school study and life. Such concerns are central to spiritual and therefore personal development. Indoctrination and education as processes cannot be neatly distinguished from each other; therefore ultimately only the goals and values of school and teacher can ensure that a proper balance is maintained between curricular prescription and personal option.

A CONCLUDING WORD

I do not pretend to have reviewed the whole field of human studies or to have constructed a complete educational theory. The task undertaken was the much narrower one of taking one value judgment, suspected of being basic to Western ideology, and demonstrating that it could be so defined as to provide normative guidelines for educational theory at many points. I may be permitted to hope that the attempt will help to mitigate man's inhumanity to children.

BIBLIOGRAPHY

As an aid to readers who may wish to follow up particular aspects of this study or certain of the ideologists with whom it deals, the following bibliographies are provided:

A. *Primary References:* Consulted works by the ten thinkers studied.
B. *Secondary References:* Other books and articles consulted with reference to the ten thinkers.
C. *Selected General References:* A few general works relating to the field of this study.

A. PRIMARY REFERENCES

Martin Buber

Between Man and Man. Trans. Ronald Gregor Smith, 1947. Reprinted London: Fontana, 1961.

Eclipse of God. London: Victor Gollancz, 1953.

For the Sake of Heaven. Trans. Ludwig Lewisohn. New York: Meridian Books, 1958.

Good and Evil: Two Interpretations. New York: Charles Scribner's Sons, 1952.

I and Thou. Trans. Ronald Gregor Smith. New York: Charles Scribner's Sons, 2nd ed., 1958.

The Knowledge of Man. Trans. Maurice Friedman and Ronald Gregor Smith. London: George Allen and Unwin, 1965.

Paths in Utopia. Trans. R. F. C. Hull. London: Routledge and Kegan Paul, 1949.

Pointing the Way: Collected Essays. Trans. Maurice Friedman. London: Routledge and Kegan Paul, 1957.
The Writings of Martin Buber. Ed. Will Herberg. New York: Meridian Books, 1956.

John Dewey

A Common Faith. New Haven: Yale University Press, 1934.
Democracy and Education. New York: Macmillan, 1916.
Educational Essays. Ed. J. J. Findlay. London: Blackie, 1910.
Experience and Education. New York: Macmillan, 1938.
"From Absolutism to Experimentalism." In *Contemporary American Philosophy*, vol. 2. Ed. G. P. Adams and W. P. Montague. New York: Macmillan, 1930.
How We Think. Boston: Heath and Co., 1910.
Human Nature and Conduct: An Introduction to Social Psychology. London: George Allen and Unwin, 1921.
The Influence of Darwin on Philosophy and Other Essays in Contemporary Thought. London: Bell and Sons, 1910.
"The Philosophy of Whitehead." In *The Philosophy of Alfred North Whitehead.* Ed. Paul Arthur Schilpp. Evanston: Northwestern University, 1941.
Problems of Men. New York: Philosophical Library, 1946.
"Reply." In *The Philosophy of John Dewey.* Ed. Paul Arthur Schilpp. Evanston: Northwestern University, 1939.
Reconstruction in Philosophy. 1919. Reprinted New York: Mentor, 1950.
Ethics (with James H. Tufts). New York: Henry Holt and Co., 1908.

Søren Kierkegaard

The Concept of Dread: A Simple Psychological Deliberation Oriented in the Direction of the Dogmatic Problem of Original Sin, by Vigilius Haufniensis. Trans. Walter Lowrie. London: Oxford University Press, 1946.
Concluding Unscientific Postscript to the Philosophical Fragments. Trans. David F. Swenson and Walter Lowrie. London: Oxford University Press, 1945.
The Journals of Søren Kierkegaard: A Selection. Ed. and trans. Alexander Dru. London: Fontana, 1958.
The Point of View for My Work as an Author. . . . Trans. Walter Lowrie. London: Oxford University Press, 1939.

The Present Age and Of the Difference Between a Genius and an Apostle. Trans. Alexander Dru. London: Fontana, 1962.
Purity of Heart Is to Will One Thing. Trans. Douglas V. Steere. New York: Harper and Bros., 1956.
The Sickness Unto Death. Trans. Walter Lowrie. Princeton: Princeton University Press, 1941.
Works of Love: Some Christian Reflections in the Form of Discourses. Trans. Howard and Edna Long. London: Collins, 1962.

Karl Mannheim
Diagnosis of Our Time. London: Kegan Paul, 1943.
Essays on Sociology and Social Psychology. Ed. Paul Kecskemeti. London: Routledge and Kegan Paul, 1953.
Freedom, Power and Democratic Planning. Ed. Hans Gerth and Ernest K. Bramstedt. London: Routledge and Kegan Paul, 1951.
Ideology and Utopia: An Introduction to the Sociology of Knowledge. Trans. Louis Wirth and Edward Shils. New York: Harcourt, Brace and Co., n.d.
Man and Society: In an Age of Reconstruction. London: Kegan Paul, 1940.
Systematic Sociology: An Introduction to the Study of Society. Ed. J. S. Erös and W. A. C. Stewart. London: Routledge and Kegan Paul, 1957.

Jacques Maritain
The Degrees of Knowledge. Trans. Bernard Wall. London: Geoffrey Bles, 1937.
Education at the Crossroads. New Haven: Yale University Press, 1943.
The Education of Man. Ed. Donald and Idella Gallagher. New York: Doubleday, 1962.
Existence and the Existent. Trans. Lewis Galantiere and Gerald B. Phelan. New York: Doubleday Image Books, 1961.
Man and the State. Chicago: University of Chicago Press, 1951.
"On Some Typical Aspects of Christian Education." In *The Christian Idea of Education.* Ed. Edmund Fuller. New Haven: Yale University Press, 1957, 173–212.
The Person and the Common Good. Trans. John J. Fitzgerald. New York: Charles Scribner's Sons, 1947.

The Range of Reason. London: Geoffrey Bles, 1953.
The Rights of Man and Natural Law. London: Geoffrey Bles, 1958.
St. Thomas Aquinas. 1930. Trans. Joseph W. Evans and Peter O'Reilly. New York: Meridian Books, 1958.
Scholasticism and Politics. Ed. Mortimer Adler. London: Geoffrey Bles, 1940.
"Thomistic Views on Education." In N.S.S.E. 54th Yearbook, *Modern Philosophies and Education.* Chicago: University of Chicago, 1955.
True Humanism. Trans. M. R. Adamson. London: Geoffrey Bles, 1939.

Karl Marx

Capital: A Critical Analysis of Capitalist Production. Trans. Samuel Moore and Edward Aveling. Ed. Friedrich Engels. London: William Glaisher, 1912. (This is the first volume.)
The Poverty of Philosophy. London: Martin Lawrence, n.d.
Selected Works. New York: International Publishers, n.d.
The German Ideology: Parts I and III (with Friedrich Engels). Ed. R. Pascal. London: Lawrence and Wishart, 1938.
Manifesto of the Communist Party (with Friedrich Engels). New York: International Publishers, 1937.

Reinhold Niebuhr

The Godly and the Ungodly: Essays on the Religious and Secular Dimensions of Modern Life. London: Faber and Faber, 1958.
An Interpretation of Christian Ethics. London: SCM Press, 3rd ed., 1941.
Moral Man and Immoral Society. London: Charles Scribner's Sons, 1942.
The Nature and Destiny of Man: A Christian Interpretation, I: Human Nature. London: Nisbet and Co., 1941.
The Nature and Destiny of Man: A Christian Interpretation, II: Human Destiny. London: Nisbet and Co., 1943.
Reflections on the End of an Era. New York: Charles Scribner's Sons, 1934.
The Self and the Dramas of History. London: Faber and Faber, 1956.
"The Two Sources of Western Culture." In *The Christian Idea*

of Education. Ed. Edmund Fuller. New Haven: Yale University Press, 1957.

Friedrich Nietzsche
The Complete Works of Friedrich Nietzsche. Ed. Dr. Oscar Levy. New York: Russell and Russell, 1964. Volumes consulted most particularly are indicated by an asterisk:

    I. Birth of Tragedy.
    II. Early Greek Philosophy.
    III. Future of Educational Institutions.
    IV. Thoughts Out of Season. i.
    V. Thoughts Out of Season. ii.
    VI. All too human. i.
    VII. All-too-human. ii.
    VIII. Case of Wagner.
    IX. Dawn of Day.
    X. * Joyful Wisdom.
    XI. * Zarathustra.
    XII. * Beyond Good and Evil.
    XIII. * Genealogy of Morals.
    XIV. * Will to Power. i.
    XV. * Will to Power. ii.
    XVI. Twilight of the Idols.
    XVII. * Ecce Homo.
    XVIII. Index.

Nietzsche: Unpublished Letters. Trans. and ed. Karl F. Leidecker. London: Peter Owen, 1959.

T. P. Nunn
"The Aims and Achievements of Scientific Method." *Proceedings of the Aristotelian Society,* New Series, 6, 1905–1906 (New York: Johnson Reprint Corporation, 1963), 141–182.
"Animism and the Doctrine of Energy." *Proceedings of the Aristotelian Society,* New Series, 12, 1911–1912, 25–64.
Education: Its Data and First Principles. London: Edward Arnold, 3rd ed., 1945.
"On Causal Explanation." *Proceedings of the Aristotelian Society,* New Series, 7, 1906–1907 (New York: Johnson Reprint Corporation, 1963), 50–80.

Alfred North Whitehead
  Adventures of Ideas. Harmondsworth, Middlesex: Penguin Books, 1948.
  The Aims of Education. London: Ernest Benn, 1932, reprinted 1959.
  Dialogues of Alfred North Whitehead. Ed. Lucien Price. New York: Mentor Books, 1954.
  Essays in Science and Philosophy. New York: Philosophical Library, 1948.
  Modes of Thought. Cambridge: Cambridge University Press, 1938.
  Process and Reality: An Essay in Cosmology. Cambridge: Cambridge University Press, 1929.
  Religion in the Making. Cambridge: Cambridge University Press, 1927.
  Science and the Modern World. New York: Mentor Books, 1958.

B. SECONDARY REFERENCES

Where titles do not suggest the ideologists under discussion, their names follow the reference in parentheses.

Abraham, Gerald. *Nietzsche.* London: Duckworth, 1933.
Adams, G. P., and W. P. Montague, eds. *Contemporary American Philosophy*, vol. 2. New York: Macmillan, 1930. (Dewey)
Allport, Gordon W. "Dewey's Individual and Social Psychology." In *The Philosophy of John Dewey.* Ed. Paul Arthur Schilpp. Evanston: Northwestern University, 1939.
Babbage, Stuart Barton. *Man in Nature and Grace.* Grand Rapids, Michigan: Eerdmans, 1957. (Kierkegaard, Nietzsche, Marx).
Baker, Melvin C. *Foundations of John Dewey's Educational Theory.* New York: King's Crown Press, 1955.
Bantock, G. H. *Freedom and Authority in Education.* London: Faber and Faber, 1952. (Mannheim)
Beales, A. C. F. "Jacques Maritain." In *The Function of Teaching.* Ed. A. V. Judges. London: Faber and Faber, 1959.
Bennett, John C. "Reinhold Niebuhr's Social Ethics." In *Reinhold Niebuhr.* Eds. Charles W. Kegley and Robert W. Bretall. New York: Macmillan, 1956.
Bennis, Warren G.; Benne, Kenneth D.; and Robert Chin, eds. *The*

Planning of Change: Readings in the Applied Behavioral Sciences. New York: Holt, Rinehart and Winston, 1961. (Mannheim)

Berlin, I. *Karl Marx: His Life and Environment.* London: Thornton Butterworth, 1939.

Brameld, Theodore. *Toward a Reconstructed Philosophy of Education.* New York: Holt, Rinehart and Winston, 1956. (Dewey, Mannheim)

Bretall, Robert, ed. *A Kierkegaard Anthology.* London: Oxford University Press, 1947.

Broudy, Harry S. "Actual Entities and the Learning Process." *Educational Theory,* 11, Oct. 1961, 217-227. (Whitehead)

———. "Book Review: I. B. Berkson, *The Ideal and the Community.*" *Educational Theory,* 9, Jan. 1959, 62-64. (Dewey)

Brunner, Emil. "The Message of Søren Kierkegaard." *Neue Schweizer Rundschau,* 38, 1930, 84-89. Trans. H. Dymale, typescript in author's possession.

———. "Some Remarks on Reinhold Niebuhr's Work as a Christian Thinker." In *Reinhold Niebuhr.* Eds. Charles W. Kegley and Robert W. Bretall. New York: Macmillan, 1956.

Buber, Martin, article on, in the week of his death, in *Time* magazine, June 25, 1965.

Burnett, Joe R. "Alfred North Whitehead (1861-1947)." *Educational Theory,* 11, Oct. 1961, 193.

———. "Whitehead on the Aims of Schooling." *Educational Theory,* 11, Oct. 1961, 269-278.

Campbell, Hugh. "Tension in the Planners: Karl Mannheim." *Australian Journal of Education,* 2, July 1958, 114-119.

Carnell, Edward John. *The Theology of Reinhold Niebuhr.* Grand Rapids, Michigan: Eerdmans, 1960.

Childs, John L. "John Dewey." *Educational Theory,* 4, July 1954, 183-186.

Clarke, F. *Freedom in the Educative Society.* London: University of London Press, 1948. (Mannheim)

Cohen, Robert S. "On the Marxist Philosophy of Education." In N.S.S.E., 54th Yearbook, part I: *Modern Philosophies and Education.* Chicago: University of Chicago Press, 1955.

Collins, James. *A History of Modern European Philosophy.* Milwaukee: Bruce Publishing Company, 1956. (Kierkegaard, Nietzsche, Marx)

Commission of the C.C. of the C.P.S.U. (B) *History of the Com munist Party of the Soviet Union (Bolsheviks)*. Sydney: Current Book Distributors, Australian Education, 1942.

Comte, Auguste. "The Positive Philosophy." In *Man and the Universe: The Philosophers of Science*. Eds. Saxe Commins and Robert N. Linscott. New York: Modern Pocket Library, 1954. (Compared with Nietzsche)

Copleston, Frederick. *Friedrich Nietzsche: Philosopher of Culture*. London: Burns Oates and Washbourne, 1942.

Crane, A. R. "A. S. Makarenko and Russian Educational Thought." *Australian Journal of Education*, 7, June 1963, 107–121.

———. "The Educational Thought of Martin Buber." *Australian Journal of Education*, 5, July 1961, 91–99.

Crosser, Paul K. *The Nihilism of John Dewey*. New York: Philosophical Library, 1955.

Curtis, S. J. *An Introduction to the Philosophy of Education*. London: University Tutorial Press, 1958. (Dewey, Nunn, Mannheim, Buber)

———, and M. E. A. Boultwood. *A Short History of Educational Ideas*. London: University Tutorial Press, 4th ed., 1965. (Dewey, Nunn, Mannheim, Buber)

Dewey, John. "The Philosophy of Whitehead." In *The Philosophy of Alfred North Whitehead*. Ed. Paul Arthur Schilpp. Evanston: Northwestern University, 1941, 641–663.

Diamond, Malcolm. *Martin Buber: Jewish Existentialist*. New York: Oxford University Press, 1960.

Djilas, Milovan. *The New Class: An Analysis of the Communist System*. London: Thames and Hudson, 1958.

Erös, John. "Book Review: Jaques J. Maquet, *The Sociology of Knowledge*." *The British Journal of Sociology*, 3, 1952, 184–185. (Mannheim)

"Existentialism and Education: A Collaborative Essay." *Educational Theory*, 2, Apr. 1952, 80–91. (Kierkegaard)

Floud, Jean. "Karl Mannheim." In *The Function of Teaching*. Ed. A. V. Judges. London: Faber and Faber, 1959.

Frankena, William K. *Philosophy of Education*. New York: Macmillan, 1965. (Dewey, Whitehead, Maritain)

Friedman, Maurice. "The Existential Man: Buber." In *The Educated Man*. Ed. Paul Nash *et al*. New York: John Wiley and Sons, 1965.

———. "Martin Buber's Philosophy of Education." *Educational Theory*, 6, April 1956, 95–104.

―――. *Martin Buber: The Life of Dialogue.* New York: Harper and Bros., 1960.
Fuller, Edmund, ed. *The Christian Idea of Education.* New Haven: Yale University Press, 1957. (Maritain, Niebuhr)
Goheen, John. "Whitehead's Theory of Value." In *The Philosophy of Alfred North Whitehead.* Ed. Paul Arthur Schilpp. Evanston: Northwestern University, 1941.
Harland, Gordon. *The Thought of Reinhold Niebuhr.* New York: Oxford University Press, 1960.
Heinemann, F. H. *Existentialism and the Modern Predicament.* London: Adam and Charles Black, 1953. (Kierkegaard, Nietzsche)
Herberg, Will, ed. *Four Existentialist Theologians.* New York: Doubleday, 1958. (Maritain, Buber)
―――. "Reinhold Niebuhr." In *Encyclopaedia Britannica*, 1963.
Hill, Brian V. "A Dash of Existentialism." *The Forum of Education*, 24, Sept. 1965, 105–114. (Kierkegaard, Nietzsche)
Hollingdale, R. J. *Nietzsche: The Man and His Philosophy.* London: Routledge and Kegan Paul, 1965.
Holmes, Brian. "The Reflective Man: Dewey." In *The Educated Man.* Ed. Paul Nash *et al.* New York: John Wiley and Sons, 1965.
Holmes, Henry W. "Whitehead's Views on Education." In *The Philosophy of Alfred North Whitehead.* Ed. Paul Arthur Schilpp. Evanston: Northwestern University, 1941.
Hook, Sidney. *From Hegel to Marx: Studies in the Intellectual Development of Karl Marx.* London: Victor Gollancz, 1936.
Horne, Herman H. *The Democratic Philosophy of Education.* New York: Macmillan, 1935. (Dewey)
Hullfish, Gordon H., and Philip G. Smith. *Reflective Thinking: The Method of Education.* New York: Dodd Mead and Co., 1961. (Dewey)
Hunt, George L., ed. *Ten Makers of Modern Protestant Thought.* New York: Associated Press, 1958. (Kierkegaard, Buber, Niebuhr)
Jeffreys, M. V. C. "Existentialism." In *Education and the Philosophic Mind.* Ed. A. V. Judges. London: Harrap and Co., 1957. (Kierkegaard, Buber)
―――. *Glaucon: An Inquiry into the Aims of Education.* London: Pitman, 1955. (Niebuhr)
―――. *Mystery of Man.* London: Pitman, 1957. (Kierkegaard, Buber, Niebuhr)

———. *Personal Values in the Modern World.* Harmondsworth, Middlesex: Penguin Books, 1962. (Niebuhr)
Judges, A. V. "Martin Buber." In *The Function of Teaching.* Ed. A. V. Judges. London: Faber and Faber, 1959.
Kaufmann, Walter, ed. *Existentialism: From Dostoevsky to Sartre.* New York: Meridian Books, 1956. (Kierkegaard, Nietzsche)
———. *The Owl and The Nightingale: From Shakespeare to Existentialism.* London: Faber and Faber, 1959. (Kierkegaard, Nietzsche)
Kegley, Charles W., and Robert W. Bretall, eds. *Reinhold Niebuhr: His Religious, Social and Political Thought.* Vol. 2 of the Library of Living Theology. New York: Macmillan, 1956.
Kneller, George F. "Education, Knowledge and the Problem of Existence." *Harvard Educational Review,* 31, Fall 1961. (Buber)
———. *Existentialism and Education.* New York: Philosophical Library, 1958. (Kierkegaard, Buber)
Koo, Gladys Y. "The Structure and Process of Self." *Educational Theory,* 14, Apr. 1964, 111–117. (Buber)
Kroner, Richard. "The Historical Roots of Niebuhr's Thought." In *Reinhold Niebuhr.* Eds. Charles W. Kegley and Robert W. Bretall. New York: Macmillan, 1956.
Laski, Harold J. *Communist Manifesto: Socialist Landmark.* London: George Allen and Unwin, 1959.
Lawson, W. "Neo-Thomism." In *Education and the Philosophic Mind.* Ed. A. V. Judges. London: Harrap and Co., 1957, 43–59. (Maritain)
Lea, F. A. *The Tragic Philosopher: A Study of Friedrich Nietzsche.* London: Methuen and Co., 1957.
Lilge, Fred. "John Dewey in Retrospect: An American Reconsideration." *British Journal of Educational Studies,* 8, May 1960, 99–111.
Lindsay, Jack. *Marxism and Contemporary Science: or, The Fullness of Life.* London: Denis Dobson, 1949.
Lindsay, Lord. "Book Review: Karl Mannheim, *Freedom, Power and Democratic Planning.*" *The British Journal of Sociology,* 3, 1952, 85–86.
Lowe, Victor. "The Development of Whitehead's Philosophy." In *The Philosophy of Alfred North Whitehead.* Ed. Paul Arthur Schilpp. Evanston: Northwestern University, 1941.
Löwith, Karl. *From Hegel to Nietzsche: the Revolution in Nineteenth-century Thought.* Trans. David E. Green. London: Constable, 1964. (Kierkegaard, Nietzsche, Marx)

Lowrie, Walter. *Kierkegaard.* 2 vols. New York: Harper and Bros., 1962.

McCallister, W. J. *The Growth of Freedom in Education: A Critical Interpretation of Some Historical Views.* London: Constable and Co., 1931. (Dewey, Nunn)

McDougall, William. *An Outline of Psychology.* London: Methuen and Co., 7th ed., 1936. (Nunn)

Martin, C. V. "The Metaphysical Development of John Dewey." *Educational Theory,* 8, Jan. 1958, 55-57.

Martin, William Oliver. "Whitehead's Philosophy as the Ideology of Consensus Theory." *Educational Theory,* 8, Jan. 1958, 1-7.

Mehring, Franz. *Karl Marx: The Story of His Life.* Trans. Edward Fitzgerald. London: George Allen and Unwin, 1948.

Millard, Richard M. "Whitehead's Aesthetic Perspective." *Educational Theory,* 11, Oct. 1961, 255-268.

Morris, Bertram. "The Art-Process and the Aesthetic Fact in Whitehead's Philosophy." In *The Philosophy of Alfred North Whitehead.* Ed. Paul Arthur Schilpp. Evanston: Northwestern University, 1941.

Morris, Van Cleve. "Existentialism and the Education of Twentieth Century Man." *Educational Theory,* 11, Jan. 1961, 52-60. (Kierkegaard, Nietzsche)

Nash, Paul; Kazamias, Andreas M.; and Henry J. Perkinson, eds. *The Educated Man: Studies in the History of Educational Thought.* New York: John Wiley and Sons, 1965. (Marx, Dewey, Buber)

Needham, Joseph. "A Biologist's View of Whitehead's Philosophy." In *The Philosophy of Alfred North Whitehead.* Ed. Paul Arthur Schilpp. Evanston: Northwestern University, 1941.

Newbury, Dorothy J. "A Note on 'The Metaphysical Development of John Dewey.'" *Educational Theory,* 8, July 1958, 186-187.

Niblett, W. R. "On Existentialism and Education." *British Journal of Educational Studies,* 2, May 1954, 101-111. (Kierkegaard, Nietzsche)

Northrop, F. S. C. "Whitehead's Philosophy of Science." In *The Philosophy of Alfred North Whitehead.* Ed. Paul Arthur Schilpp. Evanston: Northwestern University, 1941.

Nyberg, Paul. "The Communal Man: Marx." In *The Educated Man.* Ed. Paul Nash *et al.* New York: John Wiley and Sons, 1965.

Oldham, J. H. *Florence Allshorn: and the Story of St. Julian's.* London: SCM Press, 1959. (Mannheim)

Parson, Howard L. "God and Man's Achievement of Identity: Religion in the Thought of Alfred North Whitehead." *Educational Theory*, 11, Oct. 1961, 228-254.

Popper, Karl R. *The Poverty of Historicism*. London: Routledge and Kegan Paul, 1957. (Marx, Mannheim)

Ramsey, Paul. "Love and Law." In *Reinhold Niebuhr*. Eds. Charles W. Kegley and Robert W. Bretall. New York: Macmillan, 1956.

Randall, John Herman Jr. "Dewey's Interpretation of the History of Philosophy." In *The Philosophy of John Dewey*. Ed. Paul Arthur Schilpp. Evanston: Northwestern University, 1939.

Ratner, Joseph. "Dewey's Conception of Philosophy." In *The Philosophy of John Dewey*. Ed. Paul Arthur Schilpp. Evanston: Northwestern University, 1939.

——, ed. *Intelligence in the Modern World: John Dewey's Philosophy*, New York: Random House Inc., 1939.

Reyburn, H. A., et al. *Nietzsche: The Story of a Human Philosopher*. London: Macmillan, 1948.

Roberts, David E. *Existentialism and Religious Belief*. New York: Galaxy Books, 1959. (Kierkegaard)

Robertson, R. E. "John Dewey and the Given." *Educational Theory*, 8, July 1958, 182-185.

Rohde, Peter. *Søren Kierkegaard: An Introduction to His Life and Philosophy*. Trans. Alan Moray Williams. London: George Allen and Unwin, 1963.

Roubiczek, Paul. *Existentialism: For and Against*. Cambridge: Cambridge University Press, 1964. (Kierkegaard, Nietzsche)

Rusk, Robert R. *The Doctrines of Great Educators*. London: Macmillan, 2nd ed., 1957. (Dewey)

——. *The Philosophical Bases of Education*. London: University of London Press, 1929. (Nunn)

Russell, Bertrand. "Dewey's New Logic." In *The Philosophy of John Dewey*. Ed. Paul Arthur Schilpp. Evanston: Northwestern University, 1939.

Santayana, George. "Dewey's Naturalistic Metaphysics." In *The Philosophy of John Dewey*. Ed. Paul Arthur Schilpp. Evanston: Northwestern University, 1939.

Savery, William. "The Significance of Dewey's Philosophy." In *The Philosophy of John Dewey*. Ed. Paul Arthur Schilpp. Evanston: Northwestern University, 1939.

Schilpp, Paul Arthur, ed. *The Philosophy of John Dewey*. The Library of Living Philosophers, vol. 1. Evanston: Northwestern University, 1939.

——, ed. *The Philosophy of Alfred North Whitehead*. The Library

of Living Philosophers, vol. 3. Evanston: Northwestern University, 1941.
———. "Whitehead's Moral Philosophy." In *The Philosophy of Alfred North Whitehead*. Ed. Paul Arthur Schilpp. Evanston: Northwestern University, 1941.
Schlesinger, Arthur. "Reinhold Niebuhr's Role in American Political Thought and Life." In *Reinhold Niebuhr*. Eds. Charles W. Kegley and Robert W. Bretall. New York: Macmillan, 1956.
Schlesinger, Rudolph. *Marx: His Time and Ours*. London: Routledge and Kegan Paul, 1950.
Scott, Nathan A. Jr. *Reinhold Niebuhr*. Minneapolis: University of Minnesota Press, 1963.
Sellars, Roy Wood. "Philosophy of Organism and Physical Realism." In *The Philosophy of Alfred North Whitehead*. Ed. Paul Arthur Schilpp. Evanston: Northwestern University, 1941.
Stace, W. T. *The Philosophy of Hegel: A Systematic Exposition*. New York: Dover Publications, 1955.
Stewart, W. A. C. "Karl Mannheim and the Sociology of Education." *British Journal of Educational Studies*, 1, May 1953, 99–113.
Story, M. L. "Dewey and Niebuhr: A Brief Juxtaposition." *Educational Theory*, 3, Apr. 1953, 182–184.
Strain, John Paul. "An Answer to the Misconceptions of John Dewey's Philosophy of Education." *Educational Theory*, 8, Oct. 1958, 269–274.
Swenson, David F. *Something About Kierkegaard*. Minneapolis: Augsburg Publishing House, rev. ed., 1956.
Thomas, J. Heywood. *Subjectivity and Paradox*. Oxford: Basil Blackwell, 1957. (Kierkegaard)
Tibble, J. W. "Sir Percy Nunn: 1870–1944." *British Journal of Educational Studies*, 10, Nov. 1961, 58–75.
Urban, Wilbur. "Whitehead's Philosophy of Language and Its Relation to His Metaphysics." In *The Philosophy of Alfred North Whitehead*. Ed. Paul Arthur Schilpp. Evanston: Northwestern University, 1941.
Wegener, Frank C. "Alfred N. Whitehead: an Implied Philosophy of School and Society." *Educational Theory*, 11, Oct. 1961, 194–208.
———. "The Ten Basic Functions of Man." *Educational Theory*, 5, Apr. 1955, 110–117. (Whitehead)
Wieman, Henry Nelson. "A Religious Naturalist Looks at Reinhold Niebuhr." In *Reinhold Niebuhr*. Eds. Charles W. Kegley and Robert W. Bretall. New York: Macmillan, 1956.
Wild, John. "Education and Human Society: a Realistic View." In

N.S.S.E., 54th Yearbook: *Modern Philosophies and Education.* Chicago: University of Chicago Press, 1955. (Nunn)

Winetrout, Kenneth. "Buber: Philosopher of the I-Thou Dialogue." *Educational Theory,* 13, Jan. 1963, 53-57.

Wirth, Arthur G. "John Dewey in Transition from Religious Idealism to the Social Ethic of Democracy." *History of Education Quarterly,* 5, Dec. 1965, 264-268.

Wolf, William John. "Reinhold Niebuhr's Doctrine of Man." In *Reinhold Niebuhr.* Eds. Charles W. Kegley and Robert W. Bretall. New York: Macmillan, 1956.

Wylie, Joyce F. "Education and Planning for Freedom: a Discussion of the Views of Karl Mannheim." *Australian Journal of Education,* 1, Apr. 1957, 21-25.

C. SELECTED GENERAL REFERENCES

Andersen, W. E. *Ideological Education.* Unpublished M.Ed. thesis which was awarded a university medal in the University of Sydney, 1965.

Committee on the Objectives of a General Education. *General Education in a Free Society.* Cambridge, Mass.: Harvard University Press, 1945.

Judges, A. V., ed. *Education and the Philosophic Mind.* London: Harrap, 1957.

———. *The Function of Teaching: Seven Approaches to Purposes, Tradition and Environment.* London: Faber and Faber, 1959.

Nash, Paul; Kazamias, Andreas M.; and Henry J. Perkinson, eds. *The Educated Man: Studies in the History of Educational Thought.* New York: John Wiley and Sons, 1965.

National Society for the Study of Education. 54th Yearbook, Part I: *Modern Philosophies and Education.* Chicago: University of Chicago Press, 1955.

Peters, R. S. *Ethics and Education.* London: George Allen and Unwin, 1966.

Phenix, Philip H. *Philosophy of Education.* New York: Holt, Rinehart and Winston, 1958.

———. *Realms of Meaning: A Philosophy of the Curriculum for General Education.* New York: McGraw-Hill Book Co., 1964.

Wynne, John P. *Theories of Education.* New York: Harper and Row, 1963.

SUBJECT INDEX

absolutes, absolutism 47, 78, 93, 94, 103-104, 106, 110, 110n, 122, 131, 134, 142, 166, 234, 239
actual entities, actual occasions 152-158, 172
adult education 184
adventure 151, 156-157, 160, 176, 263
aesthetic education 162, 176-177, 254
aesthetic man 27, 32, 90, 134, 289
aesthetics 161, 166, 169, 172, 176, 204, 242, 254, 265, 270, 284
aims of education 89, 92-93, 104, 114, 119, 121, 132, 138, 146-147, 173-174, 176-177, 245, 246, 247, 248-249, 259, 267, 270, 271-281
analysis, modern philosophical vi, 10, 33, 35, 35n, 185, 197, 199
animals 26, 47, 48, 49, 64, 67, 69, 90, 91, 101, 134, 154, 171, 186, 189, 190, 207, 226, 260, 262
anxiety 229, 231, 265, 267
Aristotelian Society 87, 88, 151-152
art 46, 159, 161-162, 165, 169-170. *See also* aesthetics
asceticism 52-53, 108
atheism 44, 195, 211, 214
autonomy, personal 16, 34, 51, 54, 80, 122, 163, 187, 251, 270, 295

baptism 211
beauty 161, 177, 281
behaviorism x, 90, 101-103, 106, 135, 226, 227, 246, 277, 200
between, realm of (Buber) 190-191

Bible, the 35, 184, 185, 201, 224, 235, 238, 239
bourgeoisie 67, 69-71, 85, 214, 223, 228, 236, 237
Buddhism 160

capitalism 62, 66, 70, 74, 77, 107, 117, 200, 236
Cartesianism 35, 49n, 77, 155, 163, 207-208. *See also* Descartes in Name Index
categoreal scheme (Whitehead) 152-156
Catholic. *See* Roman Catholic
censorship 289
change. *See* social change
character 266, 270, 272, 273
choice, choosing 29, 31, 32, 81, 105, 244, 265, 266, 269, 276, 288, 294. *See also* freedom
Christendom 4, 13, 37, 45, 213, 214
Christian, –ity, – faith, – gospel 37, 43-44, 46-48, 50, 51-53, 53n, 71, 71n, 77-82, 94, 99-100, 104, 109-111, 118, 158, 160, 177, 181, 185, 197, 207, 210, 213, 214, 223, 225, 229, 232, 234, 237, 253, 278
Christian Socialism 71n, 222
church, –es 25, 37, 38, 204, 210, 214, 216-217, 238, 250, 276, 288
church schools 288, 289
classics in education 176, 251, 282
classless society 66, 69, 74-75, 78, 81, 173, 237
cognition, cognitive 30, 155, 156, 158, 161, 277, 279, 285, 286, 294.

311

cognition, cognitive (cont.)
    See also reason, rationalism; rationality; thinking
collectivism, –ity 3, 62, 73, 75, 81, 167, 193, 194, 198, 200, 201, 215, 216, 234, 235, 237, 244, 254
communion 247, 265, 266, 292
Communism, Communist party 60, 61, 67n, 72, 72n, 74, 75, 107, 145, 237
Communist League, the 60
community 198, 200, 201, 216, 244, 245, 249, 253, 254, 288, 289. See also group
conditioning 248, 275, 288, 289; operant – 284-285
connaturality, knowledge through (Maritain) 212
conscience 47, 142, 227, 235, 270
consciousness, human 26, 28, 49, 50, 63, 64, 65, 68, 78-81, 88, 90, 93, 134, 137, 155-158, 170, 189, 193, 209, 226, 227, 231, 234, 238, 243, 270, 279. See also self-identity
consensus ix, 114, 218, 294
Constitution of the U.S.A. 158, 213
conversion, religious 34, 81, 105, 109-110, 195, 230-231
creativity 7, 50, 54, 72, 91, 102, 106, 119, 147, 154, 156, 158, 161, 162, 163, 164, 167, 172, 249, 263-265, 267, 273, 276-277, 285, 292
crowd. See herd, the human
cultural lag 228, 233
curriculum x, 114, 121-122, 123, 149, 174, 175, 219, 248, 249, 254, 273-274, 282-286, 290

death, awareness of 29, 35, 187
democracy, –atic ix, 13, 51, 70, 99, 104, 106, 110, 111, 113, 115, 118, 119, 132, 138, 140, 141-144, 141n, 146, 160, 165, 167, 172, 174, 211, 214, 215, 218, 219, 236, 237, 238, 249, 258, 288, 289; education for – 259.
democratic charter (Maritain) 215, 218, 250, 294
despair, dread 28, 32, 34-35, 193, 203, 267

determinism, social – 62, 65, 66, 69, 70, 90-91, 94, 101, 105-106, 109, 140, 143, 154, 193, 228, 233, 253, 268
dialectical theology 224, 239, 241
dialogue vi, 186, 191, 192, 194, 195, 197, 198, 199, 223, 227, 240, 243, 246, 254, 264-270, 273, 275, 276, 287, 292
discipline, classroom – 174, 176, 292
dissent, deviancy, heretic 106, 108, 110, 115, 120, 145, 216-217, 227, 237, 239, 247, 277, 292
distancing (Buber) 189-192, 243
distinctively human, the 259, 261, 267, 269, 270, 282, 283, 291
dread. See despair
dualism 135-136, 153, 155-158, 163, 171, 173, 207, 209, 230, 243, 262

economic factor 64-66, 68, 78-79, 100, 105, 159-160, 163, 165, 193, 215, 222, 234, 237, 289
educational agencies 282, 287-291. See also schooling, mass media
educational theories ix, x, 4, 8-12; Nunn 121-122; Mannheim 122-124; Dewey 173-177; Whitehead 173, 176-177; Buber 245-248; Maritain 248-252; Niebuhr 245, 252-253; Jeffreys 253-254; Hill 259, 270, 271-295
Educational Theory 152
education of values 291-295. See also moral education
elitism 50, 51, 52-54, 55, 56-58, 67, 71n, 75, 78-82, 105, 114, 116, 123, 143, 172, 228, 233
endurance, as a category 153-156, 262-263, 270, 273
Enlightenment, the 13, 37, 158, 213, 223, 235, 237, 252
equality 51, 54, 232
Essentialism 7
eternal objects (Whitehead) 156, 158, 166, 170
eternal recurrence (Nietzsche) 45, 46, 53
eternal Thou (Buber) 189, 194

Subject Index

ethical dimension, the 27, 35, 71, 79, 81-82, 93-94, 161, 162, 165, 177, 195, 235, 239, 242, 251, 269, 270, 284, 294. *See also* morals
evil 31, 52, 54, 162, 166, 196, 208, 211, 228, 229, 231, 237, 238, 242, 244, 254, 265, 266, 270, 292
evolution, –ary theories 48-50, 78, 135, 141, 142n, 150, 154, 156, 162, 165, 166-167, 170, 172, 193
existentialism x, 14, 25, 25n, 29, 32, 35n, 36, 45, 77-78, 81-82, 153, 181, 184, 186, 188, 192, 197, 198, 201, 205, 206, 206n, 209, 212, 224, 227, 239, 242, 243, 244, 265, 266, 273, 284, 294
existential psychology 195, 224
experience v, 137, 139, 147, 156, 162, 166, 169, 171, 173-174, 177, 186-187, 188, 194, 199, 207, 212, 226, 229, 234, 242
Experimentalism 5-7, 129, 131, 132, 139, 144, 146, 147, 148

faith, religious 25, 210, 211, 281
fallen man. *See* sin, original
family 71, 73, 109, 215-216, 226, 283, 287, 290-291; – and education 250
Fascism, Nazism 45, 57, 82, 98, 103, 104, 107, 142, 145, 184, 214, 247, 275
feeling 161, 177, 188, 193, 212; education of – 253
forgiveness 71, 232
freedom, human 29-31, 47, 49, 66-69, 75, 78, 91, 98, 104, 105-106, 107-108, 109, 114, 115-116, 120, 123, 140, 146, 157, 158, 159-160, 163, 164, 167, 176, 193, 207, 208, 209, 210, 211, 213 214, 227 228, 242, 246, 251, 253, 258, 265, 270, 274, 276

general education 253, 283-284
God 28, 32, 34, 42, 44, 48, 71, 80-82, 110, 160, 162, 166, 170, 189, 192, 194-196, 206-207, 208, 210, 214, 217, 218, 225, 226-231, 234, 242
goodness, innate – 95, 95n, 161-162, 177

good, the 48, 52, 91, 162, 166, 196, 228, 238, 254
good, the common 217, 218, 244
grace, divine 207, 210, 211, 213
"great books" course 251
great society, the 39, 95n, 107, 112, 119, 194, 201, 244
Greek legacy 4, 46, 47, 48, 82, 136, 143, 158, 162, 207, 208, 225, 226, 227, 229, 252, 263, 278
group, the 38, 107, 114, 123, 124, 139, 144, 145, 164, 197, 235, 239, 264, 274, 276, 285, 286, 288, 290; group pressures 294
guilt, – feelings 197, 229, 232

habits 135, 137, 177, 246, 266, 269
hallowing of the everyday (Buber) 184, 194
Harvard Report on General Education in a Free Society 253
Hasidism 181, 183-185
Hegelian, –ism 5, 9, 14, 24, 25, 29, 32, 33, 43, 47, 50, 60, 77, 129, 130, 135, 140
Hegelians, The Young 60
Herbartian, National – Society 5, 131, 174
herd, the human 25, 50, 51, 54, 93, 195, 197
heretic. *See* dissent
historicism 73-75, 114n, 116, 237
history 13, 32, 43, 52, 63, 66, 69, 73, 78, 100, 153, 160, 165, 170, 175, 176, 193, 199, 223, 231, 233, 235, 244, 250, 265, 268, 294
hope 210
horme (Nunn) 87, 90-91
humanism, liberal – 12, 13, 42, 94, 170, 211, 238, 267; scientific – 12, 181, 214; true – (Maritain) 211-215
humanitarian ideal 158
humanities, the 149, 152, 249, 250, 253, 268

Idealism 4, 14, 43, 63, 71, 78, 88, 92, 92n, 129, 130, 152, 189, 225, 267, 289
ideological education 247, 251, 252, 291-295

ideology vii, x, 7, 7n, 8-12, 41, 61, 64-66, 69, 73, 82, 85, 96, 98, 100, 100n, 102, 104, 105, 106, 113, 117, 120, 133, 140, 145, 147, 151, 158, 159, 163, 167, 169, 173, 174, 175, 181, 193, 198, 206, 215, 221, 223, 237, 238, 239, 242, 252, 257, 259, 272, 274, 291
I–It (Buber) 186-192, 194-195, 199, 201, 208, 242, 246-247, 264, 270
imagination 151, 249
I–Me (Mead) 191, 191n
immortality 166, 172
impartiality 292
individual, defining the human 16; Kierkegaard 25-32; Nietzsche 46-51; Marx 62-69; Nunn 89-92; Mannheim 100-107; Dewey 134-141, 144; Whitehead 152-158; Buber 186-192; Maritain 206-211; Niebuhr 224-232; Jeffreys 253; Hill 259-270
individual differences 121, 163
individualism 51, 62, 85, 89, 94, 107, 140, 142, 144, 146, 159, 163, 167, 170, 193, 198, 214, 223, 228, 236, 254, 276
individuality, –ization 16, 93, 95, 109, 116, 119, 123, 137, 139, 156-158, 172, 191-192, 208-209, 225, 226, 248, 285
indoctrination 124, 252, 276, 288, 292
industrialization 3, 13, 62, 69, 107, 112, 139, 142, 150, 158, 159-160, 222, 232, 236, 239
inert ideas (Whitehead) 176, 282
informal education 130
Instrumentalism 133, 136, 143, 145, 171, 175
intellectual, –ism 31, 136, 251, 283
intelligence, human 133, 135, 137, 138-140, 141, 142, 146, 147, 174, 205, 208, 212, 219, 269. *See also* thinking; consciousness
interhuman (Buber) 197-198
International Working-Men's Association 61, 75
interregnum, the revolutionary 72, 74

I–Thou (Buber) 109, 186-192, 194-197, 199, 200, 208, 242, 245, 264, 270, 284

joy 44, 57, 162
Judaism 46, 52-53, 52n, 55, 77, 81, 82, 164, 181, 182-185, 197, 200, 207, 252, 278
justice 70, 138, 165, 216, 217, 232, 235, 237
justitia originalis (Niebuhr) 230

kvuza and kibbutz 200

labor. *See* work
language, human 158, 263, 279
League for Independent Political Action 222
learner, the 245, 286, 287
learning 174, 176-177, 248, 285-286, 293, 294
liberal, –ism 51, 72n, 95n, 97, 99, 106, 107-110, 113, 117, 119, 121, 138, 140, 148, 159, 164, 176, 181, 184, 222, 223, 224, 229, 231, 232, 234, 236, 237
liberal education 175, 176, 249-250
liberty. *See* freedom, human
life (Whitehead) 154
love 35, 38, 53, 81, 94, 196n, 197, 207, 208, 210, 217, 218, 223, 230n, 235, 240, 243, 247, 253, 254, 281
lust 229
Lutheranism 23, 224

Machiavellianism 217, 239
Manu, Laws of 56
Marxism (Dialectical Materialism) 13, 61-62, 64, 67n, 68-69, 75n, 80, 82, 98, 103, 142, 173, 214, 222, 234, 236, 237
mass media 3, 114, 283, 289
Materialism, Dialectical. *See* Marxism
maturation 269-270
meaning, realms of (Phenix) 283-284, 294
mediation (*vide* Dewey) 141, 141n
medieval, Middle Ages 4, 52-53, 107, 164, 205, 213, 214, 283

Subject Index

memory 90-91, 134, 155, 189, 227, 261-263
mentality. *See* thinking
Methodists, the 158
mind 16, 48, 91, 120, 135-137, 152, 155-157, 207, 219, 225, 225n, 229, 238, 243
moral education 81, 93, 162, 176, 177, 218, 246, 249-252, 253-254, 276, 287, 291-295
moral law. *See* natural law
morals, –ity, – sense 43-45, 47, 48, 51-54, 69, 70, 77, 80-82, 91, 107, 112, 122, 139, 140, 143, 148, 163, 165, 172, 177, 194, 195-197, 209, 212, 217, 234, 235, 251, 254, 268, 273, 278, 280
motivation 294

naturalism 14, 92, 92n, 120, 134, 162, 173, 225-226, 266, 273
naturalistic (culturalistic) fallacy 119, 243
natural law, natural order 32, 67, 90, 153, 211-213, 230, 269
Nazism. *See* Fascism
neutrality, moral 12-13, 147, 174, 214, 250, 251, 252, 260, 278, 286, 291-295
nexus (Whitehead) 153-154

objectivity, academic , scientific – 25, 29, 42, 47-48, 99, 101, 145, 148, 186, 187, 188, 191, 206, 233, 241, 263, 265, 278, 286, 292, 294
open-mindedness 143
organism, organic theories 49, 90-91, 119, 134-141, 145, 149, 151, 151n, 152, 153, 154, 160, 166-167, 170, 177, 181, 208, 226, 261
original sin. *See* sin, original
originator instinct (Buber) 246

pacifism 165, 222, 235
Paris Commune, the 1870 71-72, 72n
peace 166, 217, 238
person, –al development 16, 106, 152, 157, 191-192, 193, 195, 196-198, 197-198, 206-211, 214, 217, 241, 243, 244, 245, 246-248, 251, 272, 277, 287, 290, 292. *See also* individuality
personalism (Maritain) 215-219
personality 32, 65, 66, 103, 104, 106, 108, 110, 115-116, 120, 194, 208-210, 228, 229, 230, 242, 252, 263, 270, 274-275, 287
personality, education for mature (Hill) 274-275, 276, 277, 290, 293
personal order (Whitehead) 154-157, 167
personal relationships 3, 37, 73, 81, 108-110, 118, 186-192, 244, 247, 285
persuasion 158, 164, 167, 192
philosophers v, 47, 63, 69, 77, 106, 127, 132, 134, 152, 165, 170-171, 188, 189, 204, 228, 244, 252; – of education x, 6-12
philosophia perennis (Maritain) 205, 210
philosophical anthropology 26, 185, 186, 187, 194, 198, 241
play 285
pluralism ix, 215-219, 250, 251, 289
positivism 43, 44, 47, 75, 78, 89, 100, 120, 203, 205, 251
power, as a social principle 235, 236, 237, 239
Pragmatism 6, 13, 88, 102, 117, 132, 136, 142, 145, 146, 151n, 170, 174, 205, 218, 248-249, 250. *See also* Experimentalism
press, the 37
privacy 108-109, 276
private property 159, 163-164
problem-solving 135-137, 144, 169, 176
procedural principles (Peters) 272
processing, human (Hill) 279, 281
Progressive Education Association 6
Progressivism 6, 121, 122, 131, 133, 175, 247
proletariat 61, 67, 70, 71, 74
propaganda 247, 248, 252
Protestantism 81, 104, 105, 107, 108, 129, 184, 203, 213, 221, 222, 223, 224, 225

psychotherapy 197
punishment 285

racism 214
rationality 4, 155-158, 160, 170, 173, 177, 249, 287
rational religion 160
Realism, New –, Neo– 7, 80, 87, 88, 89, 94n, 117, 145, 151, 151n, 152, 153, 209, 211
reason, rationalism 14, 36, 43, 50, 63, 72, 77, 91, 102, 104, 105, 108, 135, 145, 170, 177, 203, 205, 207, 209, 210, 212, 213, 214, 226, 227, 229, 230, 238, 249, 252, 263, 267, 270, 278, 283-284
receiving, human (Hill) 279
reconstructionism 123, 145-146, 174
redemption 253, 267, 268, 270
reflection. *See* cognition, consciousness, thinking
reflective thinking (Hullfish and Smith) 175
Reformation, the 24, 53, 78, 181, 213, 222, 224, 229, 230, 233, 238, 239
relation, world of (Buber) 186, 189, 194
relationism (Mannheim) 101, 118
relativism 14, 78, 101, 104, 118, 131, 138, 145, 152, 170, 172, 238, 251
relativity 150, 153
religion 27, 30, 34, 35, 37, 54, 60, 64, 69, 70, 71, 77, 78, 90, 93, 99, 104, 108-111, 114, 132-133, 142, 148, 150, 156-157, 159, 160, 165, 170, 177, 181, 184, 194, 195, 201, 212-213, 227, 232, 238, 239, 242, 251, 265-268, 281, 284, 288
religious education 242, 251, 291-295
Renaissance, the 53, 213, 228, 231, 233, 234, 236, 238
responding, human (Hill) 279-280
responsibility 32, 37, 57, 65, 110, 143, 147, 160, 195, 218, 229, 245, 246, 253, 254, 269, 274, 275, 288
rhythm in education (Whitehead) 176

rights of man 211, 213, 215, 258
Roman Catholic 7, 15, 181, 184, 203, 210, 211, 215, 216, 230, 231, 238, 248

sanctity of the individual vi, ix, x, 77, 79, 177, 287, 289, 290, 292, 293, 294; defined 15; Kierkegaard 33-36; Nietzsche 51-54; Marx 69-73, 75; Nunn 92-96; Mannheim 107-111; Dewey 119, 121, 141-144, 148; Whitehead 158-162, 167; Buber 192-198; Maritain 207, 211-215, 219; Niebuhr 232-235, 238, 239, 252; Hill 257-270
scale (Whitehead) 165
schooling, public – 6-7, 121, 147, 173-175, 248-250, 251, 274, 275, 286, 287-291, 294; – administration 289-291
science, scientific method 15, 27-28, 46, 65, 73-75, 78-79, 88, 90, 116, 118, 120, 127, 139-140, 142, 144, 145, 150, 151, 152, 159, 160, 164, 165, 169, 171, 173, 175, 181, 186, 187, 192-193, 198-199, 209, 212, 228, 233, 241, 242, 244, 265, 268; scientific curriculum 282
scientific humanism. *See* humanism, scientific
Scientific Movement in Education, the 5-6
secular, –ization, –ism 132, 142, 181, 214, 215, 223, 232, 234, 237, 291; – education 249
self, – identity 16, 26, 31, 46, 49, 66, 68, 91, 94, 115-116, 117, 119-120, 134, 135, 137, 140, 156-158, 177, 187, 191, 194, 210, 211, 225n, 226, 227, 229, 230, 231, 234, 243, 245, 261-270, 276, 277, 279, 286, 287, 291. *See also* consciousness
sin, sin consciousness 28, 31, 47, 207, 222, 225, 228, 229, 230-232, 234, 239, 243-244, 253, 265, 266-267, 270, 288, 289
sin, original 95n, 210, 211, 212, 224, 229
social change 13, 63, 68, 74, 80, 95,

98, 111, 114, 115-116, 120, 123, 134, 172
social education 113, 114, 122, 174, 233, 247, 283
socialism 51, 60, 74, 146, 194, 199-200, 222, 232, 234, 236, 239
Socialists, the True 60, 63, 71
social planning 59, 74-75, 80, 98, 101, 103, 106, 107-111, 112-116, 118, 145-147; – through education 123
social science 6, 11, 62, 63, 73-75, 85, 100, 112, 114-116, 117-121, 197-198, 232-233, 234, 252, 259, 260-261, 268, 285
societies, enduring (Whitehead) 153-158, 166-167
society, as discussed by Kierkegaard 36-39; Nietzsche 54-58; Marx 73-75; Nunn 92, 94-95; Mannheim 111-116; Dewey 139, 142-144, 144-148; Whitehead 163-167; Buber 197-201; Maritain 215-219; Niebuhr 235-240
society, the great. *See* great society
sociologism (Maritain) 248
sociology of knowledge, the (Mannheim) 98-99, 100-101, 105, 106, 117, 118, 146
sorrow 162
soul, human 46-48, 50, 81, 135, 156-158, 190-191, 193, 196, 207, 208, 209, 225, 225n, 230, 231, 243, 248, 249
spirit, –ual 16, 26, 30, 34, 48, 63, 109, 114, 130, 135, 147, 148, 160, 163, 193, 208, 216, 225n, 226, 227, 228, 230, 231, 234, 242, 243, 278, 279, 283, 288, 294
spirit, marks of (Hill) 261-270, 273, 276, 281, 284, 292
state, the (political) 47, 67, 69, 164, 167, 200, 214, 215-217, 219, 237, 289. *See also* society, as discussed . . .
Student Christian Association 130
style (Whitehead) 161
subjectivity, –ism 25, 34, 34n, 35, 72, 77-78, 81, 103, 187, 206, 209, 241, 262, 265, 278, 286, 294

subject matter in curriculum 175, 268, 282-284
superman, the (Nietzsche) 49, 53, 57
synnoetics, synoptics (Phenix) 284, 294

taxonomies of educational objectives 277-281
teacher-pupil relationships 245-248, 290, 291-292
teacher, the 121, 123, 174-175, 218, 245, 246, 247, 250, 252, 253, 286, 294-295
Teachers College, Columbia University 5, 89n, 131
teaching procedures, – methods 121-122, 131, 175, 246, 248, 284-286
technology vi, 3, 13, 78, 159, 165, 170, 181, 199, 200, 232, 237, 244, 249, 251, 275, 277, 282. *See also* industrialization
testing procedures 121, 137n, 279-280
theology 26, 28, 33, 222-224
theory, educational. *See* educational theories
thinking, thought 14, 26, 29, 30, 48, 135, 136-140, 155-156, 187, 285
Thomism 203, 204-205, 205n, 206, 207, 209, 210, 212, 215, 218, 230, 241
transcendence 171, 226-227, 229, 231, 237, 238, 240, 243, 244, 263
trust 230, 232
truth, existential 27, 29, 34, 34n, 187, 195, 242
truth, nature of 27, 29, 42, 43, 70, 101, 106, 131, 138, 139, 145, 161, 170, 177, 205n, 249, 254, 281, 283

unconscious, the 49, 102
Universal Growth Theory (Wynne, of Dewey) 138
utilitarian, –ism 51, 51n, 147, 159, 283
utopianism 66, 68, 74, 107, 115, 199, 231, 234, 236, 237, 239, 244

value, theories of – ix, 12-14, 34, 43, 48, 50, 54, 57, 70, 81, 100, 102, 107, 112, 114-115, 117-121, 138, 147, 148, 153, 156-157, 158, 159, 161, 170, 171, 172, 174, 176, 218-219, 223, 271-277
vocational training 275
voluntary agencies 287, 288, 289, 291
voting procedures 216

wandering, the power of (Whitehead) 163
war 54, 55, 57, 58, 81, 165, 181, 193, 196, 266, 291
will, the, as discussed by Kierkegaard 31, 32, 35; Nietzsche 48-50; Marx 66, 78; Nunn 90-91, 121; Dewey 135; Maritain 208, 210, 212; Niebuhr 226-227, 229
will-to-power (Nietzsche) 14, 45, 48-50, 51, 55, 57, 80, 93n, 117, 228
Will To Power, as a reliable source 55n
work and labor 3, 64-65, 68-69, 70, 73, 143, 147, 193, 213, 222. *See also* economic factor, the
world, the 42, 44, 49, 63, 134, 140, 150, 153, 156, 157, 158, 161, 166, 172, 188-189, 209, 227, 231, 263, 264
worship 142, 160, 194, 195, 213

youth 114, 123, 274

Zarathustra 45, 47, 50, 56n

PERSONAL NAME INDEX

Abraham, Gerald 41n
Acton, Lord 115
Adler, Mortimer 7, 251
Aiken, Henry D. 9n
Akhnaton 164
Allport, Gordon W. 3n, 17n, 103, 137n, 140, 140n, 285n
Andersen, W. E. x, 75n, 293, 293n
Aquinas, Saint T. 181, 193, 204, 205, 206, 208, 213, 251, 276
Aristotle 54, 162, 205, 208, 213, 227n, 249, 250
Aschner, Mary Jane 284n
Augustine, Saint 181, 193, 213, 222, 224

Bacon, Francis 141
Bakunin, Michael 61, 71n, 75, 75n
Bantock, G. H. 97n, 113, 116
Barth, Karl 185, 224, 229n
Beales, A. C. F. 203n, 249n
Benda, J. 104
Bennett, John C. 221n, 237, 237n
Bennis, Warren C. 97n
Bergson, Henri 203
Berkeley, Bishop 189
Berkson, I. B. 146n
Berlin, Isaiah 59n, 61, 67, 67n, 70, 72, 72n
Bloom, Benjamin S. 277, 277n, 281, 282
Bloy, Leon 203
Boultwood, M. E. A. 92n, 146, 146n
Brameld, Theodore 123, 146, 146n
Bretall, Robert 27n, 32n, 38, 38n

Broudy, Harry S. 146n, 171n, 177, 177n
Brunner, Emil 27-28, 28n, 185, 224, 224n
Buber, Martin 15, 35, 109, 121, 181, 183-201, 208, 209, 211, 223, 224, 228, 231n, 241-254, 264, 270, 284, 286, 294
Bultmann, Rudolph 78n
Burns, Hobert W. 8
Burtt, E. A. 11, 11n
Butler, J. Donald 6n, 131n, 140, 140n

Calvin, John 229n, 237
Campagnac, E. T. 95
Campbell, Hugh 112n, 114n, 116, 116n
Camus, Albert 82
Carnell, Edward John 224n, 229, 229n
Cattell, J. McKeen 131
Clarke, Sir Fred 95, 95n
Cohen, Robert S. 62, 62n, 68, 68n, 80, 80n
Collins, James 50n, 52n
Comte, Auguste 107, 130, 241
Copleston, Frederick 46
Counts, George S. 146
Crane, A. R. 200, 200n
Cremin, Lawrence A. 6n
Crittenden, Brian S. 293n
Cromwell, Oliver 237
Crosser, Paul K. 141n
Curtis, S. J. 92, 92n, 95n, 97n, 110n, 113, 146, 146n, 151n

319

NAME INDEX

Darwin, Charles 13, 49, 50, 51n, 134, 158
Descartes, Rene v, 30, 213, 262
Dewey, Jane 130, 130n
Dewey, John 5, 6n, 9, 14, 15, 16, 29n, 94, 121, 124, 127, 129-148, 149, 165, 169-177, 197, 198, 218, 222, 223, 228, 229, 232-233, 238, 239, 240, 244, 246, 254, 269, 272, 273, 273n, 262n, 282
Diamond, Malcolm L. 183n, 185, 188n, 196, 196n, 197, 197n, 199, 199n
Djilas, Milovan 62n, 74n, 237
Dru, Alexander 23n

Eichmann, Adolph, 184
Einstein, Albert 90n
Eliot, T. S. 99n
Engels, Friedrich 60, 61, 72
Erös, John 101, 101n, 103n
Euclid 150

Feuerbach, L. A. 60
Floud, Jean 113n, 115
Friedman, Maurice 185n, 190n, 196n, 200n, 246n
Freud, Sigmund 26, 26n, 29, 49, 89, 103, 117, 197, 226, 227n, 241, 243
Froebel, Friedrich 13

Goethe, J. W. von 192
Goheen, John 165, 165n
Good, Carter V. 292-293, 293n

Harland, Gordon 233, 233n
Harris, W. T. 130
Hegel, G. W. F. 4, 14, 26, 28, 29, 33, 62, 63-64, 71, 75n, 77, 77n, 78, 93, 110, 156, 206n
Heidegger, Martin 45, 194
Heinemann, F. H. 32, 32n, 35, 35n
Henderson, Stella van Petten 6, 7n
Herbart, J. F. 5, 13, 136
Herberg, Will 191n, 203n, 215n, 222, 222n
Hill, Brian V. v, vi, vii, 8n, 290n
Hirst, Paul H. 9, 9n
Hollingdale, R. J. 41n, 52n, 55n
Holmes, Brian 140, 140n, 175, 175n

Holmes, Henry 176, 176n
Hook, Sidney 63, 63n, 80n
Horne, Herman H. 7
Hullfish, Gordon H. 175, 175n
Hume, David 119, 120, 262
Husserl, Edmund 188n
Huxley, T. H. 130

James, William 130, 133, 135, 137, 137n, 155, 166, 262
Jaspers, Karl 29
Jefferson, Thomas 223
Jeffreys, M. V. C. 221, 245, 245n, 268, 268n, 278n
Jesus Christ 31, 53, 54, 166, 192, 210, 230, 235, 254
Joad, C. E. M. 57n, 71n
Judges, A. V. 196, 196n, 246, 246n
Jung, C. J. 93n, 102

Kant, Immanuel 47, 54, 66, 98, 120
Kaufmann, Walter 26n, 31n, 45, 45n
Kierkegaard, Søren 14, 23-39, 43, 59, 77-82, 119, 121, 122, 148, 171, 177, 181, 184, 186, 187, 188n, 193, 194, 195n, 197, 201, 206, 224, 229, 245n, 254
Kilpatrick, W. H. 175
Kingsley, Charles 71n
Kneller, George F. 31n, 196n
Koo, Gladys Y. 191, 191n
Kroner, Richard 224n

Lane, Homer 122
Laski, Harold I. 71n
Lassalle, Ferdinand 61, 71n
Lawson, W. 206, 206n
Lea, F. A. 41n, 42, 44, 44n, 49n, 56n
Leibniz, G. W. 155
Lenin, V. I. U. 61, 65n, 68, 71n
Lessing, G. E. 23n
Lilge, Frederic 42n, 147, 147n, 148, 148n
Lindsay, Jack 65n
Lindsay, Lord 99n, 101n
Livingstone, Sir Richard 150
Locke, John 213, 223
Lowe, Victor 151, 151n
Löwith, Karl 13n, 38n, 53n, 77n
Lowrie, Walter 23n, 38n

Name Index

McCallister, W. J. 93n
McDougall, William 87, 87n, 88, 93n, 261
McMurray, Foster 8, 8n
Makarenko, Anton S. 73n
Malthus, T. R. 158
Mannheim, Karl 7n, 14, 15, 85, 95n, 97-116, 117-128, 142, 146, 165, 167n, 238, 239, 254, 274
Maritain, Jacques 15, 181, 185, 194, 203-219, 228, 230, 241-254, 271, 273, 273n, 275, 275n, 276, 283n, 286, 288
Maritain, Raissa 203
Martin, Clyde V. 132n, 138n
Martin, William Oliver 163n
Marx, Karl 13, 14, 54, 77-82, 98, 106n, 110, 115, 116, 142, 173, 181, 199, 228, 232, 241, 243, 254, 257
Mead, George Herbert 110, 130-131, 191
Mehring, Franz 59n, 71n, 74
Middleton-Murry, John 99n
Mill, J. S. 223, 258
Moberly, Sir Walter 13n
Montessori, Maria 89, 121, 122
Moore, G. E. 14, 119
Morris, Bertram 157, 157n, 161, 161n
Mumford, Lewis 147
Musgrove, Frank 287n

Napoleon Bonaparte 54, 56, 191
Nash, Arnold S. 104n
Nash, Paul 62n
Needham, Joseph 164, 164n
Newbury, Dorothy J. 132n
Newton, Sir Isaac 63, 150, 193
Niebuhr, Reinhold 15, 39, 181, 185, 194, 200n, 201, 209, 215, 221-240, 241-254, 269, 294
Nietzsche, Friedrich 14, 26n, 41-58, 59, 65, 71, 77-82, 93n, 104n, 107, 117, 142n, 152, 181, 183, 186, 228, 254, 257
Northrop, F. S. C. 6, 10, 10n, 118n, 119, 119n, 145, 171n
Nunn, Sir T. Percy 14, 85, 87-96, 151, 165, 254, 273, 274, 276, 276n
Nyberg, Paul 62n

O'Connor, D. J. 9, 9n, 210n
Oldham, J. H. 99n

Parkhurst, Helen 122
Pascal, Blaise 193
Passmore, John 88, 88n
Paul, Saint 160, 213, 224, 230
Peirce, C. S. 131, 136
Pericles 164
Pestalozzi, J. H. 5, 13, 89
Peters, R. S. 221, 271n, 272, 272n
Phenix, Philip H. vii, x, 275, 275n, 283, 283n, 284, 293-294
Plato 115, 156, 193, 287
Popper, Karl 73, 73n, 74, 97n, 113, 114n, 116
Price, Lucien 149n, 159n, 163n, 164, 164n, 165n
Proudhon, Pierre Joseph 60, 66

Ramsey, Paul 238n
Randall, John Herman Jr. 137n, 144, 144n
Ratner, Joseph 134n, 144, 144n, 146n
Read, Herbert 185
Reyburn, H. A. 41n
Rogers, Carl B. 285n
Rohde, Peter 25n, 26
Rosenzweig, Franz 184
Roubiczek, Paul 35n, 55n, 57n, 78n
Rousseau, Jean-Jacques 13, 92, 93, 95, 95n, 209, 213, 273
Rusk, Robert R. 90n, 92n, 94, 144, 144n, 147
Russell, Bertrand 14, 87, 87n, 88n, 129, 145, 147, 150, 151, 200
Ryle, Gilbert 136, 262

Santayana, George 140, 140n, 142
Sartre, Jean-Paul 30, 45, 82
Savery, William 136n
Scheffler, Israel 9n
Schilpp, Paul Arthur 133, 157n, 165, 165n
Schleiermacher, F. E. D. 26
Schlesinger, Arthur 234, 234n, 236n, 238
Schlesinger, Rudolph 68, 68n

Schopenhauer, Arthur 42, 44, 48, 49, 93n
Scott, Nathan A. 221n, 223, 237n
Sellars, Roy Wood 157, 157n
Simon, Ernst 199
Skinner, B. F. 284-285, 284n, 285n
Smith, Adam 60
Smith, Philip G. 8n, 175, 175n
Socrates 24, 31, 36, 192
Spencer, Herbert 84
Stewart, W. A. C. 97n, 99n, 103n, 108
Stirner, Max 60, 66
Story, M. L. 233n, 269, 269n
Strain, John Paul 10n, 132n
Strawson, P. F. 11, 11n, 16
Swenson, David 24n, 29n, 30, 31, 32n, 34, 34n, 38, 38n

Thales 177
Thomas, J. Heywood 35n
Thorndike, E. L. 5

Tibble, J. W. 87n, 92n, 93, 93n
Tillich, Paul 78n, 185
Trotsky, L. D. B. 61

Ulich, Robert 132n, 148
Urban, Wilbur 162, 162n, 166

Wagner, Richard 42, 43, 44, 55
Weber, Max 108
Wegener, Frank C. 152, 152n, 164, 164n
Whitehead, A. N. 6, 14, 87, 90n, 127, 148, 149-167, 169-177, 181, 228, 239, 242, 242n, 244, 254, 270, 282
Whyte, William H. 290
Wieman, Henry Nelson 239n
Wild, John 94n
Wirth, Arthur G. 100, 130n
Wittgenstein, Ludwig 9
Wyndham, H. S. 274, 274n, 276
Wynne, John P. 8n, 138, 138n